With Masses and Arms

WITH MASSES & ARMS

Peru's Tupac Amaru Revolutionary Movement

MIGUEL LA SERNA

The University of North Carolina Press
CHAPEL HILL

This book was published with the assistance of the
H. Eugene and Lillian Youngs Lehman Fund of the University of
North Carolina Press. A complete list of books published in the
Lehman Series appears at the end of the book.

Cover photo: "MRTA en Pucallpa," by Carlos Saavedra, *Caretas*

Library of Congress Cataloging-in-Publication Data
Names: La Serna, Miguel, author.
Title: With masses and arms : Peru's Tupac Amaru
Revolutionary Movement / Miguel La Serna.
Other titles: H. Eugene and Lillian Youngs Lehman series.
Description: Chapel Hill : University of North Carolina Press,
[2020] | Series: H. Eugene and Lillian Youngs Lehman series |
Includes bibliographical references and index.
Identifiers: LCCN 2019053597 | ISBN 9781469655963 (cloth : alk. paper) |
ISBN 9781469655970 (paperback : alk. paper) | ISBN 9781469655987 (ebook)
Subjects: LCSH: Movimiento Revolucionario Túpac Amaru—History. |
Movimiento Revolucionario Túpac Amaru—Public relations. |
Revolutionaries—Peru—History—20th century. | Women
revolutionaries—Peru—History—20th century. | Collective memory—
Peru. | Peru—Politics and government—1980–
Classification: LCC HV6433.P42 M68446 2020 | DDC 322.4/20985—dc23
LC record available at https://lccn.loc.gov/2019053597

For Mateo Gael and Micaela Renee

Contents

3

Illustrations

COLOMBIA

ECUADOR

Putumayo River

Amazon River

• Piura

Area Enlarged Below

BRAZIL

• Chiclayo

Huallaga River

• Cajamarca

N

• Trujillo

• Chimbote   Pucallpa •

• Huaraz

PACIFIC
OCEAN

• Huánuco

Ucayali River

• Oxapampa

Urubamba River

Callao •   Molinos
Lima   Jauja •   •   *Apurímac River*
            • Huancayo

Puerto Maldonado •

• Ayacucho

• Cuzco

Moyobamba •   Yurimaguas •

Rioja •

Mayo River

• Ica

Tabalosos •

Lake Titicaca

San José
de Sisa •   Tarapoto •

• Nazca

Sisa River

Puno •

Sapoosoa River

• Arequipa

• Juanjuí

SAN MARTÍN

• Moquegua

BOLIVIA

Huallaga River

• Tacna

• Tocache

CHILE

0   100   200 mi
0   100   200   300 km

Peru

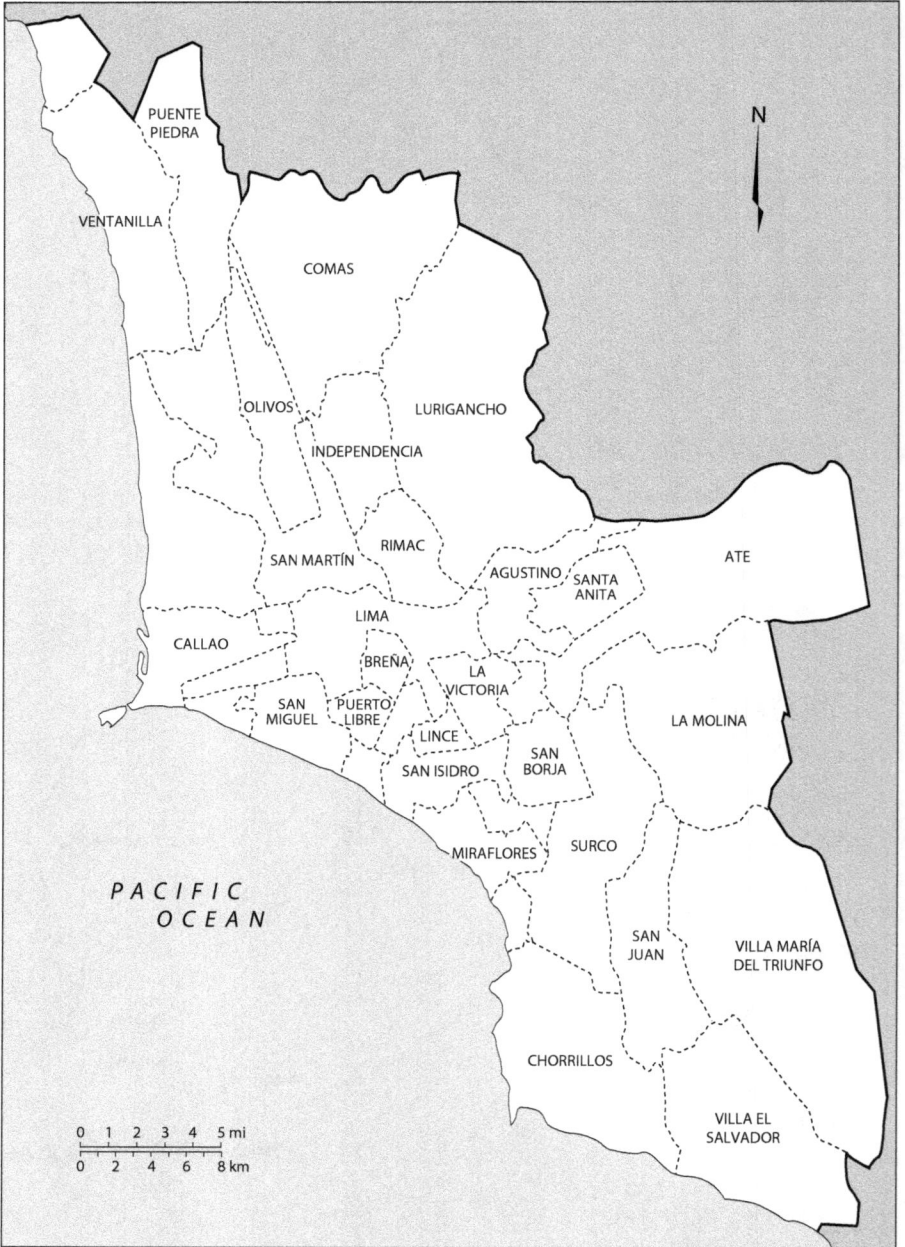

N

PUENTE
PIEDRA

VENTANILLA

COMAS

OLIVOS

LURIGANCHO

INDEPENDENCIA

SAN MARTÍN

RIMAC

AGUSTINO

SANTA
ANITA

ATE

LIMA

CALLAO

BREÑA

LA
VICTORIA

SAN
MIGUEL

PUERTO
LIBRE

LINCE

LA MOLINA

SAN ISIDRO

SAN
BORJA

MIRAFLORES

SURCO

PACIFIC
OCEAN

SAN
JUAN

VILLA MARÍA
DEL TRIUNFO

CHORRILLOS

VILLA EL
SALVADOR

0 1 2 3 4 5 mi

0   2   4   6   8 km

Lima

Acknowledgments

It has been both rewarding and challenging writing this book: rewarding in that I have benefited from the generous support of others; challenging to do justice to their wisdom and guidance. I thank my Peruvianist colleagues José Carlos Agüero, Carlos Aguirre, Renzo Aroni, Florence Babb, Julián Berrocal, Kathryn Burns, Iván Caro, Ricardo Caro, Carlos Contreras, Martha-Cecilia Dietrich Ortega, Paulo Drinot, Gustavo Gorriti, Shane Greene, Jaymie Patricia Heilman, Walter Huamaní, Lucía Luna Victoria Indacochea, Marie Manrique, Mario Miguel Meza, Diana Miloslavich, Raúl Necochea, Jorge Ortíz Sotelo, José Luis Rénique, and Tony Zapata for their many insights, conversations, and feedback at various stages of the research and writing process. Ruth Borja, Roberto Bustamante, Sebastián Chávez Wurm, Karina Fernández González, Marcelita Gutiérrez, Oscar Medrano, Pablo Rojas, Melissa Sánchez, and Santiago Tamay Silva helped me locate crucial archival records, for which I am forever grateful. I owe a tremendous debt of gratitude to Oscar Arriola, Liliana Gliksman, Nancy Madrid, Marco Miyashiro, Ricardo Noriega Salaverry, Mario Rossi, Vladimir Uñapillco, Iris Valladares, and especially Lori Berenson and Anahí Durand for putting me in contact with critical interview subjects on both sides of the political divide.

My professional community in the United States was a rock of support. At the University of North Carolina at Chapel Hill, Sharon Anderson, Joyce Loftin, Jennifer Parker, and Beatriz Riefkhol were always willing to put up with my queries, requests for administrative and financial support, and other nuisances along the way. My colleagues Fitz Brundage, Emily Burrill, Sebastián Carassai, John Chasteen, Rudi Colloredo Mansfeld, Mariana Dantas, Kathleen DuVal, Oswaldo Estrada, Joe Glatthaar, Jacqueline Hagan, Karen Hagemann, Jonathan Hartlyn, Emil Keme, Lisa Lindsay, Malinda Maynor Lowery, Susan Pennybacker, José Juan Pérez Meléndez, Cynthia Radding, Julie Reed, Marian Schlotterbeck, Tatiana Seijas, William Sturkey, Ben Waterhouse, Brett Whalen, and Luise White offered invaluable moral and intellectual support. I am most grateful to Martha Espinosa, Stark Harbour, Emma Macneil, Sydney Marshall, Danielle McIvor, Kenneth Neggy, Elizabeth Stillwell, Emily Taylor, and Diana Torres for their thoughtful comments on my penultimate draft. Ponciano Del Pino, Lou Pérez, Orin Starn, Brendan Thornton, and Chuck Walker deserve special mention for exhibiting that special blend of mentorship, scholarly exchange, and friendship. I am grateful to the UNC Institute for the Arts and Humanities for providing me with a Faculty Fellowship to work on this project. There, Jan Bardsley, Michelle Berger, Tim Carter, Banu Gokariskel, Mark Katz, Heidi Kim, Enrique Neblett, Álvaro Reyes, and Milada Vachudova provided the stimulating intellectual incubator in which many of the book's key ideas and concepts metastasized. Down the road at UNC Press, my editor Elaine Maisner helped breathe life into this project. If this book is of any value to readers, I invite them to join me in thanking Elaine for her incredible patience, guidance, and encouragement at every step of the journey.

My family and friends in the United States and Peru have always kept me going. My Peruvian family, Carlos, Karlos, Korah, María, Matías, Olenka, Pepe, Piotr, Ricardo, Teresa, Veronica, and Yolanda La Serna, offered unwavering support. My parents, Sabad and Susan, sent me off into the field with much love, encouragement, and no small amount of concern for my well-being, for which I am truly grateful. I am indebted to Carmen and Michael Betts for offering the kind of moral, emotional, and childcare support usually reserved for family. Thank you to Jonathan Woody for always being there in a pinch. Finally, I thank Jillian Joy, Micaela Renee, and Mateo Gael La Serna for enduring all the trips, late nights, drafts, rewrites, deadlines, and headaches along the way. You are my life, my heart, my soul. *Los quiero hoy, más que ayer, pero no tanto como mañana.*

Abbreviations and Acronyms

APRA   American Popular Revolutionary Alliance

CVR   Truth and Reconciliation Commission
            (Comisión de la Verdad y Reconciliación)

DINCOTE   Peruvian counterterrorism police

GRFA   Revolutionary Government of the Armed Forces

ITT   International Telephone & Telegraph

KFC   Kentucky Fried Chicken

MIR   Revolutionary Left Movement

MRTA   Tupac Amaru Revolutionary Movement
            (El Movimiento Revolucionario Túpac Amaru)

PIP   Peruvian Investigative Police

SIN   National Intelligence Service

LA UNI   National University of Engineering

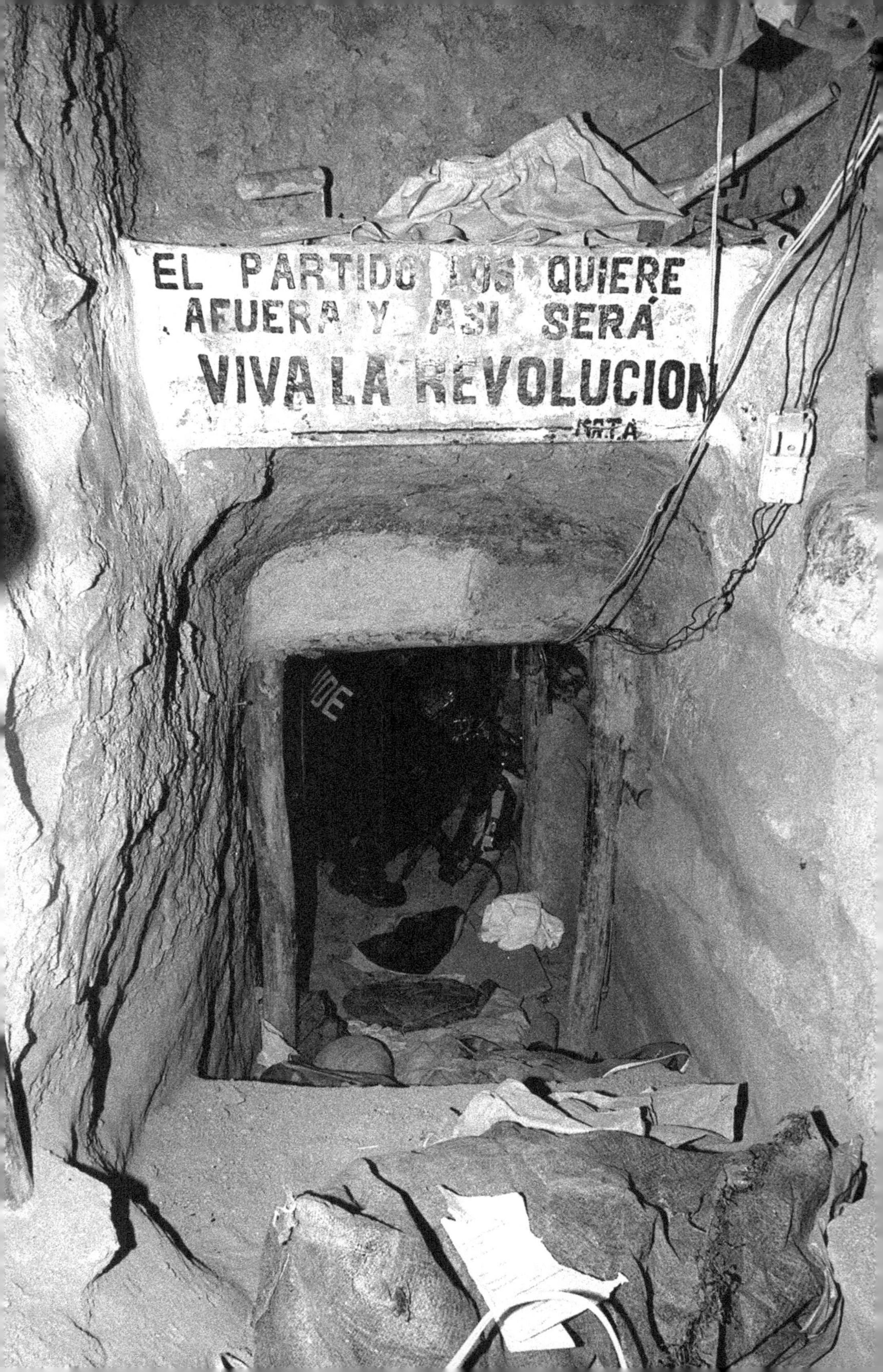
EL PARTIDO LOS QUIERE
AFUERA Y ASI SERÁ
VIVA LA REVOLUCION

With Masses and Arms

Introduction

Néstor Cerpa Cartolini awoke early on the morning of 22 April 1997. It had been 126 days since the rebel commander had led thirteen of his comrades from the Tupac Amaru Revolutionary Movement, or MRTA, in storming the residence of the Japanese ambassador to Peru, in an upscale Lima suburb. The rebels and their seventy-two hostages had been locked inside the residence with no electricity or running water since before Christmas of the previous year.

Cerpa was the last of a dying breed of rebels in 1997. The former labor organizer was an ideological purist of sorts, exhibiting an indefatigable commitment to armed struggle as the only way to achieve revolutionary change. When the voices of compromise emerged within the rebel organization, Cerpa had been among the hard-liners to stomp them out. By now, however, most of his comrades-in-arms could be counted among the long list of the rebellion's deserted, defected, detained, and deceased. All that remained were his thirteen subordinates inside the residence and a handful of guerrillas scattered throughout Peru and South America. Still, Cerpa believed that he could use the hostage crisis to negotiate his way out of his current predicament.

After calling his troops to order, Cerpa announced that they, the Tupac Amaristas, would be singing the "Anthem to the Heroes of Los Molinos."

Something's shaking in Latin America
A free country, on the horizon it is
The children of the Andes are fighting
Tomorrow it will be Socialist [refrain]

Eternal light is reserved for the guerrillas
All of whom gave their lives for peace
By their example the people will be left with
The seeds that they need to become free [refrain]

You live now and always, Tupac Amaru!
In battle you became our immortal son
Los Molinos, example of courage
In the fight for the revolution [refrain]

The hymn was a tribute to the Tupac Amaristas who had been ambushed in Molinos, in the mountains outside Jauja, during a 1989 rural campaign. Cerpa and his comrades believed that the army had given the guerrillas no quarter, massacring them even after they had surrendered. The anthem was as much a tribute to the martyrs as it was an admonishment against surrender. It was also a key component of the MRTA's political-cultural war, in which Tupac Amaristas sought to situate key moments in their insurrectionary experience within the arc of Peruvian history.

After singing the anthem, Cerpa addressed his troops, reminding them of their mission to free political prisoners.

"One hundred twenty-six days and counting since the sacking of the Japanese Embassy!" Cerpa cried.

"Never surrender, dammit!" his comrades responded in unison.

"With masses and arms!" Cerpa said, citing the MRTA slogan. "Fatherland or death!"

"Long live Peru!" they replied.[1]

Cerpa appeared melancholy on that late April morning. His mood swings had become more and more frequent, and he spent large stints holed up in bed.[2] Perhaps everything—the broken-down negotiations with the government, the four months of captivity in the stuffy residence, the grim prospects of a peaceful resolution—had taken its toll. Still, he refused to give in. As he had said on multiple occasions and repeated that morning, he would not stop until the government released his comrades from prison. There was no room for compromise. Either he was walking out of the residence a free man or he and everyone else in there were leaving in body bags. The fate of the revolution as he knew it depended on how the hostage crisis played out.

■ The MRTA ranks among the formidable Latin American insurgencies of the Cold War, similar in size, scope, and impact to Uruguay's Tupamaros, Colombia's M-19, and El Salvador's FMLN. Yet, while there has been a rise in scholarship on these other insurgencies in recent years, the full story of the MRTA has never been told.[3] Instead, Shining Path, or Sendero Luminoso, has monopolized the historiography of the Peruvian war years. Shining Path was larger than the MRTA, and its militant following and embrace of the macabre made it the focus of horror and curiosity. So much has it over-shadowed the MRTA that scholars refer to literature about Peru's political violence as "Senderology."

When Shining Path launched its insurgency in May 1980, it was still a little-known faction of the Peruvian Communist Party (although its leaders would declare it Peru's one true Communist party). Within a few years, the guerrilla group that President Fernando Belaúnde Terry had once dismissed as a small group of rustlers developed into one of the world's deadliest insurgencies. At its helm was Abimael Guzmán, a white professor who had once taught philosophy in the Andean backwater of Ayacucho. Known to his followers as Presidente Gonzalo, the "Fourth Sword" of global Marxism—behind Marx, Lenin, and Mao—Guzmán demanded absolute devotion from his followers, even while his whereabouts were unknown to but a few in his inner circle. All the while, Guzmán's guerrillas, or Senderistas, who were mostly urban, educated mestizos who received moral and logistical support from Quechua-speaking highlanders, carried out a campaign from the countryside to the cities that included nightly car bombs, selective assassinations of government officials and capitalists, ad hoc "popular trials" against party enemies, and massacres of recalcitrant peasant communities. It was against this backdrop that the scholarship on the internal armed conflict developed. Some early researchers attempted to explain Shining Path's ideology, party structure, and mysterious leader, while others sought to explain its peasant support.[4]

By 1988, just eight years into the armed struggle, Guzmán and the Shining Path Central Committee were so confident of the impending collapse of the Peruvian state that they held the party's first and only national congress to lay out their plan for seizing power. Then, just as suddenly as it rose, Shining Path fell. The group had placed so much power in the hands of Guzmán that its very survival depended on his remaining free and overseeing the insurgency from hiding. When GEIN, the special intelligence group of the counterterrorism police, tracked down Guzmán and his inner circle to their safe house in a Lima suburb in September 1992, the party was effectively decapitated.

This dramatic turn of events led to a new wave of studies in the 1990s that sought to explain Shining Path's collapse. Some scholars focused on the active role of the *rondas campesinas*, the peasant counterinsurgency militias, which had by now spread throughout rural Peru. Anthropologists offered rich ethnographies of war-torn Andean communities, highlighting their agency in driving the Maoists out of the countryside.[5] While Guzmán's capture was the coup de grâce for Shining Path, these scholars showed that the group had already been severely weakened, in large part because of the mobilization of the indigenous peasantry. Scholars of the period typically declined to highlight the role of the state or its security forces in Shining Path's downfall. To date, most accounts of Guzmán's capture are written by members of the counterinsurgency forces themselves or by sympathetic journalists.[6] Instead, scholars, human rights advocates, and some journalists devoted their attention to chronicling how the government of Alberto Fujimori, who presided over the governmental palace at the time of Guzmán's arrest, turned to authoritarianism, corruption, and human rights violations during the counterinsurgency.[7]

In 2000, Fujimori's past crimes caught up with him, and he fled the country amid a cloud of scandal. The following year, interim president Valentín Paniagua convened the Truth and Reconciliation Commission (CVR) to investigate the crimes and human rights abuses of both state and nonstate actors during the internal armed conflict. The CVR collected over 17,000 testimonies on the way to publishing its nine-volume, 8,000-page *Final Report* two years later. The CVR found that more than 69,000 people had died during the armed conflict, the vast majority of them Quechua-speaking peasants.[8] In a rare departure from other truth and reconciliation commissions that found government forces the main killers, the CVR held Shining Path responsible for the majority of the casualties (54 percent), holding state and civilian counterinsurgency forces accountable for less than half (44.5 percent) and the MRTA responsible for 1.5 percent. Aside from its shocking conclusions, the CVR offered an opportunity for civil society to discuss the war. Many middle-class mestizos and some indigenous peasants elected not to engage.[9] Still, for the first time since the war had begun in 1980, the opportunity for a meaningful dialogue existed. Some, even those who had not participated in the CVR's investigation, began to explore new ways to engage the broader public about the political violence. These expressions took various forms, entering the realms of photography, art, literature, and music.[10] The CVR opening also led to a new wave of scholarship on the war's aftermath. In recent years, scholars have conducted insightful research in the highland communities most affected by the armed conflict, exploring the politics of memory and reconciliation at both the micro and macro levels.[11] While these scholars sought to unpack the war's legacies, historians moved into the archives to make sense of its origins. Much of this scholarship picked up on historian Steve J. Stern's pathbreaking 1998 volume, *Shining and Other Paths*, an early effort to contextualize Shining Path's rise and trajectory.[12] The CVR report, and the national conversation that it engendered, made available new sources that had previously eluded historians. In addition to the open-access archive of the CVR, historians used interviews, fieldwork, and local and regional archives to reconstruct the historical antecedents and political trajectory of Shining Path's war from a regional and national perspective.[13]

Shining Path limped along after its leader's capture, splintering into Guzmán loyalists, who recognized the group's military defeat, and hard-liners who continued the armed struggle under new leadership and without Guzmán's explicit consent. Forty years after the war had begun, a severely depleted group of hard-liners continued to fight in the mostly coca-producing jungles of Peru, while the loyalists, regrouped under a would-be political party, MOVADEF, sought legal recognition and amnesty for Guzmán and other Shining Path prisoners. The efforts of Shining Path to enter mainstream legal politics met fierce resistance from both civil society and the Peruvian government, a sign that the open wounds left by the conflict still had not healed. Efforts by the right to silence Shining Path sympathizers culminated in the passing of a law against apologia, that is, any effort to deny that Shining Path was anything but a terrorist organization. As historians Paulo Drinot, Cynthia Milton, and Carlos Aguirre have pointed out, the period since the publication of the CVR's findings featured a heated contest over the narrative of the armed conflict. Within this context, Milton notes, two narrative tropes emerged. The first, "salvation memory," dominated by Fujimori's political disciples, branded the former president the hero of the fight against terrorism and denounced his critics as *terrucos* (slang for "terrorists").[14] The second trope, "human rights memory," consisted of Fujimori critics and emphasized the many human rights abuses committed under his and others' watch. Amid this heated political terrain, Abimael Guzmán penned, from prison, his own version of the party's history, always with an eye toward political amnesty.[15]

Only recently have historians attempted to revisit the war as a whole, pulling together new sources that emerged in the war's aftermath. New biographical studies have sought to explain Guzmán's apotheosis.[16] Recent works by Antonio Zapata, José Luis Rénique, Adrián Lerner, and others offer syntheses large and small of the political violence, building on the existing literature and incorporating, for the first time in some cases, interviews with imprisoned Shining Path leaders.[17]

◼ Despite the remarkable nuance and depth of analysis offered by Senderology, there are several key aspects of the Peruvian insurrection that have escaped scholarly attention. First, and perhaps most surprisingly, we do not yet have a well-developed history of the lived experience of war for those who fought it. While most studies touch on specific massacres, individuals, and communities, they tell less about the day-to-day experience of war not only for those who rebelled but also for those who participated in the counterinsurgency. This absence is due largely to the difficulties in accessing combatant voices. Unlike some other Latin American guerrillas, few Senderistas kept journals or wrote memoirs. This was due in part to the fact that many rank-and-file members spoke Quechua, a spoken language, as well as the fact that the party eschewed individualism in a practice that the late Carlos Iván Degregori dubbed the "abolition of the ego."[18] Add to this the fact that many former insurgents were still, twenty-five years after Guzmán's arrest, imprisoned and restricted by the national penitentiary system from giving formal interviews, and the dearth of Senderista perspectives becomes even more understandable. Those who had been released usually preferred not to discuss their time in Shining Path, either because they wanted to move on with their lives or because they did not want to further incriminate themselves and risk the very real possibility of more legal troubles. Those who still toed the party line were even less likely to share personal stories, sticking mostly to preapproved party talking points or deferring to the official narrative offered by Guzmán. The same problems of command structure have made it difficult for scholars to access voices from the counterinsurgency. This, coupled with scholars' ambivalence toward the perpetrators of state crimes and atrocities, has created a veritable black hole in quality scholarship on rank-and-file and junior officers.

A second underexplored topic of analysis within Senderology is the role of women and gender in the guerrilla organizations. Some of the best scholarship on women in the conflict examines the ways in which indigenous peasant women experienced it, both as civilians and as members of the *rondas campesinas*.[19] For reasons outlined above, accessing Shining Path women's voices proved far more difficult. For nearly two decades after the fall of Abimael Guzmán and his wife and second-in-command, Elena Iparraguirre, the most comprehensive portrait of Senderista women was the succinct 1993 investigation of journalist and human rights advocate Robin Kirk.[20] Only recently have historians, drawing on prison interviews and newly available archival records, begun to reconstruct the insurrectionary lives of Shining Path's women leaders.[21] We still have much to learn about the lived experiences of rank-and-file and midlevel women in Shining Path and the MRTA, as well as the gendered conduct of insurgent men and the intersections between gender, culture, and power within Peru's radical left.

A final aspect of the war that is absent from the conventional narrative is any comprehensive analysis of Peru's other major guerrilla group, the Tupac Amaru Revolutionary Movement. When the MRTA is mentioned, it is usually in passing, a kind of acknowledgment of the group's existence while admitting that a systematic treatment of the group is beyond the study's scope.[22] The exclusive media and scholarly attention on Shining Path has produced a narrative of the political violence that is both incomplete and inaccurate. Carlos Iván Degregori, once recognized as the world's leading Shining Path scholar, set the tone of Senderology by highlighting three defining features of Shining Path: its cult of death, its abolition of the ego, and its exaltation of the leader.[23] Indeed, most mainstream media coverage and some scholarly representations of Shining Path reinforced this popular image. Peruvians of a certain age remember the images captured from inside a maximum-security women's prison, where a group of Senderista inmates clad in Chinese Cultural Revolution uniforms and carrying red flags marched and sang revolutionary songs in total synchronization, hailing Presidente Gonzalo, whose idealized portrait had been plastered to one of the towering prison walls.[24] Images like these contributed to popular representations of Peru's rebels as a revolutionary enigma. If the Che Guevaras, Carlos Fonsecas, and Raúl Sendics of the world were romantic rebels fighting imperialism, capitalism, and authoritarianism, Andean rebels appeared as dogmatic, cultlike maniacs at the fringes of the global left.

In exploring the experiences of combatant women and men in the war between the MRTA and the Peruvian state, *With Masses and Arms* addresses each of the above-mentioned areas of historiographical oversight while simultaneously challenging the myth of the Andean conflict. Far from being the quasi-religious fanatics of the popular imagination, many middle- and working-class Peruvians took up arms precisely because they questioned conventional wisdom and challenged authority. For most, this recalcitrance only strengthened once they joined the rebel ranks. An exploration of Tupac Amarista women's and men's experiences thus allows us a way out of the salvation/human rights binary that Cynthia Milton identifies in her analysis of postconflict narratives. In doing so, it builds on recent autobiographical portraits by Lurgio Gavilán, a former child Senderista, and José Carlos Agüero, whose parents were Shining Path militants, which describe life inside Shining Path with refreshing intimacy.[25] We still have much to learn about the quotidian, lived experiences of combatants on both sides of the conflict.[26] This book seeks to offer new insights into these experiences by exploring the daily challenges, decisions, conflicts, insecurities, and struggles of Tupac Amarista rebels and the counterinsurgency forces who pledged to stop them.

■ As the first comprehensive history of the MRTA, *With Masses and Arms* is, first and foremost, a narrative history. Bringing together newspaper clippings and media footage; guerrilla propaganda, communiqués, leaflets, and manuscripts; classified and declassified documents of the Peruvian counterterrorism police (DINCOTE); military manuals and field reports; published and unpublished memoirs from rebel leaders, counterinsurgency heads, and victims of political violence; testimonies, interviews, and ephemera from the archives of the CVR and the Memory Place (LUM); and unreleased court records from the so-called Megatrial of MRTA leaders, the book chronicles the rebellion's major episodes, developments, and turning points. Rather than offer a blow-by-blow of this thirteen-year-conflict, the narrative follows a diverse cast of characters whose lives the war brought together in unexpected ways. It focuses primarily on rebel leaders and foot soldiers who bet their lives against the status quo and sometimes paid the ultimate price. These rebels' stories are complemented by those of members of the Peruvian government and security forces, from the heads of the counterterrorism police down to the Civil Guard watchmen in neglected jungle stations. Along the way, readers also meet some of the ordinary civilians whose lives the war swept into its orbit.

Among the people whose insurrectionary lives the book follows are two women who achieved different levels of status within the MRTA. The first, Lucero Cumpa, started off as a low-level militant in the mid-1980s, worked her way up to the Central Committee, and eventually commanded the group's guerrilla front. Despite occupying one of the most coveted positions within the rebel hierarchy, and despite being among the only women to command any guerrilla army during the Peruvian armed conflict, Cumpa has not been the subject of much scholarly attention. *With Masses and Arms* thus offers a rare portrait of a woman who rose through the rebel ranks from militant to commander, showing not only that women were present in the left's guerrilla campaigns but that they helped shape and lead them. But this is not merely a story of female agency. After all, Lucero Cumpa was the exception, not the rule. The story of this book's second woman protagonist, Esperanza Tapia, is far more representative of the experience of Tupac Amarista women inside the rebel organization. Yet, both the foot soldier Tapia and the commander Cumpa experienced gender and power in similar ways. While the MRTA publicly advocated women's empowerment and gender equality, women at all ranks of the MRTA experienced an insurrectionary culture of paternalism, patriarchy, and misogyny. Whether limiting women's access to guns, propping them up as guerrilla poster children, restricting their physical movement, or blurring the boundaries between reality and role-play, rebel men sought to exert physical and symbolic control over women's bodies. As common as these attempts to control and contain were, so too were women's efforts to contest, challenge, and cut through these aggressions. As the insurrectionary lives of Lucero Cumpa and Esperanza Tapia demonstrate, women rebels waged their own internal revolution by letting no slight go unchecked, no double standard go unchallenged. Only through these daily struggles did Peruvian women change the guerrilla patriarchy from within. For these women, the daily battles for dignity, equality, and respect mirrored what historian Michelle Chase, channeling Fidel Castro, has called a "revolution within the revolution."[27]

In bringing in a range of combatant perspectives, *With Masses and Arms* seeks neither to criticize nor to apologize, neither to glorify nor to vilify, but, rather, to tell the story of the Tupac Amaru Revolutionary Movement in all its human complexity. This human dimension would not have been possible without extensive interviews and fieldwork. Over the course of seven years, the author interviewed rebel leaders, followers, and sympathizers, both in prison and out; military and police commanders, lieutenants, and privates; victims of MRTA assaults; civilians who had run-ins with security forces and rebels; former Peruvian officials and American ambassadors; and family members of imprisoned and deceased insurgents. Fieldwork spanned the United States and Peru, with multiple trips to the Andes, the Amazon, and the coast. To protect the anonymity of most participants, identifying names and places have been altered; only the names of public figures remain unchanged. One of those figures is MRTA leader Víctor Polay Campos. At the time of the writing of this book, Polay was serving a thirty-five-year sentence under solitary confinement in a Peruvian naval prison. He agreed to an interview, but his jailors wouldn't allow it. Instead, he allowed the author access to his attorney, to his closest family and friends, and to manuscripts such as his unpublished memoirs. Interpersonal exchanges, sustained over multiple sessions and, in most cases, years, imbued these historical actors' stories with a layer of depth, empathy, and intimacy that this book endeavors to capture.

■ Focusing on grassroots insurrectionary experiences allows us to move beyond binary discussions of the global Cold War. In 2008, historians Gilbert M. Joseph and Daniela Spenser published their seminal edited volume, *In from the Cold*, in which they called for historians to move beyond superpower-centric, policy-driven narratives of the Cold War and toward a more organic history of grassroots political culture. The contributors made a case for bringing the global periphery, namely, Latin America, more squarely into a foreign-relations-centered historiography that tended to emphasize the United States and the Soviet Union. As Joseph argues, incorporating local archives and grassroots actors into studies of the period would enable scholars to move "in from the cold," thereby complicating the conventional emphasis on superpowers, policymakers, and ideology.[28] This attention to local theaters allows us to visit the political-cultural realm, which, as Spenser reminds us, is where "the state's power is deployed or contested through representations, symbolic systems, and new technologies, recognizing that the exercise of power not only flows from the policies and interventions of states but also works through language and symbolic systems in everyday practice."[29]

In Peru, the political-cultural realm became the main theater of war for both the MRTA and the state.[30] Tupac Amaristas deliberately blurred the boundaries between the symbolic and the military realms in their effort to frame the narrative of the rebellion. They constantly appropriated national symbols in an effort to paint an image of themselves as what Anthony D. Smith calls the "ethnic guardians" of Peruvian culture, identity, and history.[31] Many of their armed actions, while certainly carrying strategic and military objectives, sought to identify the state and the ruling class as hostile outsiders who would destroy the nation's cultural fabric. MRTA targets—whether individuals, institutions, buildings, or monuments—spoke a heavily symbolic language. The governments of Alan García and Alberto Fujimori were well aware of the political stakes, each drawing on its own symbols of collective memory and cultural identity in an effort to construct an image of the state as more authentically Peruvian than the enemy. The result was a civil war in which the appropriation of colors, banners, names, images, places, and other "realms of memory" went hand in hand with armed combat, thus obscuring the cultural and political spheres.[32]

The MRTA understood that, in a late-twentieth-century Cold War context, its ability to win the sympathy of a skeptical public depended on its capacity to win the public relations war. For the guerrillas, then, ink, cameras, photographs, video, and radio were weapons as powerful as guns, bombs, and tanks.[33] The MRTA frequently privileged political theater over theaters of war, putting to the test the theory that the lens was mightier than the sword. Whenever possible, Tupac Amaristas attempted to persuade, cajole, and deceive the free press into covering their actions in the most favorable light possible, always with a mind for optics. Nor was the MRTA alone in this molding of war and theater. As anthropologist Shane Greene notes, Shining Path, too, captured the popular imagination through aestheticized politics.[34]

Yet, for all their efforts, neither Shining Path nor the MRTA managed to win the hearts and minds of the majority of Peruvians, much less the armed struggle. What explains this limitation? While a number of factors contributed to the Tupac Amaristas' downfall, none was perhaps more critical than their own limited vision of what Peru was, and could become. For all the group's fixation on the past and on a narrow sense of nationalism, the agendas and priorities of the MRTA's militant, hard-line faction constantly prevailed over those of their comrades who sought to articulate a more inclusive, progressive vision of the future that responded to late-twentieth-century Peruvian and Latin American realities. Time and again, when presented with opportunities to become more inclusive, more democratic, more peaceful, and more forward-thinking, the MRTA's more nationalist, more authoritarian, more bellicose, and more backward-looking voices prevailed. This unwillingness by a few hard-liners to compromise, converse, and concede led the party into a position that was at once politically untenable and militarily unwinnable. This is the position in which Néstor Cerpa found himself on the afternoon of 22 April 1997, as he sat alone inside the Japanese ambassador's residence. What follows is the story of how he got there.

Part **1**

1

A New Generation Needs a New Name

Víctor Polay Campos quickstepped into the Banco de Credito on 28 July Avenue. La Victoria was a rough neighborhood in a rough city in a rough country in 1982. It wasn't uncommon for petty thieves lurking outside the bank to pickpocket customers before they made it off the 24th block. Others tried less subtle tactics, relieving clients of their withdrawals at gunpoint. Polay was making a hefty withdrawal himself on this late March day, but he wasn't worried about being robbed. He had grown up on the streets of Callao, Lima's twin city, and was by now, in his twenties, fairly streetwise. He was also armed with a semiautomatic rifle. Today, it was Polay who would be doing the robbing.

Polay's partner in crime was a San Marcos University student named Jorge Telledo Feria. Once inside, the two young men dashed over to the Civil Guardsman on duty and attempted to wrestle his gun from him. The guard was far more seasoned than the rookie thieves and fended them off as they attempted to pry the gun from his hands. Several bullets ricocheted off the floor; three struck the guard and another hit Telledo, who dropped dead on the spot. Only then did Polay finally win the gun. He pistol-whipped the guard, knocking him out. Weapon raised, Polay then ran over to the counter and put as much money as he could into his bags before running to the street and jumping into a getaway car. The green Fiat transporting Polay, three accomplices, and 10 million soles of stolen cash sped down Giribaldi Avenue just as the first batch of police arrived at the scene. Polay and his accomplices fired their weapons at the squad cars, buying themselves enough distance to disappear into the labyrinth of avenues, boulevards, and alleyways that made up Peru's concrete jungle.[1]

Polay and Telledo were no ordinary criminals. In fact, they didn't consider themselves criminals at all. Unlike other bank robbers, who used the spoils of their heists to line their own pockets, Polay and Telledo carried out the armed robbery in the name of a cause much greater than themselves. Their 31 May 1982 run on the Banco de Credito in La Victoria was the first armed action of the nascent Tupac Amaru Revolutionary Movement. The uncredited action proved to be the group's baptism by fire, procuring much-needed funding for the formal insurgency, which they would launch two years later under the MRTA banner. For Víctor Polay, the future leader and public face of the rebel organization, the bank robbery served as the culmination of years of political activism in the Peruvian left.

■ Historian Mario Miguel Meza argues that the political origins of the MRTA are best understood within the broader context of the history of the Peruvian left.[2] Indeed, Víctor Polay and other MRTA founders conceived of their movement in direct relation to Andean revolutions past and present. Shining Path, the Communist party that initiated its armed struggle two years before the MRTA's founding, offered not only competition for winning bodies, hearts, and minds but also a model of what to avoid. Instead, the MRTA built on previous revolutionary experiments under which many of its founders came of age. The left-leaning Velasco government of the late 1960s and early 1970s, the failed MIR (Revolutionary Left Movement) guerrilla campaign of 1965, and years of Aprista radicalism dating back to the 1930s provided both the revolutionary tradition and the political recruits for the nascent movement. Yet, for many Tupac Amaristas, these previous experiments in revolutionary politics represented a kind of failure. Instead, the rebels turned to the nation's founding fathers, to figures like José de San Martín and Tupac Amaru II. This grassroots revolutionary tradition, coupled with a broader political culture of revolutionary action in the Latin American Cold War, provided the backdrop under which the MRTA came into being.

For Víctor Polay Campos and many other Tupac Amaristas, the American Popular Revolutionary Alliance, or APRA, served as an incubator for their political maturation. Polay's father, Víctor Polay Risco, had been a founder and activist of the populist anti-imperialist party led by the gifted orator Víctor Raúl Haya de la Torre.[3] The Apristas had a well-earned reputation as rabble-rousers. In 1931, Haya de la Torre had lost a presidential bid against the military ruler Luís Sánchez Cerro in an election that many of his supporters considered stolen. Despite winning twenty-three congressional seats, the Aprista faithful took to the streets, their protests frequently erupting in violence.[4] The government responded by sacking APRA party headquarters in Trujillo, killing several people, expelling the newly elected Aprista congressmen, and eventually outlawing the party. Haya de la Torre and other party leaders went into exile, but the violence continued for another two years, with the Apristas leading an uprising in Trujillo and the government responding in kind. After an Aprista militant assassinated Sánchez Cerro in 1933, the new government of Oscar Benavides continued to crack down on the party, rounding up party militants while Haya de la Torre and other leaders went into hiding or into exile.[5] APRA existed largely as a radical clandestine party for over a decade, and its militants armed themselves and engaged in acts of sabotage and violence while simultaneously demanding a foothold in legal politics.[6] In 1948, Apristas sailors in Polay's home city of Callao staged an unsuccessful mutiny that left 65 government and mutineer forces and 175 civilians dead.[7] Into this political fray, Víctor Polay Campos was born in 1951.

Polay Risco was doing time in El Frontón, the Peruvian Alcatraz, when his son was born. As Polay's older sister, Otilia, recalled, her father spent most of her childhood bouncing back and forth "between prison and home."[8] Polay was two years old before he met his father. The little boy looked at the strange Asian man standing before him.

"Víctor," his mother said, "this is your father."

Víctor Polay Risco's family had come to Peru along with a steady wave of Chinese "coolies" at the turn of the twentieth century. A Cantonese immigrant, Po Lay Seng didn't speak a word of Spanish when he took up a job as a field hand in the hacienda Cajacay, in the department of Ancash. To avoid being deported, he married a Peruvian woman named Clemencia Risco, who gave birth to their son in 1904. They named the boy Víctor Polay Risco, a Hispanicization of the father's name, and baptized him as a Christian months later.[9] Polay Risco assimilated easily, despite being a spitting image of his Chinese father. He was a political animal, and he joined the young APRA party upon its founding in the 1930s and built a reputation as a passionate, charismatic leader. He later married fellow Aprista Otilia Campos, who hailed from Cuzco, the ancient Inca heartland.

Otilia Campos raised her four children practically as a single mother. "My mother was the anchor of the house," Polay later wrote.[10] She single-handedly ran the *ferretería*, a neighborhood hardware store. When she came home for lunch or after work in the evenings, she would cook for her four children and attend to all the household chores before putting the little ones to bed. Víctor would keep her up at all hours, having developed chronic asthma in Callao's punishingly damp seaside. Many nights, she would sit by the wheezing boy's bedside, rubbing Vicks VapoRub on his chest until he finally fell asleep.[11] Otilia Campos also took it upon herself to make sure the kids kept up with their studies, and it was she who taught young Víctor to read. Whenever her eldest son got out of line, she would pinch his ear and make sure he acted right. She didn't hit her kids, opting instead to give them the cold shoulder until they reflected on what they'd done wrong.

Despite the challenges of single motherhood, Otilia Campos did her best to keep the memory of her children's absent father alive and well in the household. When Víctor was about eight years old, a well-known painter, Macedonio La Torre, cousin of the APRA founder, crafted a lovely finger painting of Polay Risco in honor of his service to the party. Otilia Campos just knew she had to have it. This way, the kids would always be able to see their father, even when he was away. When she went to request the portrait, however, she learned that La Torre had already sold it to a wealthy Arequipan landowner. An undeterred Campos took the thirteen-hour bus ride all the way up the zigzagging Andean mountain range to the landlord's home. She fed him a cockamamie story about Polay Risco having died fighting alongside Fidel Castro in the Cuban Revolution. That painting, she said with tears in her eyes, was the only memory that remained of her late husband. The landlord couldn't help but sympathize and insisted that Campos take the painting free of charge.[12]

There were, nevertheless, long stints when Polay Risco was home. To make up for lost time, he would take his two boys and two girls to Cine Badel, Callao's state-of-the-art movie theater. Polay and his siblings marveled at the Cineplex's glass walls, which gave it a kind of Hollywood flavor. Afterward, Polay Risco might treat his children to a sandwich at the theater's cafeteria or, if they'd been really good, an ice cream or lemon meringue pie. On these days young Polay, who'd always had a sweet tooth, couldn't have been happier.[13]

Polay Risco spent most of his days consumed by politics. He did his best to rear his children to become good little radicals. "He was the one who introduced me to words like imperialism, agrarian reform, nationalization, dictatorship, democracy, industrialization," Polay wrote.[14] Following its reinstatement as a legal political party in 1956, APRA set up headquarters in downtown Lima. Polay Risco often took his children with him to political gatherings there. Every 21 February, the eve of leader Víctor Raúl Haya de la Torre's birthday, Apristas would commemorate the occasion by letting the old man speak at the party headquarters. The young Polay would spend the entire afternoon listening to the aging politician's long-winded and impassioned speeches. Once Haya de la Torre had finished talking, Polay would take his spot in line behind all the other Aprista youth, waiting to shake the hand of his political hero. Then, at the stroke of midnight, the children would run onto Alfonso Ugarte Avenue and set off firecrackers to celebrate the occasion.[15]

The Callao house became a hub of political activity, always shrouded in secrecy. "Ever since I could remember," Polay wrote, "my parents always acted mysteriously." They received visitors in hushed voices and with strange passwords, as if fully expecting to be arrested at any moment. Still a little guy, Polay would watch as his father stashed away political papers. The curious asthmatic would wait until no one was in the room and remove the papers from their stash, never quite able to decipher their full meaning.[16] After breaking bread at the dining room table, however, the adults would always loosen up. The grown-ups would gather around to *frontonearse*, that is, to share stories about their time behind bars at El Frontón and other prisons. Little Víctor and his siblings would sit transfixed listening to these tales of solidarity, near-death experiences, and escape attempts. There was *El Invisible*, the Invisible Man, an inmate at El Sexto who, while the walls were being repainted, was said to have grabbed one of the worker's abandoned caps, brushes, and paint cans, sprinkled paint all over his clothes, and walked right out the front door as if he had been a contract painter. Then there was the story of El Frontón inmates who attempted to swim through the ice-cold waters of the Pacific to the mainland, many of them drowning along the way. Polay and his siblings could recount the stories by heart, but they never tired of listening to them. For him, these were real-life tales of adventure, heroism, and political conviction that rivaled anything Dumas or Cervantes had ever dreamed up.

Polay did read his share of literature. From a young age, his father instilled in him a love of reading. Often the old man would come home with a bundle of books for himself and his kids to devour. Political newspapers like *La Tribuna*, the APRA mouthpiece, were daily sustenance, as were, for comparison, right-wing dailies like *El Comercio* and *La Prensa*.[17] Whereas some families went to church or did Bible study, the Polay Camposes spent their Sunday afternoons sitting around the dining room table reading the literary and political classics. "Everyone select a poem," Polay Risco would say after the table had been cleared. The four kids would scramble over to the bookshelf, which to them looked like the biggest library in the world, and pull down the weighty tome, *Hablemos del amor*, to select their favorite poems to read aloud. Polay had a soft spot for the great Chilean poet Pablo Neruda. When it came to novels, he also gravitated toward the Latin American classics, preferring the grittiness of Peru's own Mario Vargas Llosa to the magical realism of Gabriel García Márquez.[18]

The elder Víctor and Otilia knew that the key to success was a good education. They spent much of their hardware store earnings to enroll their oldest son in El Colegio San Antonio, a Catholic school run by Marianist priests. Polay took well to his studies, earning the admiration and respect of his teachers. The feeling was mutual, and Polay even expressed interest in becoming a priest. "What most appealed to me was the opportunity to do missionary work in the jungle or other far away places like Africa and Asia."[19] The clerics encouraged him and invited him to serve as an altar boy in the church. When Otilia Campos learned of this newest development, she went through the roof. "I didn't raise my son to be a priest!" she scolded Polay. The next thing he knew, his mother had pulled him out of Catholic school and enrolled him in Colegio 2 de Mayo, Callao's largest public high school.

While attending 2 de Mayo, Polay joined the local chapter of the Boy Scouts. There, he earned a reputation as a leader with a strong moral compass and quickly ascended to the position of scout master for the Wolf Patrol. The teenager would spend his Saturdays on the campground or performing community service with the younger scouts. All that running around did a number on his lungs, and he would often spend all day Sunday laid up in bed. This didn't bother him much since, aside from the comradery of Scout life, it got him out of having to work at the family store.[20] The young scouts were like a band of brothers. During the summers, they would walk the beach of Punta Hermosa collecting whatever trash or knickknack they found. When night fell, they would stand around a bonfire, the salty breeze tickling their numbed ears, and take turns sharing which vice they hoped to shed that summer before tossing their knickknacks into the flames so that the items, like their vices, would smolder into ash. Afterward, Polay would lead the younger scouts in song as they crowded around the fire.[21]

After graduating high school at fifteen, typical by Peruvian standards, Polay enrolled in his hometown college, the Universidad de Callao. The freshman left an impression on the APRA leadership, exhibiting his father's charisma and his mother's pluck. He joined the Comando Universitario Aprista, a selection of Aprista student leaders from universities across the capital, and was later elected by his peers as general secretary of the Mechanical Engineering Department. As his sister, Otilia Jr., recalled, Polay had earned a reputation as "Víctor Raúl's protégé," the heir-apparent to the aging party founder.[22] The reality was that Polay had some stiff competition. One of those was Alan García Pérez, the six-foot five-inch, handsome Aprista with a natural gift for public speaking. Haya de la Torre seemed to be grooming both young men, as well as a few others, for leadership in the party. In 1969, the elder statesman solicited Polay, García, and other promising young Apristas to form his Conjunctions Bureau, an elite political task force charged with traveling the country to make contact with the party's base. The bureau reported directly to the old man himself, meeting with him daily in some cases and briefing him on local conditions.[23]

■ The 1960s were a turbulent period the world over. The Vietnam War and Mao's Cultural Revolution in China gave radicals hope for a future outside the confines of U.S. imperialism and toxic capitalism. But events and players closer to home gave young Peruvian radicals their causes célèbres. The triumph of the Cuban Revolution, which had succeeded in overthrowing the right-wing, U.S.-supported dictator Fulgencio Batista in 1959, seemed to offer a blueprint for other Latin Americans living under similar conditions. Che Guevara, the Argentine Marxist who had helped Fidel Castro lead the successful guerrilla campaign against Batista's forces from the Sierra Maestra jungle, had become an international symbol of rebellion, more so after his death in October 1967 while attempting to ignite a revolution in the Bolivian Andes. Already in Nicaragua the Sandinista Front of National Liberation, a guerrilla organization known popularly as the Sandinistas, was attempting, at fits and starts, to replicate the Cuban experience. Some of the MRTA's founders had spent time in Cuba and Nicaragua during this period. The Peruvian rebels conceived of their movement both in relation to and in dialogue with these earlier experiences of the Latin American Cold War. Moreover, they drew inspiration from Che Guevara's *foco* theory of guerrilla warfare, which hypothesized that a small vanguard of dedicated guerrillas could bring about revolutionary change even if the revolutionary conditions, in the classic Marxist sense, had not fully developed.[24]

Peru had its own revolutionary experiment in 1968 after the Peruvian military carried out a coup that put General Juan Velasco Alvarado in power. Unlike most Latin American military dictatorships, the one led by Velasco leaned left, carrying out the most sweeping agrarian reform in Peruvian history and proclaiming its own revolutionary bona fides.[25] Future Tupac Amaristas embraced these top-down social reforms and even joined the revolutionary government to aid in their implementation. Others, such as Víctor Polay, remained vehemently opposed to any military dictatorship, no matter how socially progressive. Polay and other members of the Aprista youth took to the streets in late 1969 to protest what they viewed to be the imperialist policies of the junta. During some of these marches, various factions of the left had it out, with Apristas engaging in fisticuffs with Communists. Polay was arrested during one of these scuffles, his first of many brushes with the law. Fortunately, his mother intervened to get him released.[26]

This legal scare didn't stop the young militant. Three years later, he was arrested while attending another antigovernment protest at the agrarian university, La Molina. This time, no amount of wheeling and dealing could get him free. Polay claimed that his captors had tortured him and his fellow protesters before locking them away in the Lurigancho penitentiary. While doing time, Polay met a group of Trotskyites who had waged a short-lived, disastrous guerrilla war in the highlands of Jauja ten years earlier. His conversations with these men of conviction, such as Jacinto Rentería and Carlos Cerdeña, persuaded him that armed insurrection, even in its failure, could be a meaningful force for political change.[27]

All this political agitation concerned Polay's mother. Otilia Campos had always believed in her son's promise as a political leader. He could even be president one day if he really wanted to. But she didn't want him engaging in political militancy. It was too dangerous, given the current climate.

"I don't want you to end up like your father," she said.[28] And without so much as giving Polay a choice, she sent him packing for Europe. Spending some time abroad would be good for him, she reasoned, at least until the political environment died down back home.

Polay landed in Spain in 1972. He studied sociology at the Universidad Complutense in Madrid and continued to support left-wing politics. By then, the underground movement against dictator Francisco Franco had reached new heights, aided in part by the generalissimo's declining health. The young Peruvian joined clandestine organizations and participated in "flash mob" rallies in Vallecas or Cuatro Caminos, where participants fled in every direction when police arrived.[29]

In Madrid, Polay roomed with Alan García, the tall, slender activist from his days in the Comando Universitario Aprista. The two had never been close, but they found common cause in their past, decided to room together, and eventually developed a friendship. While on summer break from the university in Madrid, the roommates backpacked through Europe looking for odd jobs to sustain them during the holiday. They made quite the pair, García the lanky city-slicker with the dreamy brown eyes, and Polay the scrappy little Boy Scout with his father's slanted eyes. Hitchhiking to Switzerland, García stuck out like a sore thumb as he stuck out his thumb. The sight of the six-foot five-inch Peruvian standing on the side of the road with a suitcase fit for a small army was enough to make even the most sympathetic drivers pass them by. Finally, after going nowhere in a hurry, Polay told his roommate to hide along with his luggage behind some bushes or in a ditch while he hailed a ride. The plan worked, and only after securing passage would Polay then motion for his friend to come out from hiding and jump aboard with his oversized bag. When they finally arrived in Geneva, the two young men found work for a construction company, the lanky García pouring the concrete into the top of the tall drum while Polay pumped it from the bottom.[30] Polay enjoyed his time in Switzerland with García. During his calls home, he would rave about the rich Swiss chocolate, describing it as "the best in the world."[31]

After the summer was over, the young Apristas went their separate ways. García went back to Spain to complete his studies before returning to his native Peru. He continued to rise through the ranks of APRA as the party consolidated its power and prestige in the legal political sphere. Polay went to Paris, where he surrounded himself with other radicals and delved more deeply into leftist politics. In less than ten years, the two friends would become mortal enemies: García would be Peru's first Aprista president, and Polay would lead a small group of rebels sworn to fight his government to the death.

■ In Paris Polay severed all ties with APRA. He had very little money, having already spent much of his hard-earned summer savings. To save money, he would jump subway turnstiles to avoid paying the meager fares. "I'm surprised more people don't do that here," he told his sister about the practice.[32] It was here that Polay's radicalization became complete. The city was a Mecca of radicalism, drawing activists from around the world from every leftist camp. Many prominent Peruvian leftists had also found a home in France, and Polay joined them in Marxist study groups. He had already begun reading works by great socialist thinkers like Marx, Lenin, Trotsky, Che Guevara, and Peru's homegrown thinker José Carlos Mariátegui. These works resonated with him in ways that the Aprista writings never had. Now he found himself associating with militants in the Revolutionary Left Movement, or MIR.

The MIR was one of Latin America's many radical left parties that came of age in the aftermath of the Cuban Revolution. Countries like Chile and Venezuela would also form their own MIR parties, each with their own points of convergence with and divergence from the Peruvian party. Several of the Peruvian MIR's founding members, including Luis De La Puente Uceda and Héctor Cordero, had cut their teeth as Aprista radicals in the 1950s and early 1960s. Dissatisfied with the party's tactical turn toward the center and toward coalition building, these Aprista radicals formed the MIR in 1962. Within two years, the Mirista leadership concluded that the conditions were ripe for a full-fledged guerrilla insurgency. Their decision was hardly unique, as a number of leftist groups, from Colombia's FARC to Argentina's EGP, also decided to embrace armed struggle during the period.[33] In 1965, the Peruvian Miristas launched their armed insurgency.[34] Using Che Guevara's *foco* theory of guerrilla warfare as a template, De La Puente led the insurgency from Cuzco but failed to gain sufficient civilian support or to log any significant military victories. The guerrilla leader was killed in combat on 23 October, shortly after initiating the armed struggle.[35] After that, the insurrection stalled and was swiftly crushed. The MIR continued in various forms after its military defeat, splintering into a number of political factions, each claiming its own legitimacy and with different attitudes toward armed insurrection. Later, some of the same Miristas who had taken up arms under De La Puente in 1965 would join the core group of radicals to form the Tupac Amaru Revolutionary Movement.

Increasingly, Polay saw himself as drawing more inspiration from Miristas like Luis De La Puente Uceda than from Haya de la Torre, whatever his political gifts. In short, Víctor Polay Campos wanted to be a revolutionary, and that was a calling that the party of his parents simply couldn't support.[36] The young radical broke the news to his mother during her visit to Paris in 1975. Otilia Campos was devastated. She returned home to Callao and sat her husband down on the couch to deliver the bad news. The two sat holding hands and sobbing.[37] They had held such high hopes for their oldest son, believing that he, not Alan García, would one day become the leader of the party and the country. Now they had to accept that he would not only shun legal politics but spend the rest of his life in hiding or on the run. If he were lucky, he might grow old behind bars. If not, he wouldn't grow old at all.

Polay accepted the fate that his decision entailed. He could no longer count on his parents' financial support, much less sustain contact with them. It also meant leaving behind his friendships with other Apristas like Alan García, who would never associate with a radical like him. Víctor Polay Campos was all alone in 1975, with no friends, no family, and no place to call home. "I had to start from scratch."[38]

■ After General Juan Velasco Alvarado stepped down from the presidency due to declining health in 1975, the Peruvian military junta took a hard right turn. Francisco Morales Bermúdez, the new head of the regime, scaled back most of the progressive reforms initiated by his predecessor and instituted a period of increased repression against all opposition. It was during this time that Polay joined the MIR and returned to Peru determined to bring down the dictatorship. Back in Lima, he helped set up "self-defense brigades," armed groups of militants pledging to defend workers and shantytown dwellers against state security forces.[39] Three years later, he joined the Unidad Democrática Popular, a militant faction of the MIR intent on employing all forms of oppositional politics—from legal measures to armed conflict— to force radical change.[40] By then, the political climate in Peru had gotten so polarized that the military had no choice but to relent. The junta announced a return to democratic elections and the creation of a constituent assembly, and in May 1980 Peru held its first free elections in a dozen years.

Many Peruvians treated the democratic transition as a victory for the left. Due in large part to its tireless activism in the face of dictatorship, the left had now earned a place at the negotiating table. Even the Peruvian Communist Party fielded candidates for congress. Building on this momentum, a diverse group of academics, activists, and politicians formed Izquierda Unidad, or United Left, a big tent coalition and political party designed to harness the energies of the many competing leftist groups.[41] Others met the democratic transition with skepticism or outright hostility. Many Miristas took a wait-and-see approach to the transition. They embraced elections as a positive step but continued to mobilize workers, peasants, and shantytown dwellers, all the while pushing an agenda of armed insurrection.

Only Shining Path declared all-out war on the state. Originally a splinter of the Peruvian Communist Party, Shining Path launched a guerrilla insurgency on the very eve of the 18 May elections in an event commemorated in party folklore as the Initiation of the Armed Struggle, or ILA (by its Spanish acronym). The Senderistas began with fairly unremarkable operations, burning down municipal buildings in remote highland communities, hurling Molotov cocktails at government buildings in Lima, and occasionally attacking poorly guarded Civil Guard stations.[42] They earned early sympathy in Quechua-speaking villages by holding "popular trials" against supposed enemies of the party. These enemies usually consisted of other peasants who had committed social faux pas, such as adultery or cattle rustling, as well as abusive landlords and town officials. Typically, the Senderistas would bring the accused out to a crowded village square and ask the villagers to decide their fate. During the early months of the insurgency, the accused might endure a flogging or be paraded naked on a donkey before being admonished not to repeat the alleged offense. In some cases they were expelled from the village altogether.[43] These early actions earned

Shining Path a good deal of support in the Andes and within urban leftist circles.

As the war progressed, however, the party's more extreme beliefs and practices came to the surface, giving even the most sympathetic observers pause. In December 1980, for instance, Limeños awoke to the sight of hanging dogs, which had been affixed to lampposts throughout the city with signs attached to them denouncing Chinese leader Deng Xiaoping as a "Son of a Bitch." It was a reference to "running dogs," a term popularized under Mao to refer to unprincipled people who, like dogs blindly chasing anyone with food, would sell out to imperialism. If the symbolism of this political theater hit home with Maoist hard-liners, it struck almost everyone else as gratuitous and macabre. Shining Path also began stepping up the violence against civilians at this time. On Christmas Eve of 1980, the Senderistas killed a landlord named Benigno Medina in the mountains outside Pujas. From that point forward, "popular trials" resulting in death became a staple of Shining Path's guerrilla campaign.[44]

Shining Path's escalation of violence, together with its inflexible stance toward indigenous cultural, political, and economic practices, led to a breakdown in its relationship with the peasantry. By early 1983, some Andean communities began forming their own civilian militias, the *rondas campesinas*, to push the guerrillas out of the countryside.[45] This violent rejection by the very population they sought to liberate provoked an extreme reaction by the Senderistas. The guerrillas responded by massacring refractory villages and butchering any peasant who stood in their way.[46]

The Senderistas believed their actions justified. As far as Abimael Guzmán and company were concerned, the peasants were not civilians but military targets, having joined forces with the counterinsurgency. Few outside the party shared this logic, and many would-be Senderistas saw the guerrillas' campaign against the peasantry as beyond the pale. This, coupled with Guzmán's demands for his followers' total submission and his unwillingness to compromise even with other leftists or members of his own party, led many aspiring revolutionaries to follow a different path.[47]

Víctor Polay hoped to be part of that alternative. In July 1980, just two months into Shining Path's Andean insurrection, Polay joined a group of leftists from the MIR and the Partido Socialista Revolucionario (Revolutionary Socialist Party) at a Unitary Conference. The idea was to put aside ideological differences and infighting long enough to wage an armed revolution of their own. They knew they would have to act fast if they were to have any chance of competing with Shining Path's rapidly expanding insurgency. For the next two years, this small group of revolutionaries, headed by Luis

Varese, Carlos Urrutia, and Hugo Avallaneda, continued to engage in efforts to mobilize their base, all the while seeking to create the necessary conditions to launch a vanguard revolutionary party. Then, in early 1982, two years into the democratically elected government of Fernando Belaúnde Terry, the young militants decided that, as Polay later put it, "all that theorizing would do us no good if we didn't start putting our ideas to practice."[48] The time for revolution had come.

It was a decision that leftists in other Latin American countries had long since reached. The previous two decades had witnessed an unprecedented rise in armed vanguard parties throughout the Americas. In the Southern Cone countries of Argentina, Brazil, Chile, and Uruguay, where large swaths of the population were concentrated in one or more cities, the guerrillas had developed an alternative strategy to Che Guevera's rural *foco* theory. These countries witnessed, beginning in the 1960s and into the 1970s, the onset of urban insurgency, with bombings, kidnappings, and plainclothes shootouts now regular features of Latin America's Cold War insurrectionary tool kit.[49] Using these insurgencies as a model, the MRTA would develop its own urban insurgency from the capital of Lima, where more than a third of the national population was concentrated. In doing so, the Peruvian rebels collaborated directly and in person with Chilean Miristas and Uruguayan Tupamaros.

On 1 March 1982, the Peruvian radicals convened to devise an action plan and to settle on a name for their vanguard party. As Polay and others in the group hailed from the MIR, they believed that this name should prevail. The MIR, after all, was the name of the guerrillas of 1965, in whose name they fought. It was also the name of the guerrillas of Chile, with whom they shared political affinity. Predictably, the Partido Socialista Revolucionario members rejected the idea, pointing out that such a move would effectively relegate their party to a secondary status. During the ensuing debate, a peasant activist named Miguel Meza took the floor. He advocated cutting the metaphorical cord from the older generation of the MIR. "If we really want to be consequential with what we say," Meza said, "if we want to effectively jumpstart the armed struggle, then we need a new generation with its own name. I propose we call ourselves the Tupac Amaru Revolutionary Movement."[50]

Few could argue with that logic. Tupac Amaru II occupied a coveted place in Peruvian collective memory. The eighteenth-century rebel claimed to be a direct heir to Tupac Amaru, the last Inca to be defeated during the Spanish conquest. On 10 November 1780, this second Tupac Amaru, whose real name was José Gabriel Condorcanqui, launched a rebellion of mostly Quechua-speaking Andeans from his native Cuzco. The rebellion spread far and wide, encompassing not just indigenous highlanders but also Peruvian-born whites, blacks, indigenous, and mixed-race people from Cuzco to modern-day Bolivia. Spanish authorities finally captured and executed Tupac Amaru, together with his wife and second-in-command, Micaela Bastidas, in Cuzco's cobblestone plaza in May 1781.[51] In the years following Tupac Amaru's violent rebellion, the word *Tupamaro* became synonymous with bloodthirsty treason. Not until the twentieth century did the name take on a more revolutionary connotation. Most famously, Uruguay's Tupamaro guerrillas reclaimed the insurgent name as a badge of honor.

In Peru, Tupac Amaru had earned a place among Creole patriots like José de San Martín and Simón Bolívar as a founding father. The MIR of De La Puente Uceda invoked Tupac Amaru in their guerrilla campaign of 1965, claiming to be picking up the martyred Andean's banner. Following the 1968 coup that put Juan Velasco Alvarado in power, the colonial *kuraka*, or ethnic leader, became the keystone of the military regime's "great arch" of state formation.[52] Velasco's Revolutionary Government of the Armed Forces, or GRFA, used Tupac Amaru's name and likeness in government propaganda, speeches, memorials, and social reforms in an effort to rebrand the state as his revolutionary heir.[53] Anthropologist Enrique Mayer explains: "Everything revolutionary and nationalistic during the Velasco regime had the name Túpac Amaru. New statues, plazas, and streets were dedicated to him in every city. The Ministry of Agriculture and its agrarian reform posters had Túpac Amaru on them. Expropriated haciendas with aristocratic Spanish names were renamed after him, and even the state-run food distribution system had a stylized stencil symbol of Túpac Amaru with a black-brimmed, tall top hat and a stern face."[54] Tupac Amaru continued to occupy state discourse even after the GRFA took a conservative turn. After installing Francisco Morales Bermúdez as president in 1975, the GRFA rebranded Tupac Amaru as a reformist. Morales Bermúdez's principal legislation, El Plan Tupac Amaru, undid many of Velasco's social welfare programs in the name of the revolutionary icon.

Naming their movement after a 200-year-old rebellion made perfect sense to the MRTA's mostly mestizo rebels. In invoking Tupac Amaru, they could stake a claim to Peru's rich revolutionary past. The present-day Tupac Amaristas would thus be fighting the war begun in 1780, picked up in 1821 during the wars of independence, revisited in the short-lived MIR insurgency of 1965, and illegitimately appropriated by the military state in 1968. This obsession with historical memory was present in the very first meeting of the rebel group, and it would come to define both the insurgency and the state counterinsurgency throughout the coming conflict.

2

Gone in 90 Seconds

The district of Villa El Salvador occupied a unique place in Peruvian history. In 1971, 3,000 Andean migrants had descended on the sand flats to the south of Lima in search of new homes. After a bloody confrontation with police that left one squatter dead, the left-leaning government of Juan Velasco Alvarado drew up a new settlement, divided in a grid pattern by sector, group, and block. That settlement was Villa El Salvador. By the mid-1980s, Villa El Salvador had become Peru's most famous shantytown, known as much for its grassroots organizing and communal works projects as for its inhabitants' consistent poverty. This reputation made the district an ideal target for the MRTA's first armed action.[1]

Police at the Civil Guard station in Villa El Salvador had been on heightened alert since about four o'clock on the afternoon of 22 January 1984. Around that time, unidentified assailants knocked down an electricity tower, thrusting the shantytown on the outskirts of Lima into darkness. Anticipating a nighttime attack, the Civil Guard doubled its forces at the station and sent additional officers to patrol the streets. When night fell, the ten guards at the station took their posts at the windows and on the rooftop. It was pitch black except for the faint flickering of the candles they had placed throughout the building.

The attack came suddenly. At around ten o'clock, as many as fifty rebels from the MRTA's Micaela Bastidas squadron fired on the front door of the station from their positions inside the surrounding houses and behind construction sites. Fidel Tello Leva, the corporal who had been guarding the door, exchanged gunfire with the assailants for several minutes before falling injured with three bullets to the torso. Two bystanders, a man and a woman who happened to be passing by, also took stray bullets. The Micaela Bastidas assailants engaged the police for thirty-five minutes before finally withdrawing.[2]

And so ended the first armed action of the MRTA insurgency. Rebel attacks on police stations mounted in the following months.[3] Like many of the MRTA's early targets, police stations represented more than just a military mark. They were also, in the eyes of Tupac Amaristas, emblems of state abuse against Peru's most vulnerable citizens. According to the MRTA Central Committee, police had abused women, children, peasants, and the urban poor in places like Villa El Salvador. This made them fair game for targeting.[4] Police stations were just one of several symbols of state abuse. In the coming months, Tupac Amaristas also targeted government officials, museums, and the former Inca heartland of Cuzco, all in an effort to establish themselves discursively as the legitimate guardians of the Andean nation.

■ If, according to the MRTA talking points, police had abused the poor physically, the government had done so economically. During the opening months of the insurgency, Tupac Amaristas made a point of targeting government officials whose policies they believed threatened the livelihood of the country's most vulnerable social classes. Economy Minister Carlos Rodríguez Pastor was a fitting example. Despite being born, raised, and educated in Peru, the minister had strong ties with international banks and had spent many years living in the United States. This made him as good as American in the eyes of the rebels. Indeed, many on the left denounced Rodríguez Pastor's neoliberal policies as an antinationalist gift basket to North American bankers that would do nothing but devastate the popular classes.[5]

These criticisms were not entirely unfounded. The neoliberal reforms undertaken by the Belaúnde administration resulted in higher gasoline and food prices as well as a devaluation of the Peruvian sol. In response, the country's largest labor union announced a general workers' strike for 22 March 1984. The week leading up to the strike featured mass marches and demonstrations by the urban poor. Hoping to placate the popular classes,

Rodríguez Pastor stepped down as minister of economy the day before the strike. The damage, however, had already been done. The strike went on as planned, and the MRTA leadership had already resolved to "hit the minister for his antipopular platform."[6]

The hit took place within days of Rodríguez Pastor's resignation. The ex-minister was in his Monterrico residence preparing an economic brief for his successor the night of 26 March when three columns of the MRTA's Luis De La Puente Uceda squadron, named after the Mirista who had died during the doomed 1965 guerrilla insurgency in Cuzco, scurried across the golf course bordering the minister's home toting high-caliber automatic rifles. Eighty meters away, a squad car guarded the front of the minister's house. Sergeant Carlos Sarmiento and his two lieutenants, Pascual Reyes and John Vicuña, had been chatting outside the car when the rebels opened fire, shattering the window and peppering the body of the vehicle. The policemen took cover behind a nearby tree. Reyes promptly unloaded all twenty-five rounds of his machine gun on the rebels. Armed only with a six-shooter, Vicuña did the same. After firing several rounds of his own revolver, Sergeant Sarmiento ordered Vicuña to return to the patrol car and call for backup. Out of ammo, Vicuña lay flat on the ground and crawled toward the car as rebel bullets whistled past him. Once inside the vehicle, the lieutenant hugged the floorboard and nervously radioed central command.

"This is it," Vicuña thought. "This is how we die."

No sooner had Vicuña returned to his cover behind the tree than the Tupac Amaristas redirected their attack toward the main residence, firing thirty-two rounds on the house. Ten minutes after opening fire, the subversives retreated across the green. Sarmiento and his men ran directly into the house, where they found the ex-minister and his family shaken but unharmed.[7] Still, the rebels touted the attack as a success. Killing Rodríguez Pastor had never been the objective. Instead, they had wanted to establish themselves as a kind of economic watchdog of the Peruvian poor. Rodríguez Pastor was, as one MRTA publication put it, a "*gringo* sent by international financial interests to do their bidding in our country." In hitting the house but not the man inside it, the Tupac Amaristas were putting the Belaúnde administration on notice.[8]

■ Not all the MRTA's early actions involved high-stakes shootouts. At various moments throughout the insurgency, the Tupac Amaristas reappropriated key realms of memory that harkened back to Peru's national mythology. In mid-1984, a rebel column raided the museum of Huaura. The museum was ripe with historical symbolism, serving as the very house from which independence leader José de San Martín issued his proclamation of Peruvian independence. The three items the rebels took from the museum were equally significant. The first was San Martín's silver saber. The second was the republic's first coat of arms, the Orden del Sol. The third was the original flag carried by San Martín's Army of the Andes. The subversives broadcast their appropriation of these items in a special supplement to *Venceremos*, their official mouthpiece, displaying half-page images of the confiscated relics. The article included a brief historical synopsis of San Martín's arrival to Lima in September 1820 and establishment of the inaugural flag a month later. Thanks to the heroic work of the Tupac Amaristas, these symbols of national liberation were now back where they belonged: in the hands of *el pueblo*. The article closed with a page-long excerpt from San Martín's proclamation of independence, underscoring the liberator's famous phrase: "Free or dead, but never slaves!"[9] The rebels considered the possession of these items an important victory in their symbolic war against the state. Artifacts in hand, the rebels would, literally and metaphorically, pick up the banner of the nation's independence heroes in their second war of national liberation.

The rebels also sought to appropriate Cuzco itself. Considered the center of the universe by the Incas, the former capital served as the religious, administrative, and military center of the Inca empire, Tawantinsuyo, and remained so until the Spanish conquest. With its rich pre-Columbian history and archaeological marvels, Cuzco was considered a national patrimony. But it was not only Cuzco's preconquest legacy that attracted the rebel leadership. Cuzco also symbolized indigenous resistance and rebellion. It was there that Manco Inca led the first armed resistance to Spanish rule in the mid-sixteenth century. Manco's son, Tupac Amaru, the last Inca of Peru, led a rebellion of his own against the Spaniards, a rebellion that would lead to his 1572 beheading in Cuzco's main square.[10] Two hundred years later, the *kuraka* José Gabriel Condorcanqui would take the name of the fallen Inca before leading, together with his wife Micaela Bastidas, the bloodiest uprising in Peruvian colonial history. Cuzco remained a hotbed of unrest well into the republican period. Peasant land invasions and uprisings in Cuzco received national attention in the 1960s.[11] In choosing to base its rural campaign in Cuzco, then, the MRTA aligned itself metaphorically with the Incas and their rebellious descendants.

This view reflected a common conception of *peruanidad*, or Peruvianness, in which the country's mestizo majority reclaimed a romanticized Inca past while simultaneously ignoring or expressing contempt for Andean peoples and culture.[12] Most mestizo Limeños had never lived in the Andes or had much contact with indigenous highlanders. When indigenous peasants migrated to the coast, they experienced overt discrimination from their mestizo neighbors. It is not surprising that these attitudes of racial superiority carried over to the MRTA, which was made up almost entirely of urban mestizos. Even while harkening back to an idealized Andean past, MRTA rebels made little effort to recruit Andeans, learn indigenous languages or practices, or seek the political input of the highland peasantry. Rather than invest the time in building up a relationship with Andean highlanders, learning their lifeways, and incorporating them fully into the movement, the mestizo rebels hoped to win their hearts and minds by simply setting up a guerrilla *foco* in the Peruvian countryside.

The job of establishing the Cuzco *foco* in late 1984 fell to sociologist Luis Varese. Varese was a longtime leftist who had been active in the Sandinista revolution in 1970s Nicaragua. Upon returning to Peru, he became a functionary of the left-of-center military government of General Juan Velasco Alvarado. When conservative elements within the regime deposed the ailing Velasco in 1975, a disillusioned Varese left the ranks of the government. Varese was among the original founders of the MRTA in 1982, bringing his Revolutionary Socialist Party into the upstart organization and serving on its founding Central Committee.[13] The Central Committee charged Varese with locating a hacienda in Cuzco from which to build a guerrilla camp. Transporting weapons to and from the Paucartambo estate proved a most difficult task, but Varese's column managed to do so before establishing two more guerrilla camps in the zone. It did not take long for Cuzco's authorities to learn of the guerrillas' presence in the city. They promptly dispatched a Civil Guard patrol to raid Varese's camp, arresting one guerrilla and embarking on a manhunt for the others.[14]

When Víctor Polay learned of the Cuzco debacle, he was beside himself. He believed that Varese had jeopardized not just the rural guerrilla operation but the entire insurgency by not keeping a low profile. Reunited in the city, he persuaded the Central Committee to demote Varese to the rank of common combatant.[15] It was a politically savvy move on Polay's part. In addition to sending a clear message of the fate that awaited anyone whose commitment to the revolutionary cause wavered, the move consolidated Polay's power and influence within the MRTA's administrative structure. Although he did not officially outrank his other comrades in the Central Committee, Polay emerged as the group's de facto leader.

Polay's next task was to deal with the fallout from the Cuzco debacle. Although the Civil Guard raid produced only one immediate arrest, more soon followed. In December, police captured nine additional members of the Cuzco column along with an important weapons arsenal.[16] Worse, no one had heard any news regarding the fate of the captured Tupac Amaristas beyond intelligence reports that the rebel organization had been "significantly reduced."[17] Many on the left agreed, making statements such as "The Tupacamarus are finished" and "They won't recover from this." Yet, while Polay and his comrades in the Central Committee acknowledged that the Cuzco raid dealt a "major blow" to the insurgency, they were not yet ready to concede defeat.[18] Polay and his comrades resolved to take "decisive action" to force the state's hand.[19] The action, Polay knew, needed to be bold enough to capture the imagination of the Peruvian people and send a message that the MRTA was alive and well. Who better to deliver this message than the media?

■ The most popular news program in late 1984 was *90 Seconds*. The show had captivated viewers thanks to the investigative journalism of its award-winning reporter Vicky Peláez.[20] Peláez left her Lima home the morning of Saturday, 8 December, to head to the Channel 2 studio. She made a quick stop at her favorite salon to pick up a perfume order.[21] As she left the salon, a young man in blue jeans, sneakers, and a white T-shirt walked up and asked for a moment of her time. When Peláez obliged, he came in close, pressed a revolver to her, and whispered for her to remain calm and follow him. Presuming a robbery, she looked toward her colleagues for help, only to discover that Percy Raborg, her cameraman, had also been apprehended by other subjects. She pleaded with her assailant not to harm her, explaining that she was a journalist with a small child and a modest income. The young man explained that he was a member of the Tupac Amaru Revolutionary Movement and that if she cooperated no one would get hurt. He ordered her into a red car parked in front of a nearby restaurant.[22]

Raborg was already in the car, along with a couple other Tupac Amaristas, when Peláez got in. The rebels handed them newspapers and told them to open them up and bury their heads inside as if they were reading. With their victims' faces covered, the Tupac Amaristas drove away down Benavides Avenue, toward Paseo de la República. After a few minutes, the car came to a halt.[23]

"Vicky," one of the rebels said. "I'm going to hand you some tape to wrap around your partner's eyes."[24]

The sound of her name startled her. This was not a random act, but a kidnapping. After wrapping her and Raborg's eyes in tape, the rebels ordered them to put on sunglasses to avoid suspicion. Peláez's eyes welled up with

Néstor Cerpa Cartolini, 1985 (photo by Carlos Saavedra, *Caretas*, with kind permission)

tears behind the tape. Her legs shook uncontrollably. She thought of her son, who had just had his birthday the day before. Would she ever see him again?

Finally the car stopped, and the rebels led Peláez and Raborg into a guerrilla safe house, where several more Tupac Amaristas were waiting. The insurgents removed the tape from their captives' eyes. All of them were hooded and armed; at least one was a woman. The insurgents instructed the reporters to take a seat before bringing out a television set and setting it on the floor.

"Make yourselves comfortable," one of the rebels instructed, turning on cartoons.

As Peláez and Raborg sat in front of the TV, another Tupac Amarista handed each of them a plastic cup filled with soda. After a while, a heavy-set man walked up to Peláez. That man was Néstor Cerpa.[25]

■ Born in 1953, the year of the birth of Fidel Castro's 26th of July Movement and the death of Josef Stalin, Néstor Cerpa Cartolini came from a humble working family in San Cosme, a shantytown in the hills above Lima. In the mid-1970s, he took a job at the textile factory Cromotex to pay his way through college, joining the factory workers' union. In early 1979, the last year of military rule under General Francisco Morales Bermúdez, Cerpa joined his coworkers in a labor strike to demand a living wage and constitutional guarantees. It was the stocky twenty-five-year-old's first real experience with labor organizing, and it brought production to a halt. On the brink of bankruptcy, the owners fired the striking workers and opened a new factory at a different location. All that remained was for the owners to ship the machines from the old factory to the new. One early February morning, Cerpa and his fellow union workers occupied the old factory. The government responded by sending in police to clear the building on 4 February. When the workers refused to budge, police opened fire, killing labor leader Hemegidio Huertas and five others.[26] Cerpa watched his friend and mentor die before police arrested him and forty-three of his coworkers. The state tried him for inciting a riot and sentenced him to prison at Lurigancho.[27]

When Cerpa got out of prison seven months later, he began looking for a way to avenge his fallen coworkers. The only real option for aspiring revolutionaries in 1980 was Shining Path, the Communist party that had already begun its insurgency in the highlands of Ayacucho. Cerpa had several friends who had already joined the Maoists. He considered joining and consulted some Chilean friends who had been active in their country's MIR. These militants implored him to resist joining such an authoritarian party and instead to consider Víctor Polay's incipient revolutionary movement, a much better fit for a young syndicalist like himself. Cerpa took their advice to heart and joined the MRTA in 1984, when the insurgency was still in its infancy.

Later that year, the brown-skinned Lima cell leader stood unmasked, with his slicked-back hair, stubby goatee, and prescription sunglasses, before the *90 Seconds* reporter Vicky Peláez. What Peláez was going to do now, Cerpa said, was interview his hooded comrades and record a message in which they read their manifesto to the Peruvian people. Peláez would introduce the segment and conduct the interview, and Raborg would film it. The film would then air during the normal programing of *90 Seconds*.

Cerpa led Raborg to a room where the filming equipment had already been set up and asked him to verify that it was adequate for filming. After squaring away the details of the filming, a hooded militant stepped in front of the camera. It was Víctor Polay, although he didn't reveal his true identity at the time. Polay would serve as the group's anonymous spokesperson, addressing the media personally with a black bag over his head. As Raborg's camera rolled, Polay read a statement denouncing the torture of his captured comrades. Once he had finished, the guerrillas sent his videotaped message to the producers of Channel 2 along with a communication explaining that they had two reporters in their custody whose liberty depended on the network airing the videotape. The producers responded promptly, promising to air the manifesto during the regularly scheduled program.[28]

The Tupac Amaristas gave their captives some bread, chicken, and soda to snack on while they awaited the start of the news program. Before the show aired, Channel 2 reported about the developing situation and asked viewers to stay tuned. When the program went live, however, the recording never aired. Having learned of the situation, the Belaúnde administration had blocked the video's airing. Now the fate of the two reporters was in the hands of Polay, Cerpa, and their comrades.[29]

Polay decided not to punish the reporters. Since the news network had met its end of the bargain, he would let them go, but not before they interviewed him. He clarified that the MRTA was completely independent of Shining Path. Unlike the Senderistas, his group fit within Peru's revolutionary tradition: "We feel that the Tupac Amarista insurgency, the guerrilla struggle in our country, is nothing more than the culmination of the 400 year struggle of our people against domestic and foreign oppressors. . . . Our conception and perspective feed off the very entrails of our history."[30]

Polay went on to discuss the Tupac Amaristas' mission to battle hunger and misery and to wrest power away from the dominant classes that historically oppressed the people. He identified his movement with that of revolutionaries past who fought against Spanish oppression in Peru—revolutionaries like Manco Inca, Juan Santos Atahualpa, Micaela Bastidas, Simón Bolívar, and, of course, Tupac Amaru. But the MRTA also saw its roots in more modern insurgencies, such as the Aprista uprisings of 1932 and 1948 and the more recent guerrilla campaign of the MIR.[31] True to his word, Polay let the reporters go after the interview. Before daylight the following morning, the rebels left Peláez and Raborg, safe and unharmed, near Callao's Jorge Chávez International Airport, where they were later picked up by local police to be returned to their families.[32]

■ The kidnapping of Vicky Peláez taught the Tupac Amaristas the important role that public relations could play in a modern insurgency. All major newspapers covered the incident, and Polay's interview dominated the television news cycle for the next forty-eight hours. Vicky Peláez gave interview after interview retelling the story of her capture and, equally important, her safe release. The papers asked what was on everybody's mind: Who were these rebels, and what were they fighting for? In doing so, these outlets put the Tupac Amaristas on the political map. If most Peruvians had never heard of the MRTA before this, they now knew who the rebels were and what they stood for. And what they stood for was justice for the Peruvian people. "With Masses and Arms," went the rebel slogan, "We Will Prevail!" Just because they had weapons, however, didn't mean they would always use them. As the Peláez kidnapping demonstrated, the rebels could capture the public imagination through spectacular actions that inflicted minimal or no physical harm on civilians or police forces. In this modern war over the very meaning of *peruanidad*, pen and lens would be their greatest weapons of all. From that point forward, the MRTA made capturing media attention—through any means necessary—a priority in the insurgency.

This media attention enabled the Tupac Amaristas to highlight their differences with Shining Path. If the Senderistas took their ideological cues from Mao's China, the MRTA offered Peruvians a more homegrown style of insurgency. The symbols that the Tupac Amaristas appropriated tied them to a pantheon of heroes from the Andean nation's revolutionary tradition. By targeting police and government officials, the Tupac Amaristas presented themselves as ethnic guardians, protectors of Peru's downtrodden masses. This carefully crafted narrative gave aspiring revolutionaries a clear choice. If Shining Path was violent, uncompromising, and foreign, the MRTA would be humane, just, and Peruvian.

At least that was the plan in the beginning. By the end of the war, the Tupac Amaristas would succumb to a campaign of car bombs, hostage taking, civilian assassinations, and guerrilla warfare that would render them indistinguishable from Shining Path in popular opinion. For the time being, however, the MRTA's messaging payed off, and many young radicals who might otherwise have gravitated toward the Maoists wound up joining ranks with the MRTA. Among those would-be Senderistas was a young woman from Comas named Lucero Cumpa.

3

La Cumpa

The U.S. military armed, trained, and abetted Latin America's armed forces throughout the Cold War. Many of the scorched-earth counterinsurgency campaigns that Latin American militaries carried out in the mid-1980s came straight out of Fort Bragg, North Carolina, and Fort Benning, Georgia, as well as the School of the Americas in the Panama Canal Zone. It wasn't uncommon for U.S. military personnel to be seen in Latin America, training and working alongside some of the most ruthless counterinsurgency commanders in the region. Given this high level of collaboration between U.S. and Latin American militaries, it stands to reason that the Tupac Amaristas would come to resent the U.S. military top brass. In the mid-1980s there was one American colonel who provoked the ire of the MRTA more than any other. His name was Colonel Sanders.

Just after 8:00 P.M. on 20 May 1985, a column of Tupac Amaristas stormed into the Kentucky Fried Chicken (KFC) on Miraflores's Arequipa Avenue. Submachine guns raised, the rebels ordered the customers to lie on the floor. After dumping gasoline all around the dining area, they ordered the civilians to get up slowly and exit the building without making a sound. The Tupac Amaristas then set fire to the dining area and left as quickly as they had arrived. As the restaurant went up in flames, the cooks, who had been hiding in the kitchen during the assault, had no choice but to crawl out the back windows to freedom.[1]

The attack on the Miraflores KFC was one of seven simultaneous attacks on KFC fast-food chains in the capital that evening. These assaults made up part of the MRTA's early campaign to target symbols of American imperialism. The Tupac Amaristas saw the United States as the most recent and destructive empire in a 400-year history of colonialism, first under the Spanish, then the British, and now the Americans. This legacy of colonialism, movement leaders insisted, was responsible for the state of misery, poverty, and oppression under which the Peruvian people historically lived. Indeed, rebels considered Yankee imperialism "the greatest enemy of our people."[2] Who better symbolized this legacy of imperialism than the Colonel? As with American foreign policy itself, KFC had tentacles in over eighty countries worldwide. The fact that President Belaúnde's nephew owned three of the fried chicken restaurants only reinforced the perception of untoward association between the Peruvian government and U.S. capital.[3]

KFC was just one of several symbols of U.S. imperialism that landed in the rebel crosshairs. On 11 April 1985, after attacking the U.S. Embassy dispatch on Alfonso Ugarte Avenue, the guerrillas went on to attack a Diners Club, the Summer Institute of Linguistics International, the ITT (International Telephone & Telegraph) building, and the offices of Citibank and Kodak. As far as the rebels were concerned, these businesses represented the tangled web of U.S. military and economic intervention. "These actions," the MRTA declared in a related communiqué, "express our people's rejection of the imperialist presence in our country, as well as our aversion to the provocative and war-mongering politics of the Reagan administration." For the MRTA, simply to denounce imperialism was not enough. Rather, the guerrillas felt it necessary "to combat imperialism in practice, in actions."[4]

Within Tupac Amarista historical memory, the resistance to imperialism was rooted in an idealized indigenous past. It began with the Spanish conquest of 1532, when foreigners first colonized the Incas. Manco Inca had been the puppet ruler of the Incas following the Spanish conquest in the early sixteenth century. After leading an aborted siege of Cuzco, Manco Inca retreated to the jungles of Vilcabamba, where he held court for seven years before a group of trusted Spaniards betrayed and killed him.[5] Two hundred years later, an Andean man who went by the name of Juan Santos Atahualpa arrived in the lowland jungles of Tarma and Jauja professing to be the descendant of Inca rulers. Building up an army of mostly Asháninka natives, Juan Santos Atahualpa led a violent uprising that shook the colonial order. Although the uprising succeeded in expelling Spanish missionaries and settlers from the region for centuries to come, it failed to spread beyond the region, and Juan Santos was believed to have died sometime after. The

.

Tupac Amaristas saw their revolutionary namesake not just as heir to this tradition of indigenous rebellion but also as the forefather to Latin American independence. "Tupac Amaru," read one of the MRTA's first public manifestos, "was the great precursor who with arms fought for our independence which was achieved years later by [Simón] Bolívar, [José de] San Martín and [José] Martí."[6] Seen in this way, the mestizo guerrillas conceived of their insurgency as the latest manifestation of a centuries-long indigenous struggle against colonialism. "We believe that we are fighting for a second and definitive independence," a hooded Tupac Amarista told the media in 1985. "Yesterday [the struggle] was [against] Spanish colonialism. Today it is against North American imperialism. The MRTA is no more than the continuation of that struggle."[7] It didn't matter that few Andeans actually joined the insurgency, much less led it. Evidently, the mestizo rebels did not see that their selective appropriation of indigenous history and symbols was itself a form of colonialism.

If the United States was the enemy, anyone who aligned with the Americans was necessarily unpatriotic. At the top of the MRTA's list of imperialist sellouts was President Belaúnde and his cabinet. One of the MRTA's first public manifestos, published in 1984, called out President Belaúnde for failing to stand up to the gringos. "On bended knee [the president] has accepted the mandates of North American imperialism, bringing shame to a country by appointing lackeys like [Manuel] Ulloa and [Carlos] Rodríguez Pastor [as ministers of economy]." Since Belaúnde took office in 1980, read the manifesto, "the word Country or Peru has become a blasphemy in the mouth of the viceroy [Belaúnde] and his royal visitors [cabinet]."[8]

The problem with Belaúnde's cabinet, the MRTA asserted, was that it was more American than Peruvian. Yes, these ministers were Peruvian, but, as Víctor Polay told reporters, "they think in North American, they speak in North American, they raise their children in the United States, they study in the United States, they live their lives in the United States."[9] Take the energy minister, Pedro Pablo Kuczynski. In 2016, Kuczynski would become the oldest president of Peru before resigning two years later amid a cloud of scandal. The controversy that brought down the man later known by his acronym, PPK, involved bribery, quid pro quo arrangements, and the acceptance of illegal advisory fees from a foreign company. None of this would have come as a surprise to Polay, who in 1985 already had PPK pegged as an imperialist sellout. In "exonerating" $600 million of "imperialist enterprises" in Peru, Polay said, "the minister had committed a monstrous crime . . . greater than any crime committed by any Peruvian in our country, because those 600 million dollars represent many children who will die.

They represent many jobs, many homes and a better future in this country. It's with this crime in mind that we can't permit them to continue massacring our people."[10] The juxtaposition of the energy minister and the Tupac Amaristas could not have been clearer. Despite PPK's nationality and his position as a top government official, the Tupac Amaristas labeled him as an ethnic outsider. This differed greatly from the Tupac Amaristas, who self-identified with "our country" and "our people."

■ Lucero Cumpa was a getaway driver for the KFC attacks of 20 May 1984.[11] A romantic might conclude that Cumpa was destined to be a Tupac Amarista. María Lucero Cumpa Miranda was born on 10 November 1964, November being the month that Tupac Amaru II initiated his rebellion against the Spanish crown, and she grew up on a street in Comas named after the eighteenth-century rebel. Even her name had a special meaning. *Cumpa*, her surname, was the word that modern-day Tupac Amaristas used to refer to one another, a rebel shorthand for "comrade."

José Cumpa Carrillo, Lucero's father, was a doctor who delivered her at birth. A member of the Christian People's Party, a center-right political party based on the principles of Christian Democracy, José was socially and politically conservative. María Miranda Mercado, Lucero's mother, was ten years older than José and over forty when she bore him his first child. Pregnancy was difficult for María, and she almost died during childbirth. Her health recovered, but her relationship with José never did. The two separated when Lucero was just two years old.[12]

María raised her daughters to be good Christians who looked out for the welfare of others. "Everything she had she shared," Cumpa recalled. When Cumpa was a girl, her mother would take in homeless kids from the street, giving them food and shelter for as long as it took them to get back on their feet. As she didn't have much, this often meant María and her daughters sacrificing their own food. "If there's enough food for three," María would tell her daughters, "there's enough for four. And if there's enough for four, there's enough for five."

Cumpa didn't realize just how bad her family had it until she saw the way others lived. As a child, she would walk barefoot to her aunt's house with Príncipe, her spotted white lab, nipping at her heels. Her aunt had married a man of means and lived in comfort. The couple had it all: a big house, a big car, fancy toys for the kids, and servants to wait on them. Cumpa, who couldn't even afford shoes, didn't understand why some people enjoyed this kind of privilege while others went hungry. María believed her daughters could improve their conditions by staying in school. This came naturally to Cumpa, who attended Comas's Colegio Jesús Nazareno and got stellar grades, breaking down in tears if she ever got less than a perfect score.

Her introduction to politics came at a young age. During her visits with her father, he would prepare political slide shows in the hopes of swaying her toward his more centrist political position. Cumpa, who had always had the intellectual curiosity of an alley cat, would listen intently. Rather than jump into a political party as some youth did, Cumpa decided to learn as much as she could about all perspectives before making a decision. At thirteen, she moved with her mother and sister to La Victoria, another poor district, to live with her half-brothers. Her brothers were leftists from the Patria Roja, or Red Fatherland, political party. Whenever they weren't around, she would sneak into their rooms and read their leftist magazines. "I would just take the magazines—they didn't give them to me. They were none the wiser," she said. Other times, she would tag along with her older sister, who had been taking classes on Marxism at the University of San Martín de Porres. When her sister transferred to the Universidad Nacional Mayor de San Marcos, Peru's flagship public university and one renowned for the left-wing views and activism of its faculty and students, Cumpa would sit in on the lectures to learn new perspectives.

By the time she was fifteen, Cumpa, too, identified as a leftist. She read Darwin's *On the Origin of Species*, and began to question her family's religious conventions. Once she tried to get a rise out of her aunts by challenging the origin story of Adam and Eve. According to science, she told them, all humans had descended from monkeys.

"Mary!" the scandalized aunts cried. "What kind of nonsense are you filling your child's brain with?"

Despite being a devout Christian herself, María didn't seem to mind her daughter's iconoclasm.

"You may not go to mass," she told Cumpa one day, "but you are more Christian than your aunts."

Having her mother's full-fledged support was incredibly helpful. When she applied for college at fifteen, no one in her family thought she had a chance.

"She's not getting in," her cousins prognosticated behind her back, loud enough for her to hear. "Who's she kidding?"

Only her mother expressed confidence. She would get in, María assured her, and she would place first. And that's exactly what she did.[13]

Cumpa was sixteen when she enrolled in the National University of Engineering, La UNI, in 1981. Like many universities in Lima in the early 1980s, La UNI was a hotbed of leftist student activism. She began exploring her options to see which group would be the best fit. One day, an old high school friend invited her to attend a lecture on women's issues at Lima's César Vallejo University. Cumpa agreed, but when she got there, she quickly realized that she had been tricked into attending a Shining Path meeting.

"I came here to listen to a talk," she blurted out, interrupting the speakers. "This is a party meeting!"

With that, Cumpa stood and left the classroom. It wasn't that she didn't share the speakers' vision of social justice or their dreams for creating a better society. When Shining Path launched its insurgency in 1980, Cumpa, still a high school student, didn't necessarily object.

"Maybe they're onto something," she mused. She even believed some of the Senderistas were "heroic youths."[14]

It didn't take long for her to change her mind.

"What's China got to do with the Peruvian revolution?" she wondered. Better yet, "What does an expression as macabre as a dead dog hanging from a post have to do with Peru's liberation?"[15]

It all struck her as foreign and strange. "Everything [with Shining Path] was imported from abroad, from Maoism and [outside] revolutions," she recalled. "They didn't look at the Peruvian reality, assimilate to the characteristics of our own idiosyncrasies, our own culture, our own social classes, our own way of life and living."[16] She believed that a homegrown revolution should have a Latin flavor, like the one led by Che Guevara and Fidel Castro in Cuba more than two decades prior. Shining Path clearly wasn't that. She would continue to explore her options.

She began looking for other students who sought a more Latin American rebellion—one that honored the tradition of other Latin American revolutionaries like Simón Bolívar and Che Guevara. Like many Latin American students at the time, Cumpa became enamored with Che's *Reminiscences of the Cuban Revolution* and the notion of a grassroots guerrilla insurgency. She began associating with other students who shared this conviction.

One of those students was Fernando Valladares. Cumpa had first met Valladares in a college-prep class at César Vallejo academy in 1980, before she entered La UNI. They only spoke once, when Valladares asked Cumpa if he could borrow a copy of *Caballo Rojo*, a magazine of the leftist newspaper *El Diario Marka*. At the time, Cumpa didn't even know Valladares's name, but he already had two things going for him: he was handsome, and he was a leftist. Cumpa couldn't help but notice, however, that the young man always wore the same two outfits, both of them featuring a light jacket and pants.[17] When Cumpa entered La UNI a year later, there was Valladares, wearing the same two simple outfits. The two engineering majors ended up taking some of the same classes. Cumpa was working on a written assignment in class one day when she felt a light tap on her shoulder.

"Lucero," Valladares asked, "can I borrow your eraser?"

Lucero tried her best to hide her surprise as she handed over the eraser. "He knows my name!"[18]

After that, Cumpa put on the charm offensive. She became increasingly flirtatious toward the fashion-blind boy from Ancash hoping to crack his shell of shyness, but he never let on that he was interested. After several weeks, she finally got her signal. It wasn't the most feminist come-on—in fact, it was downright sexist—but Cumpa wasn't exactly a feminist. Valladares had been sitting with a group of young men when she walked by, hoping to catch his eye. Evidently she did, because he let out an unexpected catcall whistle.

"Who did that?" Cumpa barked, her scowl transforming into a smile. "I'd like to thank him!"[19]

This flirtation soon developed into romance. It helped that Valladares was also a militant intent on changing the world. In 1983, he and Cumpa joined Juventud Rebelde (Rebel Youth), a militant group of the MIR. The group was dominated by men, but Cumpa, the only woman in her chemical engineering major, was used to being outnumbered. As she later explained, the men treated her "almost" like an equal. They appreciated her input and her commitment to the cause, but they also adopted a paternalistic attitude. One of the problems had less to do with the men's behavior than it did with that of Peruvian patriarchy more broadly. Whereas most young men and even teenage boys could come and go from their homes as they pleased, university-aged women had to abide by strict curfews and always let their parents know their whereabouts. This made it hard for women like Cumpa to participate in militant activities that were designed to be off the grid in the first place, and militant men were not sympathetic.

"That's when I entered my existential crisis," Cumpa recalled. She had to reevaluate her priorities. Her grades had been suffering since she began her militancy, and now her family was breathing down her neck. Her choice was either to abandon the cause and return to a sense of normalcy at home and in her studies or to jump in with both feet and never look back. She chose the latter. "If I die, I die, and that's that," she told herself. The hardest part was "breaking the physical lasso" connecting her to her family. She believed this decision to be harder for women than for men. "Women," she explained, "are inclined to give life, and now we had to be willing to take it away."

Cumpa's "existential crisis" was typical for MRTA women. Unlike the men, women had to contend with a patriarchal, Catholic family structure that rendered mobility difficult. Gladys, a Lima college student who joined the MRTA in 1986, faced a similar situation. Like Cumpa, Gladys had always questioned authority. "I have a rebellious streak," she admitted years later. "I don't like when people try to tell me what to do." That inclination toward rebellion led her to the MRTA. Gladys started as a low-level militant, painting party slogans on walls at night while still attending classes by day. However, as she soon discovered, even this minimal level of activity was unsustainable due to her overbearing home life. "I would come home at midnight, and my mom would always pick a fight, telling me that this isn't a hotel: 'This is a home, not a hotel!' And I would just go straight to bed."[20] Things got worse for Gladys when she became romantically involved with a member of the MRTA underground. "My mother had always instilled in me that the first man [I slept with] in my life would be my eternal partner until death do us part." Now, she felt pressure to move in with the man who took her virginity, even if she wasn't ready to become a full-time rebel. "All these things led me to determine, 'I'm leaving, I'm leaving.' . . . I left home. I left the university. Everything. I just left."[21] Gladys joined her partner in the rebel underground and became a clandestine Tupac Amarista until her 1990 arrest.

Lucero Cumpa took a similar path. She started off as a low-level militant in the MIR Rebel Youth, painting walls with revolutionary graffiti. VVV— "Vive, Vuelve, y Vencerá"—was the slogan of the day, heralding that Tupac Amaru II "Lives, Returns, and Will Prevail!" By now, the MRTA was in its opening throes and emerging as an autonomous movement. Valladares, her partner, would eventually join the young movement and take on a leadership role in the Lima underground and encourage Cumpa to join as well.

When her mother, who generally supported her intellectual and political independence, began to restrict her mobility, Cumpa did what many radical women did at the time: she lied. As part of her initiation into the movement, she had to attend a mandatory crash course in political and military militancy in 1984. To get out of the house, she made up a story that she hoped her mother would believe.

"I'm going on a field trip with the university. I'll be back on Sunday."

"Okay," María replied.

The course was a combination of military and ideological training on the outskirts of Lima. During Cumpa's first lesson, the instructor, a Chilean Mirista, handed out guns so that the students could know how to hold them. It was the first time Cumpa had held a gun. She held it in her hand, gently eased her hand across the trigger, and—

Bang!

The pistol misfired, narrowly missing the instructor as he walked by. Not only did she nearly kill the Chilean, but the shot could have ruined the whole operation. All it would have taken was a phone call from one of the neighbors for police to come and arrest the whole class. As penance, she had to perform sentry duty and read Che Guevara's writing about the importance of properly handling munitions.

The cadets also had to perform simulations of combat situations. One of the drills involved disarming police officers without bloodshed. For this, Cumpa played the role of the police officer while another student acted as the attacking guerrilla whose objective was to disarm her. Before the drill, Cumpa strapped one of her two guns to her leg. Before she could put the other gun on her other leg, the instructor leaned in and told her to put it inside her waistband, betting that the assailant wouldn't dare look for it there. Cumpa did as told. Sure enough, when the drill began, the assailant grappled with Cumpa, removing the first gun from her leg but failing to locate the second. He was about to pin Cumpa to the ground when she removed the weapon from her waistband, flipping around and forcing him to tap out. Now it was Cumpa's turn to be the attacker. She quickly disarmed her opponent, even after he had stuck one of the guns very deep inside his own waistband. Annoyed, the comrade demanded a do-over, no doubt embarrassed that he had twice been bested by a woman. The instructor would have none of it, telling the cadet that he lost fair and square.

At the conclusion of the training, Valladares convinced Cumpa to stay behind one more night with him. When she returned home, her mother was notably worried and more than a little suspicious. She had already called Cumpa's classmates and professors, who said that they weren't aware of any field trips. María was waiting in the doorway when Cumpa arrived a day late.

"You weren't on a field trip," María said.

Cumpa came clean, causing a familial scandal complete with tears and screams. Her brothers, themselves leftists, were livid. They blamed Valladares for indoctrinating their little sister.

"I'm turning him in!" one threatened, marching toward the front door.

María stood in the doorway, spreading her arms and legs.

"Stand down," she ordered. "You'll do no such thing! She is my daughter. If anyone has a right to turn her in, it's me—and I'm not going to do it!"[22]

That ended the discussion. Although Cumpa's brothers would keep a close watch on her from that point on, they couldn't do anything to stop her. After that, Cumpa began stepping up her militancy.

On 23 October 1984, the anniversary of Mirista guerrilla Luis De La Puente Uceda's death, Cumpa joined a rally in Lima's 2 de Mayo plaza. During the rally, some of the protesters clashed with police, hurling rocks at the officers. Afterward, she and a small group of militants volunteered to paint the slogan "With Masses and Arms" along the walls of the busy Wilson Avenue. She was mid-brushstroke when one of her fellow militants alerted her that the police were coming. She dropped everything and ran, but the officers caught up to her. One of them, still agitated after the confrontation with students earlier in the plaza, took out his aggression on Cumpa and her comrades. "The guy was the devil," she recalled, describing the grisly way he beat her over the head and body with his baton. After she submitted, the officer pulled her by the hair into a squad truck. As the police transported her and her comrades to the Alfonso Ugarte precinct, they continued to beat them relentlessly. "All I could do was protest."[23]

By the time she got to the station, Cumpa could already feel the lumps forming on her head; her torso was beginning to bruise. As part of her training, she had learned what could await women rebels if captured, but nothing could prepare her for what she was about to face. That night, "the devil" isolated the blindfolded and handcuffed nineteen-year-old in her own cell and gang-raped her with his colleagues. According to Cumpa, policemen continued the torture throughout the night, appearing every so often to try to beat a confession out of her.[24]

"Talk, dammit!" one screamed. "What group do you belong to?" When Cumpa didn't answer, he decided to up the ante, pressing his gun to her head and pulling the trigger. The gun fired with a loud bang, and Cumpa thought she was done for. "I can't explain it," she told the Truth Commission some twenty years later: "That feeling of certain death."[25]

It was a psychological game. The officer had loaded the gun with blanks to intimidate her. Afterward, he left her alone in the cell. As she lay there blindfolded and bound, she could hear the sobs of her comrades in the nearby holding cells. It was after midnight when the policemen moved her into another police car. When she arrived at the new station, they led her into a locker room and stripped her of her clothes and her dignity. She stood there shaking, trying her best to count the number of men in the darkness of her blindfold while the drops from the leaky showerhead drizzled on her head. It seemed like there might have been eight.

"We're going to fuck you up," one of them taunted. Cumpa trembled, preparing for the worst.

After several tense moments, a voice called out to the policemen, bringing the commotion to a halt. The man appeared to be a superior officer. He walked up to Cumpa.

"Get dressed," he ordered.

Cumpa tried her best to get her clothes back on in the darkness. Afterward, the officer led her out of the locker room and into his office. He had her sit down and removed her blindfold. "He was an elderly man, from the countryside. He didn't say a word, but I felt like he was my protector." The man just sat there, not saying a word. Moments later, a lieutenant walked up and smacked Cumpa across the face.

"Fucking terrorist! Your kind are nothing but a bunch of Ayacuchan pariahs," said the lieutenant, referring to the cradle of the Shining Path insurgency. "I hope you die, dammit!"

Before the lieutenant could continue, the office telephone rang. The officer had instructions to transfer the suspect to DINCOTE, the famed counterterrorism police headquarters. "Saved by the bell," Cumpa remembered.[26]

Once she was in DINCOTE custody, the torture stopped. Fortunately, one of Cumpa's neighbors who lived across the street from her mother was a commander in the Peruvian Investigative Police (PIP). The neighbor owed his life to Cumpa's mother. Years earlier, he had been one of the street youths whom María had taken under her care. It was thanks to María's charity that he now had a steady job and a roof over his head. More than a neighbor, he was like family, and he thought of Cumpa as a niece.

When the neighbor learned of her arrest, he marched over to the police station and gave the officers a good dressing-down.

"My niece is innocent!" he yelled, demanding to see her.

When he finally got a moment alone with his young neighbor, he pulled her close and lowered his voice.

"I don't care if they beat the shit out of you. You are to tell them nothing. Nothing! Do you understand?"

The teenager stood there incredulously. "Okay."

Cumpa heeded her neighbor's advice, and after nearly a month in custody the police finally let her go.

It was at that point that Cumpa decided to come clean with her mother. She was going to be up to things that María best not know about.

"Some nights I might not come home until 2 in the morning," she said.

After that, her mother grew gravely ill. Her brothers blamed María's frail condition on Cumpa. She had caused her mother all this pain and anguish. It was all her fault. Maybe they were right.

Cumpa would cry herself to sleep at night, when María wasn't looking. She loved her mother and hated to see her suffer, but she also believed that she was fighting for something much bigger than her family. After three weeks of agony, she finally made up her mind.

"Mom," she said, "I can't go on like this."

Her mother, still bedridden, simply replied, "I know." With that, María gave her daughter her implicit blessing. Cumpa shouldn't worry about her. She should do what she had to do. "That was when I learned what love is," Cumpa said of the encounter.

After graduating from the training school, Cumpa left home and dedicated herself full time to rebel activities. She married Valladares, her cell leader, and carried out local actions in the city, like the assault on KFC. Often she served as the getaway driver while her fellow Tupac Amaristas attacked targets.[27]

Metaphorically speaking, men were the ones in the driver's seat. While the MRTA publicly advocated women's empowerment and gender equality, women at all ranks of the organization experienced a quotidian culture of paternalism, patriarchy, and misogyny in which men sought to exert physical and symbolic control over women's bodies. Yet, as quotidian as these attempts to control and contain were, so too were women's efforts to contest, challenge, and break through these aggressions. For women like Lucero Cumpa, daily battles for dignity and respect were as common as their military battles. Even after she took control of her own column, made up of four men and one other woman, Cumpa found it difficult to earn the respect of Tupac Amarista men. Her first action as column leader in 1985 exposed this gendered double standard. Armed with submachine guns, Cumpa and her comrades stormed the market in her home district of Comas, distributing revolutionary leaflets and playing a prerecorded tape cassette about the MRTA insurgency on the loudspeakers before fleeing the scene. Sitting in the yard of a Chorrillos prison more than thirty years later, Cumpa recalled the shock of Fernando Valladares, her cell leader and husband, when she returned from the action.

"So? How did it go?" Valladares asked in a tone anticipating bad news.

"Good," Cumpa said.

"Good? Nothing happened?"

"No, nothing," Cumpa replied, shrugging it off.

According to Cumpa, however, Valladares refused to believe that she had pulled off the action without a hitch. It was not until he read about the attack in the newspaper the following morning that he finally conceded the point. Cumpa attributed her husband's unwillingness to accept her report of success to his gender bias. Even though she was his wife, he didn't think her capable of leading a rebel column. Yet, as Cumpa recalled, he never questioned his men's stories of military success.[28]

Cumpa recalled another occasion in which her husband exhibited his gendered assumptions. As she prepared to lead another incursion in the capital, Valladares handed Chino, her subordinate, two rifles.

"Why does he get two and I only get one?" Cumpa asked.

"Because you're a woman," Valladares said, explaining that Cumpa was too weak and fragile to carry two rifles into battle.

Cumpa insisted that Valladares hand her two rifles so that she could demonstrate the ease with which she carried them. It was only after performing this demonstration that he relented, handing her Chino's second weapon.[29] This constant, daily struggle for women rebels to prove that they belonged, that they were just as capable as men in battle, became part of women's insurgent experience. These women were fighting for more than just Peru's liberation. They were also pushing a progressive social agenda that subverted the patriarchal order. Confronting sexism within the insurgency was a way for them to challenge the MRTA to be more inclusive and equitable as well.[30]

4

Capture the Flag

His instructions were clear. *La República* journalist Mario Campos was to stand outside a predetermined café at 9:00 A.M. on 16 August 1985 holding the latest edition of the weekly political magazine *Caretas*. Campos arrived early so as not to leave anything to chance. At nine o'clock sharp, a thin young woman walked up and smiled.

"Mario Campos?"

Campos affirmed. The woman told him to act naturally and follow her into a nearby vehicle. Once inside, she handed him a pair of black sunglasses.

"Put on these glasses," she instructed, "and keep your head down."

Campos obeyed. The lenses had been blacked out so that he couldn't see anything. After the car pulled away, his reporter's instincts kicked in, and he began asking questions about what was going to happen to him. He received no reply. Moments later the car stopped, and two other subjects entered and sat beside him.

"They're your colleagues," the young woman explained.

This set Campos's mind at ease. Later, he would learn that the passengers who joined him on that blind ride were from United Press International and Reuters. The three passengers sat in silence as the car zigzagged through the bustling city. Finally the car came to a halt, and their escort allowed them to remove their shades. Looking around, Campos confirmed that he was in a garage, surrounded by a group of armed rebels in olive green hoods. Embroidered in bold, just above the eyeholes, were the letters M.R.T.A. The Tupac Amaristas led the reporters to a room with yellow walls and a high ceiling and instructed them to take their seats in a row of chairs. Campos and his colleagues waited for two hours as more reporters, each one hand-picked by the guerrillas, filed into the room.

Posters of three revolutionary heroes—Ernesto "Che" Guevara, José Carlos Mariátegui, and Luis De La Puente Uceda—hung on one of the walls. Next to these, the Tupac Amaristas had mounted two flags. The first was the battle flag of independence hero José de San Martín, the very one they had stolen from a museum in Huaura the previous year. The second was the red and white flag of the MRTA bearing Tupac Amaru's likeness. The Tupac Amaristas had positioned a small, three-person table in front of the flags. There, under the symbols of Latin American and Peruvian revolution, they would hold their first press conference.

It was nearly noon when Víctor Polay and a small entourage emerged from another room dressed in baggy olive green jumpsuits. The pointed corners of the bags they wore over their heads gave them the look of real-life Batmen. Polay took his seat at the center of the conference table, two rebels on either side. Several other hooded Tupac Amaristas stood beside the table, their gloved hands positioning their submachine guns across their torsos like a presidential sash. That at least one of the armed guards was a woman speaks to the guerrillas' understanding of the optics. They wanted to show the world that the MRTA empowered women, even though in reality very few women carried out armed actions at this stage in the insurgency.[1]

After all the players were in place, Polay, still anonymous under his hood, proposed a truce with the newly elected president, Alan García. The Aprista leader, Polay said, had vowed to fight for Peru's popular classes, against imperialism, and in defense of democracy. In electing García to the presidency, Peruvians had demanded this of their government.[2] "We believed that APRA had triumphed due to the will of the people," Polay later explained, "so out of respect for that popular mandate, which was expressed in the voting booth, we declared a cease-fire."[3] But the rebel leader made it clear that this was not an unconditional rapprochement. If García failed to live up to his populist campaign promises, the MRTA would hold him accountable and resume military actions against the government. In the meantime, the group would continue to wage war on nonstate actors and members of the previous administration.[4]

In refusing to demilitarize completely, the Tupac Amaristas missed their first real opportunity to put their social democratic discourse into practice. Polay's statement acknowledged that the Peruvian people, now five years into a bloody civil war, had used the ballot box to seek a more populist, social-justice-oriented democracy. Yet rather than interpret the election results as a sign of a war-weary people's rejection of armed insurgency, the guerrilla leadership doubled down on political violence. For a movement so intent on distinguishing itself from the more violent and authoritarian Shining Path, the MRTA's decision not to disarm in late 1985 betrayed an unwillingness to embrace the democratic process at a time when the majority of Peruvians were resting their hopes in it.

Little did the president-elect know that the man behind the mask was his former college roommate. In fact, when the Peruvian Investigative Police reported on rebel activities the following year, Polay wasn't even listed as one of the MRTA's ten most important leaders.[5] There was a long-standing rumor that Abimael Guzmán, leader of the fearsome Shining Path, had spared Arequipa his wrath out of respect for his birthplace. Was this Polay's way of giving his old travel companion a pass? Probably not. For the rebels, the cease-fire was never about real compromise; it was about the appearance of compromise. Had the rebels wanted to negotiate a truce with the government, they could have laid down arms or issued a statement declaring their desire. Instead, they staged an act of political theater, complete with rendezvous points, blindfolds, guns, and secret hideouts. It was sensationalist journalism at its best, and it would paint an image of a guerrilla group that was open to dialogue. Whether or not that dialogue ever came to fruition was at best a secondary concern.

The Tupac Amaristas relied heavily on national symbols to drive home their point. Polay spoke underneath the very emblems of Peruvian (and Latin American) revolutionary history. The central position that the independence flag occupied during the press conference had a twofold effect. First, it brought into question the power of the state. If the state could not defend its most sacred emblem, what did this say about its ability to govern and protect the citizenry? Second, it legitimized the insurgency. Unlike Tupac Amaru, who, by virtue of his failure to defeat the Spaniards, was at worst a traitor and at best a failed revolutionary, San Martín's patriotic accolades were unimpeachable. When one of the reporters in attendance asked what it meant for the MRTA to have such relics in its possession, Polay fired off an impromptu history lesson. In order to comprehend the MRTA's current struggle, he said, one needed to understand Peru's revolutionary tradition. It was a tradition inaugurated by Tupac Amaru 200 years prior and later picked up by San Martín and other leaders of the Peruvian revolution. "This," he explained, "is why we assume the symbols, the heroes, the traditions and the messages [of the independence movement] as part of our own history." For the past 150 years, Peru's leaders had "prostituted" the country's original flag, sword, and coat of arms, stripping them of their revolutionary significance. Not anymore. "The time has come for the people to reclaim these symbols."[6]

Never mind that the real José de San Martín was from modern-day Argentina, an accident of history that patriots were willing to overlook. Or that he had declared independence prematurely, at a moment when Spanish authorities and forces had already retreated to the Andes. Or that he had left Peru a dejected man, having failed to persuade Simón Bolívar to join forces with him in a final push into the royalist-controlled highlands. The real San Martín set sail for Europe well before the patriots' final victory at the battle of Ayacucho.[7]

None of this mattered to the Tupac Amaristas. What mattered was that San Martín declared Peruvians free from Spanish rule. The flag symbolized this proclamation. Now the banner was in the possession of a new group of insurgents who were also fighting to liberate their countrymen from oppression. In possessing the flag of San Martín, then, the rebels infused their insurgency with a sense of moral and historical purpose. As the legitimate heirs to this revolutionary legacy, as the ethnic guardians of the Peruvian nation, the rebels reserved the right to punish the García administration should it fail to live up to its electoral promises.

■ As expected, the García administration refused to engage in talks with the rebels before they demilitarized. Instead, it made the reappropriation of these captured symbols a primary objective of the counterinsurgency. The day after Polay's press conference, Germán Ruíz Figueroa, commander general of the army, presided over a military ceremony in the very plaza dedicated to San Martín. In his speech, the general maintained that the army of the republic was the only rightful army in Peru, having been established by José de San Martín himself 164 years earlier to the day. As was the case with San Martín's Peruvian Legion of the Guard, the modern army was equipped with "steely cohesion and superior morality" and was fully prepared to "assume the responsibilities that circumstances demand." The general invited Anselmo Marini, the Argentine ambassador to Peru, to say a few words. After expressing his deepest sympathies for the loss of the three artifacts from Peru's national patrimony, the ambassador produced another replica of San Martín's sword and offered it to Ruíz Figueroa. The general received the sword with much fanfare, hoisting it over his head with both hands for all to see and photograph.[8] Although the state had failed to recover the actual sword stolen by the Tupac Amaristas, the ceremony accomplished two things. First, it offered a competing narrative to the one offered by the rebels, a narrative in which the state, personified by the republican army, appeared as San Martín's legitimate heir. Second, it neutralized the symbolic impact of the rebel's appropriation of the historic artifact.

It was a minor victory. Even though the state had managed to replace the sword with another replica, the actual saber remained at large. So did the other stolen items. If the state really wanted to reclaim its legacy as the republic of San Martín, it would need to dispossess the rebels of the artifacts. In short, it would need to capture the flag. Each time the rebels wielded the banner was a reminder of their symbolic victory over the state. Without the flag, the state had no control over the historical narrative. Without the narrative, it lacked legitimacy. This real-life game of "capture the flag" would continue to define Peru's internal armed conflict for a dozen years.

The Tupac Amaristas also went to great lengths to memorialize 4 November, the anniversary of Tupac Amaru's 1780 rebellion. Each year, the guerrillas commemorated the anniversary by detonating bombs, plastering rebel graffiti on public buildings, and draping the rebel flag bearing Tupac Amaru's likeness on public spaces.[9] They also operated their own radio broadcast, aptly named "Radio 4 de Noviembre." Alberto Aguilar was one of the technicians in charge of the rebel radio. The former engineering major would park his car at the highest point of whatever district he wanted to hear the broadcast and set up his one-man radio station. After removing the television interference devices, high- and short-wave radio equipment, and solar-charged batteries from the car, Aguilar would snake the ten-meter-long antenna up a tree to blend in with the surroundings. He would then take out a cassette tape containing the prerecorded broadcast, pop it into the transmitter, and press "play."[10]

The first broadcast of "Radio 4 de Noviembre" occurred at 4:40 P.M. on 16 May 1986. And it aired on television. Viewers who had tuned in to Channel 5 to enjoy a soccer match between the Peruvian and Venezuelan national teams watched the image on their screens slowly fade to black. Moments later, the energetic voices of a young man and woman interrupted the silence on the screen.

"You are now listening to 'Radio 4 de Noviembre,' voice of the Tupac Amaru Revolutionary Movement!"

The broadcasters reminded listeners that 4 November was the date of Tupac Amaru's rebellion against the Spaniards. As the voice of truth, insurgency, and liberation, the clandestine radio program offered Peruvians a new weapon in the fight against the dominant classes, imperialism, and the "traitorous government [that] seeks to silence the aspirations of the people." The broadcasters signed off with the rebel motto: "With Masses and Arms, We Will Prevail!"[11]

The Tupac Amaristas considered their rebel radio a public relations success. Once again, their savvy use of the media—in this case, their own—helped them deliver their message directly to the public. It also furthered their symbolic war, explicitly connecting past and present through the appropriation of 4 November. These actions, the guerrillas hoped, would legitimize the rebellion in the eyes of the Peruvian people, showing it to be the continuation of a much longer struggle for social justice.

The actions of the rebels in the first two years of the insurgency sought to drive home this message. In 1985 alone, they carried out eighteen assaults in which they stole goods from local retailers and redistributed them to the urban poor. "The time has come," read a June issue of the rebel mouthpiece *Venceremos*, "for the people to take what is theirs and punish the businesses that have gotten rich at the expense of our hunger."[12] These Robin Hood actions outnumbered all other armed attacks—car bombs, assaults on police forces, robberies of weapons arsenals—combined.[13] For the next three years, the guerrillas raided food trucks, marketplaces, retail stores, high-end restaurants, luxury hotels, and factories throughout Peru's major cities. In the process, they lifted thousands of pounds of chicken, milk, cooking oil, rice, bread, and other staples for redistribution in urban shantytowns.[14]

Meanwhile, the MRTA's war on imperialist symbols continued. In early April 1986, the Tupac Amaristas bombed the offices of IBM, the Peruvian-American Cultural Institute, and two Citibanks, all on the same night.[15] By the end of the month, they had added another Citibank, the Peruvian-American Institute, Diners Club, ITT, Kodak, the U.S. Embassy, and the Summer Institute of Linguistics International to their list of U.S. targets.[16]

The embassy itself was heavily guarded and nearly impossible to access, let alone damage. The ambassador's residence, however, was a different story. The mansion was located in the heart of downtown Lima on the busy Arequipa Avenue, nestled between a spattering of gas stations, restaurants, and public parks. Built in 1942 by a French architect, the building emulated the classic Spanish manors of the colonial period, with lavish balconies jutting out over the sidewalk below. The interior was just as elaborate, with large skylights overhead and a back parlor with large framed windows surrounding an imposing fireplace. The building was well fortified, its walls composed of a tightly wound chain-link fence embedded skeletonlike inside a thick slab of concrete to prevent swaying or collapse of the walls in the case of earthquakes. Or bombs.[17]

One morning, a red Toyota pulled up to the square of the USAID mission across the street from the residence. A team of Tupac Amaristas hopped out of the vehicle, quickly set up a mortar launcher, and aimed it at the mansion.[18]

The first mortar hit the roof, blowing a hole there and sending fragments shredding part of the exterior. The second mortar flew over the house and got caught in the high chain-link fence on the outside. The mortar dangled by a fin but never detonated. Nor did the third, which landed squarely on the driveway. The fourth mortar exploded on the street.[19]

Then, just as quickly as they had come, the Tupac Amaristas loaded the vehicle with their grenade launcher and sped away. The entire assault transpired in a matter of seconds, so quickly that Alexander Watson, the U.S. ambassador, didn't even realize that his house was under attack. Yes, the explosion was loud, and yes, it shook the entire house, but such explosions were common in late-1980s Lima. It seemed as if every night Shining Path was setting off car bombs or blowing up power lines, draping the city in darkness.

"It sounded and felt like a bomb exploding a few blocks away," Watson later recalled. It was only after his butler, Alfredo, came running into his room that he realized his home was the target.

Washington immediately dispatched a team to investigate the incident. The mortars, it turned out, were of Spanish manufacture and Portuguese labeling. Watson interpreted this as evidence of a possible Havana connection. Cuban Communists had recently intervened in the liberation struggle in Angola, and they could have acquired the weapons in the Portuguese-language country before funneling them to the MRTA. The ambassador never did confirm this theory. What he did know was that the attack had virtually no chance of inflicting any bodily harm on him or his family.[20]

"I was the most protected guy in the country," he said, noting that not even President García was as safe as he was.[21] Perhaps that was overstated, but no one could deny that Watson was well protected. In addition to occupying one of the most fortified residences in Lima, he benefited from a fourteen-man security detail twenty-four hours a day, seven days a week. Everywhere he went, he traveled in a bulletproof Cadillac accompanied by a robust motorcade.[22] The guerrillas would have known this, which is why Watson did not consider himself the target. "The MRTA probably didn't expect to kill anyone," he said, "but they wanted to make a [symbolic] attack."[23]

For the insurgents, attacks against the U.S. Embassy were never about bringing individual diplomats to justice for alleged crimes. Rather, these actions were designed to strike at the symbols of Yankee imperialism. Elsewhere, the MRTA had condemned the U.S. bombing of Libya, the Contra war in Nicaragua, and the invasion of Grenada.[24] By striking at the emblems of Yankee imperialism in Peru, the insurgents conveyed a message of solidarity with victims of U.S. aggression worldwide. Thus, even though the attacks against the U.S. Embassy produced no major injuries, casualties, or military setbacks, the Tupac Amaristas considered them political successes. This explains the letter that the MRTA National Directorate sent Watson's predecessor, David Jordan, following an earlier attack on the residence. "Your worst fears have come to pass," read the letter, which bore the insignia of Tupac Amaru and the letter V. "What awoke you abruptly at 5 A.M. was the explosion of 60 kilograms of dynamite on your doorstep, which symbolizes the protest of 20 million Peruvians against the terrorist and genocidal politics of your president, Ronald 'The Kid Killer' Reagan." The letter went on to clarify that the MRTA held nothing against the American people, but that it objected to the imperialism of the U.S. government, whose military interventions in Central America and Libya, which had resulted in the deaths of dozens of innocent children, only served to unite the people of Peru and Latin America.[25]

The State Department usually tried to downplay these attacks. Following the MRTA hit on Ambassador Watson's residence, the embassy press secretary issued an official statement explaining that the ambassador had been enjoying breakfast with his wife and daughter at the time of the assault and that, although rattled, the three remained unharmed and in good spirits. In fact, Watson was alone with his three-year-old daughter, who had just crawled into bed with him at the time of the attack. His wife, who had been out of the country at the time, returned to Lima just as the security team was completing its investigation. After briefing Mrs. Watson about the incident, the young security officer asked her if she had any questions. She had only one.

"Who was the woman having breakfast with my husband?"[26]

■ It didn't take long for the Tupac Amaristas to conclude that their own government was more American than Peruvian. When, months into his presidency, President García reneged on his campaign promise to break diplomatic ties with the United States over the Contra war in Nicaragua, the

MRTA denounced him as an imperialist demagogue, hailing the actions of the "heroic Central American people" who suffered the "brutal aggression of imperialism."[27] In May 1986, the clandestine newspaper *Venceremos* ran a cover story listing the numerous infractions that García had committed since the MRTA announced its cease-fire less than a year earlier. Prime among these transgressions was the normalization of diplomatic and economic relations with the United States. As proof, the paper printed a photograph of a smiling Aprista shaking hands with the "Yankee Deputy Secretary of State" John C. Whitehead.[28]

Three months later, the Tupac Amaristas held another clandestine press conference announcing an end to the cease-fire. Standing in front of the same icons under which he had declared a truce a year earlier, Polay, still anonymous under his hood, maintained that the García administration had broken its promise to the people, abandoning the nationalist, social-democratic principles upon which the APRA had been founded and upon which the president had been elected.

The guerrillas had never really laid down arms. Yes, they had avoided targeting key symbols of state authority since declaring a truce in August 1985, but armed actions against nongovernment targets had continued uninterrupted for the past year. It is unlikely that the García administration would have accepted anything less than total disarmament anyway, and Polay surely knew this. He must also have known that no democratically elected government, no matter how populist or well intended, could have eradicated poverty, subverted the capitalist order, and broken economic ties with the United States in just one year. The so-called cease-fire was never more than a publicity stunt designed to make the MRTA appear more reasonable and open to compromise than both the government and Shining Path. By setting an impossible threshold for the Aprista government and refusing to halt all military actions, the rebel leadership had intentionally set up the 1985 cease-fire for failure. Notwithstanding its rhetoric, the MRTA's renewal of military operations against the state in mid-1986 was a fait accompli. War, if it was ever off to begin with, was back on.

5

The Alliance

Middle-class Limeños spent the final hours of 1986 in crowded houses, nightclubs, and apartment buildings. In the *pueblos jóvenes*, shantytown dwellers burned effigies representing the year gone by.[1] For the Andean nation, 1986 had been a rough year. Inflation, unemployment, and the national debt had skyrocketed. Both the MRTA and Shining Path had taken over the capital, stepping up their actions and threatening political stability.

No one could have been more relieved to welcome the New Year than Alan García. A year and a half into his presidential term, the middle-aged Aprista had overseen the worst of the crises, and 1987 represented an opportunity to start anew. García was all smiles when he arrived at APRA party head-quarters shortly after midnight. More than 2,000 guests greeted him with warm applause. After waving to his supporters and shaking a few hands, he made his way over to the main hall, where the top APRA leaders had lined up to wish him a Happy New Year. Several toasts later, he joined his followers in a rendition of the party anthem, "Marsellista Aprista." Then, maintaining all appearances of spontaneity, he grabbed a guitar and entertained his guests with a series of melodies from the folkloric *criollo* tradition. García remained at the gathering until a little after one in the morning. After attending a small after-party with close friends and acquaintances, he and his wife retired for the evening.[2]

For others, the night was still young. Most parties, dances, and nightclubs kept their doors open well into the morning hours, taking advantage of the temporary suspension of the citywide curfew. As late as seven in the morning, thousands of people could be seen stumbling out onto the streets of Lima in the hopes of returning home for a few hours of shuteye before heading off to work or the beach.[3] No one seemed to notice when a small dark car with no plates pulled up alongside the council building of the beach town of Chorrillos shortly after daybreak. Three or four Tupac Amaristas quickly piled out of the car and placed small bundles at various points of the government building before boarding the vehicle and speeding away. Moments later, multiple dynamite blasts ripped through the council building, sending pieces of glass, wood, and concrete in every direction. Police arrived on the scene within minutes of the detonation, but the damage had already been done.[4]

The smoke had not yet cleared in Chorrillos when another explosion sounded off Lima's main drag, Paseo de la República. Moments earlier, rebels had fired automatic weapons on Republican Guards inside the Board of Elections office. The ensuing firefight provided enough of a diversion for another suspect to park a red Volkswagen in front of the building and walk away unnoticed. The car belonged to the minister of economy's public relations chief, Carlos Ortiz Ocampo. It had been stolen from outside Ortiz's residence only hours earlier. Once the driver of the stolen vehicle had reached a safe distance, it burst into flames, knocking the license plates clean off the bumper. Disoriented from the blast, the guards fired on the suspects as they fled on foot. One of the alleged assailants caught a fatal bullet to the back of the head, but the others escaped in a pair of getaway cars.[5]

The New Year's Day operation continued the MRTA's renewed campaign against the state. Each target represented a different entity that the insurgents believed had been compromised under the García administration. There was the government, represented by the town council building. There were the abusive security forces, personified by the Republican Guards. Finally, there was democracy itself, represented by the Board of Elections, and the presidential cabinet, embodied by the car of the ministry of economy's public relations chief. All were entities that the rebels saw as corrupted and in need of a good cleansing. The attack was just one of several hits on government buildings after the rebels' unilateral ending of their ceasefire.[6] The bombings also sent another message to the president. If 1986 was a year of broken peace, 1987 would be a year of war. Once again, historical and national symbols would play a central role in this renewed battle, and both the state and the rebels would go to great lengths to reclaim these symbols.

No entity better symbolized state power than the government palace. The president's cream-colored, neobaroque residence occupied an entire side of Lima's main plaza, on the very grounds that conquistador Francisco Pizarro once called home. The Tupac Amaristas symbolically renewed their war on the state by attacking the building the day after announcing the end to their self-imposed truce.[7] Exactly a year later, they returned for more. This time, a group of insurgents driving a red Ford with tinted windows circled the Vía de Evitamiento before firing two consecutive mortar rounds onto the presidential palace. The projectiles ripped holes through the palace, but nobody was harmed during the attack. Nevertheless, the rebels touted the attack as a major victory against the state.[8] Peruvian counterterrorism police, or DIN-COTE, claimed that this latest attack had been the work of the newest member of the MRTA leadership, a young sociologist named Alberto Gálvez.[9]

■ Alberto Gálvez Olaechea had grown up in Chaclacayo, a sunny district in the foothills between Lima and the Andes. Both of his parents were from the provinces and spoke Quechua, although they never spoke it around their children. When she was with her sisters, Gálvez's mother would sometimes switch to the Incan language so that her kids didn't know what they were saying, but otherwise she reared them in Spanish. His father had migrated from the highlands of Huancavelica, but Gálvez never knew he spoke Quechua until much later in life.[10] Gálvez's father had received some technical training, which allowed him to gain employment in construction and irrigation.

Little Alberto was a source of much grief for his mother. Always mischievous and with a rebellious streak, he would defy her wishes and pick on his little sisters. In the summer of 1961, when his father was packing for one of his long work trips to the countryside, his mother threw up her hands.

"Take the boy with you," she said. "I can't deal with him anymore." His father, always softspoken, simply shrugged. And so the nine-year-old hopped into his dad's truck and joined him on a road trip down to the border of Ica and Huancavelica. They didn't say much, as his father had never been one for small talk. Still, Gálvez appreciated the adventure. His father was supposed to check on an irrigation channel that pumped water from a nearby lake into the Chincha valley. The truck bounced along the highway until the paved road finally reached an end in the middle of the rolling mountains, next to a big blue lagoon.

"Wait here," his father said.

Gálvez sat in the truck, watching his father walk away along with a coworker, his silhouette getting smaller and smaller until it had disappeared from site. He sat there for hours, surrounded by the rolling pampas and the big blue lagoon, not a person in sight. Gone were the nasal cries of street peddlers, the honking horns, the rumbling buses. The silence was deafening to his chapped ears. He watched the ducks waddle by and the occasional mountain animal meander past, seemingly oblivious to his presence. "It was absolute solitude," he remembered. As the afternoon turned to dusk, the icy mountain air began to compress his body, filling his lungs with cold. He remained alone in the mountains for six hours before his father returned, finally relieving him of his anxiety. The old man made no excuses, no apologies. He simply started the ignition and drove on to the next site. The trip left a tremendous impact on young Gálvez. It was the first time that he learned of life outside the Lima bubble and of the sacrifices that his father made to put food on the table. "That was when I learned the value of hard work," he recalled.[11]

He returned from his summer trip and settled back into his normal routine. He never really liked school, nor did he get the best grades. He always learned more in his conversations with other students and teachers outside the classroom. As for his formal education, "It taught me to read and write, and that's about the only thing useful I got out of it."[12] His grades were still good enough to get him into college. He enrolled in La Cantuta in 1970 and once again found himself spending more time philosophizing and socializing than in class. As a student, he never stood out. "I was mediocre," he admitted, "middle of the road." He was mesmerized by the ability of great *indigenista* writers like César Vallejo and José María Arguedas to turn a phrase and tell a captivating story about life in the highlands. Gálvez was a gifted writer in his own right, and he was much more comfortable expressing himself through the pen than the spoken word.

In August 1970, during his freshman year at La Cantuta, he attended a Latin American Studies conference organized by the Institute of Peruvian Studies. The event brought the best and brightest scholars and practitioners from throughout the Americas, including a keynote by none other than Peruvian president Juan Velasco Alvarado. The progressive general was mid-speech when a group of women in the back of the room raised their voices, causing a commotion. Gálvez looked back at the women, still not sure what was going on. They appeared to be clamoring about the government's holding of guerrilla leaders in prison. Among those in custody were Hugo Blanco, leader of the recent Cuzco rebellion, and Héctor Bejar of the short-lived 1965 MIR insurgency. When security headed to the back of the room to restore order, a professor named Alfredo Torero rose from his seat.

"Mr. President," Torero said, "may I take the floor?"

Gálvez watched in amusement as the color vanished from the face of José Matos Mar, the nation's most prominent sociologist and the director of the institute. He was losing control of the situation, and all the press was there to chronicle it.

"Sit down, Dr. Torero!" Matos Mar ordered.

There was no stopping the professor, who calmly walked down the aisle toward the president. With all the commotion still going on in the back of the room, Torero stood before the president's podium and began what appeared to be an impassioned speech. Gálvez couldn't hear a word of it, only leaning forward to watch as the professor gesticulated passionately for his audience of one. When he had finished delivering his soliloquy, Torero quietly returned to his seat and order was restored.

Gálvez later learned that the whole episode had been orchestrated to give the leftist professor an impromptu audience with the dictator. Evidently Torero had pleaded for the commander in chief to grant amnesty to the political prisoners, who after all had been fighting for the very social programs that Velasco advocated. Four months later, Velasco pardoned all political prisoners.

The episode left a profound impact on the bespectacled freshman. This small act of political theater had been bold, well organized, decisive, and, apparently, effective. The protesters had shown that sheer drive and determination, not to mention the unwitting participation of a captive audience of journalists, could make a political impact. After that, Gálvez joined the MIR youth.

Among his first assignments as a militant was to organize the fishermen, teachers, and factory workers in Chimbote, a port town up the coast. Gálvez would spend summer vacations organizing in the anchovy-producing port. During the school year, he would take the six-hour bus ride up the coast on Friday afternoons, remain there until Sunday evening, and return on the redeye bus so he could make it back to the capital for his university classes. Maintaining this regimented schedule was difficult, however, and he found himself attending fewer and fewer classes. By 1973, he had all but given up on his studies and dedicated himself full time to party militancy. He also immersed himself in Marxist literature, which counterfeiters now copied and resold for pennies on the dollar. In his youthful hubris, Gálvez believed that his generation would bring about Peru's socialist liberation through the barrel of a gun. He spent the remainder of the decade helping the MIR build up its base of support among workers and teachers. In the mid-1970s, he helped organize teachers and agricultural farmers in San Martín, a department in the northern Amazon. His organizing brought him in contact with Néstor Cerpa's Cromotex union on the eve of the 1978 factory workers' massacre. Cerpa, still a novice labor leader, didn't think much of the goateed mestizo, writing him off as yet another armchair revolutionary. It would be years before they would meet again as fellow MRTA leaders.[13]

Gálvez's ascension to a leadership position within the revolutionary left happened almost by accident. To commemorate the death of guerrilla leader Luis De La Puente Uceda, the MIR organized a political convention in downtown Lima on 23 October 1979. On a good day, these gatherings might bring in 300 people. This time, however, the organizers went for broke, pitching a large circus tent near the national stadium with room for 3,000 participants. Much to their surprise, the tent filled to capacity, bringing in all the rising stars of the left. There was Carlos Tapia, the young economist and future member of the CVR. There was Nelson Manrique, who, in addition to becoming one of the country's most prominent historians and an expert on the political violence, also happened to be Gálvez's first cousin. Manrique was joined by fellow historian Alberto Flores Galindo, who would go on to write the best-selling book on Peruvian history *In Search of an Inca*. And then there were the anthropologists, among them Carlos Iván Degregori and Rodrigo Montoya, who defined the field for a generation. What united these future powerhouse scholars was a passion for intellectual exchange and radical change. The twenty-five-year-old Gálvez, who had never fancied himself a scholar, felt eclipsed by these emerging thinkers.

When the time came to nominate candidates to be the party's new general secretary, Gálvez wasn't surprised to see Carlos Iván Degregori's name submitted for consideration. The curly-haired anthropologist had spent time in the field, living among the poorest of the poor in the Andes. In Ayacucho, he had taught alongside Abimael Guzmán, the future leader of the Shining Path guerrillas. He was also among the smartest people in attendance that day, which was saying something, considering the company. As party procedures went, Degregori needed to have an opposition candidate against whom to run.

When someone submitted Gálvez's name, he couldn't believe his ears. By now, Degregori, Flores Galindo, Manrique, and Montoya were household names, up-and-coming scholar activists defining their fields and the left. Gálvez was not. "I wasn't very well known before the convention," he confessed. Nor was he particularly comfortable with the limelight. He much preferred to be behind the scenes, coordinating actions and writing opinions, not in front of the cameras or on center stage. But it was his way with the pen that got Gálvez on his comrades' radar screen in the first place. Before the convention, he had written an essay in which he placed the Peruvian political climate within the broader global context. The essay demonstrated the young militant's firm grasp of leftist history, discussing the Russian, Chinese, and Cuban revolutions with sophisticated analysis. Earlier in the convention, Gálvez had read his essay to the assembled militants in the form of a lecture. The Miristas were riveted and gave him an extra two hours after his thirty minutes had expired to deliver the remainder of his talk. After he had finished, the comrades lined up to congratulate him on a job well done. Years later, he still couldn't explain his feat. "I don't know, I guess I was in rare form that day."

That moving speech was enough to earn him the nomination for general secretary versus Degregori. "I still didn't think I was going to win," Gálvez admitted, but he thought it would be good to "see what I was worth." The 300 or so voting members gathered around a conference table to cast their votes publicly. As a gesture of goodwill and comradery, Gálvez voted for Degregori. The anthropologist returned the favor, and when all the votes had been tabulated, Gálvez came out ahead by a single vote. Almost overnight, the twenty-five-year-old college dropout had gone from no-name to leader of the nation's largest revolutionary movement.[14]

As general secretary, Gálvez immediately went to work building up "all forms of struggle," a common strategy among the Latin American left that combined grassroots organizing, electoral politics, and armed insurrection. Although Gálvez believed that revolutionary violence was necessary in order to compel societal change, he excelled at political strategy and social mobilization. In the early 1980s, a time when Shining Path had launched its Maoist People's War, Gálvez made frequent visits to the jungles of San Martín, where he had spent some time organizing the previous decade. There, he sought to renew contact with the older generation of Miristas in agricultural towns like Juanjuí, only to learn that they had grown tired of waiting for the armed struggle and joined Shining Path instead. Undeterred, he began recruiting teachers and students in the bustling jungle town of Tarapoto into the MIR.

When some members of the MIR split off to join ranks with the newly established MRTA in 1982, Gálvez demurred. After the 1985 elections, however, the MIR leader realized he needed to change course. On one hand, the United Left, an umbrella political party of progressives and leftists, had succeeded in gaining a foothold in the legal political sphere. On the other hand, Shining Path had emerged as an armed guerrilla force that was picking up steam with every destructive turn. If the MIR didn't act fast, it would be left behind. As far as Gálvez was concerned, the only viable alternative was to join forces with the MRTA. Aside from the fact that the Miristas had more in common with the MRTA than with Shining Path in terms of strategy and goals, many of the Tupac Amaristas were former Miristas themselves.

Perhaps, he surmised, an alliance would help catapult the MRTA to the same level as Shining Path, or at least close to it, thereby rendering a total victory of the left all the more plausible in this watershed historical moment.[15]

When he brought the proposal to the MIR leadership, the reception was less than favorable. "Most of the MIR comrades were not on board with the alliance," Gálvez recalled. They raised their objections, claiming that he was being shortsighted. No good would come of a merger with an existing guerrilla group. No matter how good the Tupac Amaristas' intentions, no matter how generous their overtures, the Miristas would always be relegated to a second-class status within the movement. Instead, these detractors argued, the Miristas should bide their time and take up arms on their own terms, at a time and place of their own choosing. But Gálvez persisted. He cajoled, pleaded, and pressured his comrades, spending all his hard-earned political capital in the process. "I had to apply a fair degree of pressure," he recalled. He lost several allies over the decision, but in the end, he succeeded in persuading the remaining comrades to take a leap of faith. He led by example, jumping into the deep revolutionary waters with both feet, never looking back. "I think it was the right thing to do at the time," he said nearly thirty years later.[16]

In late 1985, Gálvez and Víctor Polay rendezvoused in Sandinista-controlled Nicaragua to hash out the details of the merger. The MIR and MRTA leaders crashed at the Managua home of a leftist friend and talked and talked and talked. "It was the most time we ever spent together," Gálvez said of the trip.[17] While the main topic of conversation was the alliance, they also talked politics, history, and a good deal about their families and personal lives. The two leaders came away from the days-long retreat with a mutual respect and a resolve to build a better nation together.[18]

When they returned to Peru early in 1986, Polay and Gálvez began working toward the formal consolidation of their political parties. By December, they had worked out the full details of the alliance. The MIR would be folded into the MRTA. To ensure parity, the National Directorate, the main leadership body in the rebel hierarchy, would consist of three Tupac Amaristas and three Miristas, with Polay and Gálvez occupying two of the six seats. Below this would be the Central Committee, consisting of ten members from each group. They would also slowly fade out the Mirista name, attributing early attacks to the MRTA-MIR and eventually, by the end of 1987, adopting the sole name of the MRTA. And so it was that Alberto Gálvez became a Tupac Amarista.[19]

■ The newly fortified MRTA continued to focus on acts of symbolic and historical import. A favorite target of the rebels was Néstor Cerpa's old textile factory, Cromotex.[20] The rebel commander never forgot his fallen factory brothers, and he used his influence in the MRTA as a vehicle to commemorate their sacrifice. Guerrilla propaganda described 4 February 1979 as "one of the most glorious pages in the history of the Peruvian working class."[21] Although vastly outnumbered, the workers had confronted the "repressive forces that removed them by blood and fire from the Cromotex factory." The six workers who died that day made the ultimate sacrifice for a better Peru: "With the blood that they generously spilled, they showed us that against the arbitrary and irrational actions of the dominant classes there is no other path for our people but the frank and decisive struggle to change the established order."[22]

As long as Cerpa was alive and active in the MRTA, chances were high that the rebels would stage a commemorative attack against Cromotex on the anniversary of the massacre. On that day in 1987, at seven in the morning, Cerpa led fifteen Tupac Amaristas into the Cromotex factory located along the third kilometer of the central highway, Ate. Vitarte.[23] Roughly 200 workers had already arrived when the insurgents split into several squadrons, each one flanking out to the guard posts and subduing the watchmen on duty. A woman in her early twenties led the squadron assigned to the front gate. She carried a submachine gun and appeared to be in charge of the group. Upon seeing the guerrillas, some of the guards reached for their weapons, but the insurgents knocked them into submission. Once inside, the squadrons dispersed throughout the factory, rounding up workers and managers and escorting them to the main patio.

"Everyone on the floor!" the woman ordered while her comrades pointed their weapons at their hostages.[24]

Five Tupac Amaristas remained with the employees and administrators while the other ten placed dynamite packages in the administrative office and warehouses. When the insurgents returned to the patio, they did not run away as they usually did after planting explosives. This was an important anniversary and a significant symbolic target. By bombing the managers' offices, as the MRTA explained in the leaflets the rebels scattered throughout the factory, the armed group was communicating its "repudiation of the [capitalists] responsible for the massacre of the Cromotex workers."[25] Cerpa didn't leave anything to chance. He and his comrades waited silently in the patio until eight bundles of dynamite detonated in the offices. Before departing, the Tupac Amaristas left behind leaflets reiterating the significance of the Cromotex massacre in the guerrillas' interpretation of history, signing off with "Glory to the Heroic Workers of Cromotex! With Masses and Arms! Country or Death! We Will Prevail!" Only then did the rebels exit the factory. Once outside, they jumped into two trucks and sped away.[26] They would return a year later to do it all over again.[27] By revisiting symbolic vengeance on Cromotex each year, then, Cerpa's rebels sought to carve out the strike and massacre into national mythology as an important moment in the country's revolutionary history.

Cromotex was just one of several symbols of oppressive capitalism that the Tupac Amaristas targeted. The rebels also sabotaged public buses, high-end restaurants, banks, and jockey clubs, often leaving dynamite packages that, once exploded, sprinkled MRTA-MIR leaflets like confetti.[28] This was all part of a concerted effort to show that the Tupac Amaristas and the MIR were now working together, united on the side of the Peruvian people against Yankee imperialism.

One symbol that the García government had yet to reclaim was the battle flag of San Martín. For the past three years, the Tupac Amaristas had touted their cloth trophy, hoisting it almost mockingly over their heads during underground press conferences. The flag, it turned out, had been in Lucero Cumpa's possession all along.

6

Captured

Lucero Cumpa looked around. Where was she? Three of the walls were concrete slabs. The fourth wasn't a wall at all. It was just a row of iron bars. Yes, she was inside a prison cell! How did she get there? She didn't remember having been arrested, and she didn't feel like a prisoner. She looked down and noticed that she was wearing blue jeans.

Cumpa opened her eyes, still disoriented. She was in her bed in her safe house on Madre Selva Street in Salamanca. She breathed a sigh of relief. It was just a dream.[1]

A lot had changed since her husband, Fernando Valladares, had been arrested two years prior. Cumpa had proven a reliable and trustworthy militant. Not only had she kept the battle flag of independence leader José de San Martín safely tucked away in a box inside her urban hideaway, but she had demonstrated good leadership and sound judgment while in control of her own cell. Now, in mid-1987, she was head of political operations for the entire capital.

Maintaining a relationship with her imprisoned husband wasn't easy. Valladares had always wanted a child, and now that seemed unlikely. He had to settle for writing letters to Cumpa and hoping that they would reach her without compromising her whereabouts. Desperate to see her husband, Cumpa decided to visit him in prison. This was not as uncommon a practice as one might think. In fact, many MRTA women took advantage of prison visiting hours to see their partners. These Tupac Amaristas counted on a patriarchal police culture that still didn't suspect women of subversive activity in 1987. As long as they played the role of the doting wives and girlfriends, they could get past security without raising any red flags. Of course, this was dangerous, and they always ran the risk of being detained on site; but it was a risk that some women were willing to take.[2] Cumpa was one of those women. One day in 1987, she asked her superior, Peter Cárdenas, for permission to visit Valladares in prison.

A tall, slender white man of Swedish descent, Peter Cárdenas was among the MRTA's founding members. Together with Víctor Polay and the Afroperuvian political operative Hugo Avallaneda, Cárdenas rounded out the MRTA's Lima-based troika: *El Chino, El Negro, y El Gringo*, or "The Chinaman, The Black Man, and the White Man," in the uncharitable Peruvian lexicon. Both inside and outside the organization, Cárdenas had a reputation as a ruthless hitman, earning him the nickname "the Sicilian," supposedly for his gangster ways. That he sported a trimmed brown beard with a distinguishable patch of white hairs on the right side of his chin only contributed to this image. But as Leo, one of Cárdenas's Lima combatants, explained, his actions truly solidified his reputation. Leo recalled an incident early in the insurgency when a comrade named Edy began questioning the blue-eyed leader's resolve, referring to him as a *pituco*, a yuppy, behind his back. When Cárdenas discovered this, he assigned Edy as his partner for an upcoming attack on the Civil Guard station on the corner of Ayllu Avenue and Yerbateros. All the combatants, Leo and Edy included, were nervous as they sat in the parked car before the action. "I still get goosebumps thinking about it," Leo admitted more than three decades later. Not Cárdenas. When the moment for the operation began, he grabbed a briefcase and calmly walked across the street toward the police station, set the briefcase on the roof of a parked car, removed the submachine gun and tripod from inside it, and opened fire on the building. Only then did Edy, Leo, and the others follow suit. After their retreat, Edy found Leo and offered his apologies.

"Much respect for the Gringo," Edy said.[3]

These and countless other stories from both Tupac Amaristas and the media solidified Peter Cárdenas's reputation as a cold-blooded assassin. Yet, as Cumpa and others close to him knew, behind his Hollywood hitman mystique, he could also be a teddy bear. With a little persuasion, she was sure he would come around on the prison visit.

Cárdenas resisted at first. "Absolutely not. Out of the question."

Cumpa didn't take no for an answer. She appealed to his sympathies, explaining that Valladares was miserable and showing him the letters her husband had written. She assured him that she had already thought of everything. All her papers were in order. She would arrive with a lawyer. She would go in with the other wives and be out at the end of visitation hours, and Cárdenas would be waiting like clockwork. What did he have to lose?[4]

Cárdenas put off her pleas at first. Then, one day, he was driving Cumpa to a location and suddenly pulled over. A few seconds later, Hugo Avallaneda, the other Lima commander, boarded the car. Cárdenas filled Avallaneda in on Cumpa's request. If they were going to approve such a measure, he wanted to have the support of the other Lima commander. Avallaneda listened as Cumpa detailed all the precautions she had taken.

"You guys know me," Cumpa said, "I'm reliable."

After a few moments, Avallaneda opened the car door.

"You decide," he told Cárdenas before getting out and shutting the door.[5]

Cumpa looked at Cárdenas.

"You know [the National Directorate is] going to kill me," he said, "but fine!"

Cumpa could hardly contain herself and wrapped her arms around him.

"But if you're even one second late . . . ," Cárdenas warned, never finishing the sentence.

Cumpa understood the risks. That September, she showed up at the prison and registered as a guest. She could be quite charming, and she chatted up the guards and smiled often to mask her inner terror. After clearing the inspection area, she walked over to the MRTA cellblock. The guerrillas were performing one of their daily hymns to keep up morale, clapping rhythmically as they chanted revolutionary slogans. When they saw their fellow Tupac Amarista walk by as a visitor, some of them were so incredulous that they nearly stopped clapping. Cumpa kept her eyes downcast until she located Valladares on the fourth floor of the pavilion. After exchanging embraces, the young couple disappeared into Valladares's cell.

According to Cumpa, it was two minutes to six when she arrived at the prearranged meeting place outside the prison, where a nervous Cárdenas awaited to take her back to her safe house.[6]

Weeks later, Cumpa stood in her bathroom looking at the test result: she was pregnant. The first person she called was her mother.

"Mom, I'm pregnant."

There was a momentary pause on the other end of the line before María asked, "Are you happy?"

The question nearly brought Cumpa to tears. "I'm so happy!"

"Then I'm happy, too."

That was all the validation she needed.

Cumpa's pregnancy changed her entire outlook on life. "Before that moment, I was ready to die" for the cause, she recalled, "but now I needed to survive for my child's sake."[7]

Cumpa knew her condition could be a liability. In addition to the physical demands of her militancy, she could lose the baby if she were ever captured and tortured by police. Not wanting to take any chances, she hid the test even from her two roommates—both of them women—and continued business as usual.

Recently, the Central Committee had decided to increase revenue for the insurgency by kidnapping wealthy capitalists and ransoming them for cash. This strategy had proven useful for guerrilla groups elsewhere in Latin America. In Colombia, the FARC had been performing this task for years, and their guerrilla army had only expanded as a result.[8] As with the FARC, the MRTA justified this tactic by denouncing its victims not as civilians but as capitalist enemies responsible for the nation's misery. As such, any extortion of their families was fair game. Few in the mainstream media or society actually shared this sentiment. Instead, most saw the targeting of civilians as further evidence of what historian Nelson Manrique dubbed the "Senderization" of the MRTA.[9]

The task of deciding whom to abduct first fell to Lucero Cumpa. Always looking to prove that women were as competent as men, the pregnant twenty-two-year-old assembled a team made up mostly of women to scout potential targets. They settled on the Japanese Peruvian industrialist Julio Ikeda. For the better part of a month, Cumpa's team tailed Ikeda, studying his every move. Then, on the morning of 26 September 1987, they made their move. Ikeda and his twenty-two-year-old son, Julio, had just pulled out of their garage in Lima's Surco district. As the Ikedas turned onto the street, Cumpa pulled her cream Datsun in front of them, cutting them off and forcing Ikeda to slam on the brakes. Before Ikeda could react, four Tupac Amaristas dressed in all black and carrying submachine guns got out of the car. Ikeda put the car in reverse, but a pickup truck cut him off. Out hopped two more rebels dressed in black. The assailants stormed Ikeda's car, firing three warning shots into the air before pulling him from the vehicle and forcing him into the pickup truck. The remaining rebels ran on Ikeda's car and instructed his son not to move.[10] Just then, a residential security guard who had overheard the commotion pulled up and removed his gun. The rebels fired warning shots into the air, and one of the bullets struck a passing taxi driver. The guard took cover, at which point the Tupac Amaristas boarded Cumpa's car and sped away.[11] Hours later, the rebels called Ikeda's brother and demanded 45 million intis, the equivalent of 1 million U.S. dollars, for his release.[12]

Police identified Cumpa right away as the operation's mastermind. After a thorough investigation, agents tracked her down to her safe house and put a tail on her. Cumpa was none the wiser, going about her business with normal caution. When a comrade whom she was supposed to meet on the morning of Saturday, 24 October 1987, didn't show up at the rendezvous point, she simply headed back to her safe house. She didn't even notice the plainclothes agents trailing her from a distance. When she was on Salamanca Avenue, a vehicle pulled up alongside her, and a team of agents jumped out. The agents quickly cuffed and blindfolded her before pushing her into the back of a squad car. Cumpa lay facedown in the backseat with a gun to the back of her head as the car pulled up to her house. As she lay there, she could hear the gunshots and screams from inside the house as the agents raided the home. She began second-guessing herself. In hindsight, she could clearly remember seeing the civilian-dressed agents. Why had she so willfully ignored the signs? She had let her guard down, and now she would pay the price.[13]

The agents found no sign of Ikeda inside. As it happens, the industrialist had been in the custody of another team in Jesús María, which promptly released him unharmed once they had gotten word about the raid.[14] What the agents did find inside the home was a positive pregnancy test and the original battle flag of José de San Martín.

It wasn't until she arrived at the precinct that Cumpa realized she had been captured by DIVISE, the missing persons police. Inside, she saw two other women prisoners in a cell. On closer inspection, she could see that some of their family members had been locked away with them. This gave her a tremendous scare. It was one thing for her to be in jail, but she did not want to jeopardize her family. Later, she would learn that the agents had in fact attempted to arrest her mother, María, and had even put her in their squad truck, but that her neighbor, the same police officer who had bailed her out during her early days of militancy, had intervened to get María released. "It was all a tactic to pressure us, to hit us where it hurt most and force us to play ball," Cumpa explained.[15]

As she sat in her isolated second-floor cell, she looked down and noticed that she was wearing blue jeans. That was when she realized her dream had finally come to pass. "My subconscious was trying to warn me, but I ignored the signs!"[16]

Cumpa would always deny her involvement in Julio Ikeda's kidnapping. The evidence, however, was not in her favor. In her apartment, police found the weapons used in Ikeda's kidnapping as well as copies of his ID and photographs of his family members. They also claimed to have obtained confessions from Cumpa and her comrades.[17] As far as Cumpa was concerned, however, any confession should have been inadmissible, given that it occurred under duress. The agents, she said, called them "scientific interrogations," but make no mistake about it, "It's torture."[18]

These torture sessions took place in one of the offices inside the precinct. According to Cumpa, her torturers were brutal. They hung her by her arms with a rope, tied her feet and plunged her face into a bathtub filled with excrement and detergent, and delivered body blows. It was during these sessions that the agents broke her right arm. The worst, she said, was that they knew she was pregnant. In between sessions, she would talk to her still-flat tummy. "Daughter," she said, divining that her unborn child would be a girl, "you're coming into this world alive and I'm going to be right here with you. You and I are getting out of this hell-hole together."[19]

One day, after a particularly grueling torture session, a DIVISE policeman walked into the cell and removed her blindfold.

"Look what they've done to you," he said, handing her some food. "I had to participate in your torture session. We're ordered to watch."

"Well," Cumpa said, "that's how they harden you. You guys get off on it."

The policeman explained that he didn't take any pleasure in her torture. Before leaving the cell, he asked, "If you saw me in the street, would you kill me?"

"Why would I kill you?" Cumpa asked. "I'm no judge. I have no authority to decide your fate. If your conscience is clear, that's good, and if not, you'll know."[20]

According to Cumpa, she and her comrades were in such bad shape when they were handed over to the counterterrorism police several days later that even DINCOTE officials commented on the abuse.

"What did you do to them?" one DINCOTE official asked his colleagues when he saw the women. "A little more and they wouldn't have made it."[21]

The courts found Cumpa guilty of the kidnapping and locked her away in Lima's maximum-security prison, Canto Grande. There, she found her husband, Fernando Valladares, waiting for her. When they first met, he gave her a warm embrace. He didn't appear mad, scared, or even disappointed. The only emotion Cumpa could detect was joy. Somehow he had gotten word that she was with child. Even in their imprisonment, the two shared a brief embrace, a fleeting moment, to celebrate new life.[22]

■ The most prized possession police found in Cumpa's home was the missing battle flag of independence hero José de San Martín. The flag had been a source of great shame for the government since the Tupac Amaristas had stolen it from a Huaura museum three years prior. During a press conference in which the banner hung in the foreground, a police official communicated his satisfaction in having recovered "this patriotic symbol of great historical value."[23] Six days later, police turned over the flag to Alan García in a ceremony inside the Salón Dorado of the presidential palace. After receiving the bicolor banner, the president proclaimed, "This simple act has great solemnity and symbolism because it represents the recuperation of our most important symbol that expresses all of our illusions and which must never be allowed in the hands of those who invoke destruction and murder."[24] Thanking the security forces for their fine service in defense of the country against "the social ill that is terrorism," García explained that it was of vital importance that the nation preserve its symbols, particularly during such difficult times. From that point forward, he promised, the flag would remain inside the presidential palace. To complete the ceremony, the president invited the superior director of the police force into his office, where they hung the flag together.[25]

The independence banner wasn't the only flag over which the opposing sides battled. Equally important was the national triband. Consisting of two vertical red stripes surrounding a single white vertical stripe, the Peruvian flag was adopted shortly after the founding of the republic in the early 1820s. For official purposes, the ensign appears with a coat of arms in the center of the white band. While the design of the coat of arms may vary, it always includes three symbols: a vicuña, the national animal and wild cousin to the llama, situated in the upper left corner; a chinchona tree, Peru's national flora, which rests to the immediate right of the camelid; and a cornucopia overflowing with coins, representing the country's mineral wealth.

The rebel flag of the MRTA was nearly identical to the Peruvian flag, but with a twist. The rebels had replaced the crest of the national flag with the likeness of their revolutionary namesake, Tupac Amaru. The barrels of two rifles framed the cacique's serene face and adjoined beneath the neck to form the letter V, for *Venceremos* (We Will Prevail). Underneath the weapons were the letters M.R.T.A. By fusing the foremost symbol of the nation with that of their rebel hero, the Tupac Amaristas hoped to present their armed group not as a terrorist organization, as the state, media, and mainstream society liked to portray it, but as an army of national liberation.

Whenever they carried out successful armed actions, the rebels left behind the banner as a sort of revolutionary calling card.[26] Sometimes, flag planting, or *banderamientos*, in the guerrilla lexicon, was the primary objective. In November 1987, rebels commemorated the 207th anniversary of the Tupac Amaru rebellion by draping no fewer than fifteen MRTA flags throughout Lima's shantytowns. To ensure that the flags remained in place, the Tupac Amaristas set up booby traps of bombs around the flags. In Lucero Cumpa's home district of Comas, militants mounted the rebel flag on a monument of Tupac Amaru and decorated it with a floral arrangement as an homage to their namesake.[27]

The MRTA flag was a thorn in the side of administration officials. They saw it not as an adaptation of the national ensign but as a treacherous defacement of the nation's most sacred symbol. State officials insisted that, despite having the same base design, the MRTA flag was most definitely not the Peruvian flag. Luis Giampietri, admiral of the navy and future vice president of the republic, emphasized this point during a 2012 interview.

"[The Tupac Amaristas] had a distinct flag," Giampietri said. "It has two crossing rifles and the face of Tupac Amaru. In other words, it wasn't the flag of the state. The state never recognized them as a [national army]."

But wasn't the MRTA banner just the Peruvian flag with a different logo?

"No," Giampietri scoffed, pointing out the difference in the coat of arms. It was the coat of arms that made the national banner official. It was what made it Peruvian. Taking up any other banner, no matter how similar to or inspired by the national flag, was tantamount to treason. Asked how he had felt whenever he saw the Tupac Amaristas raise the rebel flag, the admiral sighed. "Namely, that they are traitors to our country."[28]

Whenever security forces encountered the flag, they made its removal from the public sphere a top priority. They, too, understood its powerful symbolism, and as long as it remained in public view, it represented a threat to the authority of the state.

■ In recent months, a special investigation unit within DINCOTE had been tailing Alberto Gálvez Olaechea in the hopes of capturing the rebel leader. A freshly minted major named Marco Miyashiro headed up the unit. A Japanese Peruvian from the twin city of Callao, Miyashiro had previously been a member of Víctor Polay Campos's Boy Scout group. In those days, Miyashiro had considered his fellow Asian Peruvian "an excellent young man with a strong capacity for leadership." Miyashiro recalled that when Polay's father was released from prison, he and the other scouts held a party to celebrate. Polay explained to the boys the difference between political prisoners and common criminals, ensuring them that his father had been the former.[29]

Now, more than twenty years later, Miyashiro found himself heading up the unit responsible for catching MRTA Directorate member Alberto Gálvez

Olaechea. Miyashiro's agents believed they had collected enough evidence to convict the cerebral thirty-three-year-old. In addition to linking him to the attack on the presidential palace, they connected him with a car bomb on Paraguay Avenue, stolen food trucks in El Agustino and Collique, and another undetonated bomb at the Jorge Chávez International Airport.[30] That Gálvez lived a semipublic life made him easy to tail. The goateed leader had secured a press pass at the left-wing weekly *Cambio* and sometimes appeared at the paper's Lima office. He also routinely visited other suspected guerrillas in restaurants and cafés throughout the city.

Miyashiro's unit went in for the arrest on 7 August 1987, detaining Gálvez as he boarded his car outside his Magdalena home. Inside, the agents uncovered a chest filled with internal documents that, according to Miyashiro, "enabled us to learn a number of details about the organization and operations of the MRTA that we never knew before."[31] It was enough to earn Gálvez a twelve-year sentence in the newly installed maximum-security prison, Canto Grande. More important, the Gálvez case opened a new path of investigation that would lead to more busts. "That investigation," Miyashiro said, "formed the building blocks of the MRTA-related analysis, study, and research that would sustain me for years to come."[32]

The loss of Alberto Gálvez Olaechea dealt a major blow to the MRTA. It was the most high-profile capture to date, for either the MRTA or Shining Path. The other MRTA leaders were still at large, and despite one DINCOTE chief's claim that Néstor Cerpa's "days were numbered," finding the former union leader proved easier said than done.[33] What police didn't realize was that Gálvez had already helped lay the groundwork for a new phase of guerrilla warfare that would go on with or without him. A year earlier, as Gálvez was working out the details of bringing his MIR into the fold of the MRTA, he, Víctor Polay, and other Central Committee members had convened the First Unified Plenary Session to evaluate the situation of the movement in the country. By then, the political violence had spread throughout the country, as both Shining Path and state counterinsurgency forces had stepped up attacks on civilians and enemy combatants alike. Although the MRTA had now established itself as a formidable guerrilla force in the city, it had still not managed to gain a foothold in the countryside. Polay believed that the time had come to organize a rural guerrilla front.[34] Gálvez concurred, and he knew just the place to launch it. His MIR had already established a base of support in the northeastern department of San Martín, a small agricultural department in the Amazon basin. The Miristas counted on a network of students, teachers, and peasants throughout the Lower Huallaga River, and the Tupac Amarista neophyte was confident that it could be mobilized quickly and efficiently should the MRTA start a guerrilla front there.[35]

Gálvez believed San Martín to be an ideal setting in which to launch a guerrilla operation. The department had served as a strong base of support for Peru's largest peasant union, the Peasant Confederation of Peru. In the years leading up to the insurgency, the Agrarian Federation of the Greater Jungle had gone head-to-head with the Peruvian government, organizing massive strikes and roadblocks throughout the department. Sanmartinenses also had experience with militancy. Students, teachers, and workers had already organized a regional Defense Front, and some peasants had formed militias as part of a wider movement in civilian defense known as the *rondas campesinas*.[36] Gálvez's MIR had been alongside these peasant activists every step of the way, forming meaningful political, legal, and logistical support. If called upon, he believed the peasants would support the MRTA.

Gálvez would be arrested before the planned insurrection ever came to fruition. By that point, however, the wheels were already in motion. As general commander, Polay personally oversaw the formation of the front in the Amazon.[37] After arriving, he scouted the area for an ideal location from which to launch the rural campaign.

Part **2**

7

The Heroic Guerrilla

Although he was just a boy in 1987, Daniel Bravo had seen his fair share of mobilization. His father, Peter, had serenaded him with stories of Mirista martyrs and Caribbean communists. A peasant organizer in San Martín, Peter helped organize rural workers to fight for a fair price for rice, the main staple in those parts of the jungle. Peter would take Daniel with him during organized rallies, political meetings, and protests, hoping the experience would teach the brown-eyed boy the importance of political activism and collective bargaining.

In 1982, when Daniel was eight, Peter took him to a location outside the town of Tabalosos, where the peasants had already blocked the major highway connecting the northern and southern parts of the department. At night, Daniel camped alongside the highway with a group of women and children while the men occupied the main road. He huddled together with his brother against the pavement and drifted to sleep under the jungle canopy.

He awoke at four in the morning to the sound of gunshots. He sprung to his feet and ushered his brother into the brush for cover. Women screamed, children cried, and people scattered in all directions as the shots rang out. Daniel and his brother ran to the house of his grandmother, who lived in a straw hut nearby. Peter came by the house later that morning covered in blood. Daniel was horrified, thinking his father was dying. Only after some initial confusion did he realize that the blood didn't belong to his father. Peter had been carrying the dead. A short while later, another peasant came running to the house looking for Peter.

"We found more dead!" the peasant shouted.

Peter dropped everything and headed toward the door.

"Follow the march," he told Daniel before leaving. "That will lead you back home. Go back to the cooperative."

Daniel saddled up a horse and joined the mass of protesters headed up the mountain. Peter didn't return that day; he was arrested while attending to the dead and wounded. Only later would Daniel learn what had happened that morning. The government had sent in police to clear the highway. When the peasants refused to budge, authorities opened fire, killing six and wounding many more.

The Tabalosos massacre marked a watershed moment for peasants in San Martín. From that point on, they agreed that if they were to continue mobilizing, they would need to arm themselves. After that fateful night, Daniel noticed graffiti along the walls of huts throughout the community. *El MIR Vuelve*, "The MIR Returns," read the cryptic paintings. Daniel had heard stories of the Peruvian rebels from his father, but he didn't quite know what these paintings meant. How could a defeated rebellion return?

He soon noticed the presence of family friends—young men, all of them— who continually came in and out of the cooperative, bathing in the communal well and patrolling the area at night. The young men were good to Daniel, giving him special attention whenever they came around; one even gave him a dictionary so he could build his vocabulary.[1] Daniel had taken to calling these men *tíos*, uncles, a term of endearment connoting a kind of familiarity in their strangeness. "We called them all *tío, tío*," he recalled, "but none of them were from around here, they were all from the coast." One night, a *tío* came to his house a bit out of sorts, his clothes covered in paint. The young man hurriedly stripped down and burned his clothes before continuing on his way. Apparently, he had been painting rebel slogans along the highway and had wanted to destroy the evidence. The following year, the *tío* returned, this time with a group of other *tíos*, all carrying guns. With Peter's permission, the militants would go out into the fields behind the co-op to engage in target practice and training drills. When the *tíos* came, Peter would go out and search for places where they could camp out—caves, mountains—with Daniel always tagging along. Daniel would fetch them water for their training.

One day in 1987, Daniel was out playing in the field when his older sister, Yasi, stopped by unannounced. She was barely twenty and newly wed, and her visits these days were infrequent, so Daniel left his friends behind to see what she wanted. It was their father. He had died suddenly. The official cause was a heart attack, but Yasi had her doubts. She said that Peter had called only the night before to check on her. He told her, rather cryptically, that he was fine and that she need not worry about him. Locals found his lifeless body the next day. Yasi suspected that Peter had been murdered by union busters. She told her mother that she would take Daniel back to live with her and her husband in Tarapoto until things smoothed over.

■ Although the rural campaign would be characterized by guerrilla warfare, Víctor Polay's forces never abandoned their symbolic war, anointing it "Tupac Amaru, Liberator," in honor of their Andean namesake. The jungle, of course, had none of the great monuments, cemeteries, and artifacts that had made the cities such a playground for iconographic appropriation. Instead, the rebels turned the calendar into their theater of war, timing their assaults to commemorate major moments in Peruvian and Latin American revolutionary history.

It was not by accident that the rebels launched their rural campaign on 8 October 1987, the twenty-year anniversary of the death of Che Guevara in Bolivia. Hailing their offensive "For the Heroic Guerrilla," the name given to the anniversary by the global left, Polay and company set their sights on Tabalosos, the site of the 1982 massacre witnessed by the young Daniel Bravo. In doing so, the rebels hoped to appropriate the Tabalosos tragedy for their own revolutionary cause. Before launching the attack, the guerrillas proclaimed, "Che Lives! Guerrilla warfare isn't dead."[2]

The Tupac Amaristas decamped on foot, marching for days. As they approached Tabalosos, they intercepted several trucks and ordered the drivers to take them the remainder of the way. This practice of kidnapping truckers would be a favorite of the Northeastern Front. The drivers dumped Polay and his comrades in front of the main plaza, a stone's throw from the police station. As commander, Polay was among the first to breach the building, catching the sentries off guard and ordering them to stand down to avoid a bloodbath. Most of the officers surrendered or fled as the rebels stormed the building.[3]

After securing the police station, Polay held an impromptu rally in the town square and described his insurgency as a social democratic revolution in defense of justice and peace. The authorities, he said, had a responsibility to honor their promises to the people. Afterward, he conversed with town leaders while his men redistributed food from commandeered trucks. Once the rally had ended, he ordered his men to set their police captives free.[4]

Polay was proud of his accomplishment, and he wanted to make it known what it signified for the Peruvian people. He told reporters a month later, "8 October is a day that will be recorded in history. It is the date of the rebirth of the guerrillas in Peru. We took by force Tabalosos, a town very dear to us."[5] What made Tabalosos so dear to the rebel leader was its role in local historical memory. This was the site of the peasant mobilization that Daniel Bravo's father had spearheaded, the site of police violence against civilian protesters. In taking this town, Polay's troops had effectively reclaimed the town for the Tupac Amaristas, the true ethnic guardians of the people of San Martín.

Next, Polay wanted to seize a large town to demonstrate to Sanmartin-enses and the country that the Northeastern Front was a force to be reckoned with. Over the next several weeks, he traveled throughout the department, meeting with militia, labor leaders, and community organizers to gauge the local populace's receptivity to the MRTA's presence. During these travels he decided to sack Juanjuí, a midsized town of more than 25,000 inhabitants in the middle of the jungle. Before his arrest, Alberto Gálvez had already made some inroads in Juanjuí and believed the townspeople would be receptive. Moreover, the local police force had a reputation for abusing the populace, so capturing the police stations could send a message of justice.[6]

Unlike the smaller Tabalosos, Juanjuí had three police stations, one for each major branch of the force. By Polay's count, the local police force numbered more than 100. However, his sources assured him that most of these forces patrolled the countryside, leaving the police stations understaffed and vulnerable to outside attack. But the police were not the only obstacle. Shining Path had penetrated the northern jungle and regularly operated in the Huallaga River that ran alongside the outskirts of the cacao-producing town. By now, the Maoists had a reputation for violence and authoritarianism, and despite having common cause with the MRTA, they had no interest in forming a rebel alliance. If anything, they viewed the Tupac Amaristas as a threat to their larger political and territorial interests in the region. In short, establishing a guerrilla base in Juanjuí would mean going to war with Shining Path.[7]

After returning to his base of operations, Polay gathered the other three commanders of the Northeastern Front. He informed them about the intelligence he had gathered on Juanjuí and explained that he had personally scouted the town.

"It's the ideal city," he said.

The other commanders, which included the heavy-set Néstor Cerpa, concurred, approving a course of action involving seventy guerrillas and dozens of civilian militia. The primary objective would be to take over the police stations of the Civil Guard, Republican Guard, and Peruvian Investigative Police, or PIP. Once secured, the rebels would seize the airport, the telephone company, and the roads leading in and out of the town in order to cut off communication and transport.[8]

On 6 November 1987, the day of the assault, the rebel army, clad in olive fatigues and rubber boots and armed with automatic rifles, submachine guns, short-range handguns, and mortars, descended upon the sleepy jungle town.[9]

It was Bronco's turn to guard the front of the Civil Guard station that morning. Bronco's lieutenant had stumbled in drunk at 2:00 A.M., headed straight to the back of the station, and passed out on a cot alongside three of his men while Bronco and his partner secured the front door. It was nearly 4:00 A.M. when the bronze-complected corporal noticed a truck slowly making its way down Callao Street. When the vehicle reached the plaza, dozens of uniformed men jumped off and scattered throughout the plaza, taking up positions throughout the square. Bronco squinted to get a closer look.

"Who are those guys?" he asked.

His partner, an older corporal named Jorge Cieza Lachos, gazed at the men for a few seconds.

"They're terrorists!" Cieza Lachos exclaimed.

Before Bronco could react, the rebels opened fire. He took cover as the rebels closed in, cocking his rifle slowly and quietly so as not to give away his position. His body was so consumed with adrenaline that he didn't realize he had been hit. A bullet had ricocheted off the ceiling, grazing his right cheek and severing a piece of his left pinky on the way down. He was bleeding from the face and finger, but he was too rattled to notice. He carefully aimed his rifle at one of the rebels and pulled the trigger, but the gun didn't fire. In his effort to keep perfectly quiet, he had cocked his gun so gently that the bullet never chambered.

Panic set in. His vision began to blur, and he lost the ability to think straight. To make matters worse, the guerrillas were now launching mortars at the building. He ran to the back room only to find it abandoned. Apparently, the sleeping lieutenant and his men had escaped through the back door as soon as the firefight began. Another policeman had snuck out through an escape hatch. Blood oozing down his face, Bronco ran out the back door and sought cover behind a nearby home. He had escaped with his life, something that couldn't be said of his partner Cieza Lachos, who received a fatal wound to the stomach.[10]

The Tupac Amaristas took over the three police stations, the airport, and the telephone company, cutting off all communication with the outside. Polay oversaw the operation from his command post near the main square. After his men seized the buildings and blocked the major roads, he got on the megaphone and addressed the curious townspeople. According to Polay, the Juanjuinos greeted him and his comrades eagerly. Hundreds of young men and women volunteered to join the rebel ranks, while others offered political and moral support. Mothers showered the Tupac Amaristas with food and clothing to take with them on their long journey. "The support from the population and its identification with the MRTA were unyielding," Polay claimed.[11]

While it is possible that the rebel leader overstated the level of enthusiasm he and his comrades received that day, there is little doubt that at least some townspeople welcomed their presence. Indeed, when some of the Juanjuinos learned that Néstor Cerpa was holding a wounded policeman named James John Trisolini at the PIP station, they demanded that Cerpa submit the officer to mob justice. Cerpa refused, instead ordering his men to drive Trisolini to the airport and radio-in his condition so that he could receive proper medical attention. On the way there, the rebels came across a police vehicle and handed Trisolini over to his colleagues, who took him without incident and escorted him to the hospital.[12]

The Tupac Amaristas remained in Juanjuí for nearly five hours, conversing with the locals and redistributing anything of value that they had confiscated in the attack. Of course, they retained all weapons from the police stations for themselves, nearly doubling their arsenal in the process. Still, Polay's forces did not miss an opportunity to turn their military victory into a symbolic one. In addition to the appropriation of the police stations, Polay's troops defaced the local symbols of state power, vandalizing, burning, and even dynamiting a number of government offices. At 9:00 A.M. they finally loaded into the beds of five pickup trucks and left town.[13]

It was early afternoon when the guerrillas reached their next target: the small community of San José de Sisa. Before the rebels arrived, some of the townspeople sounded the alarm, and police fled. When the trucks rolled into town, they encountered nothing but the gazes of curious townspeople who peered out of their doorways or climbed onto the rooftops to catch a glimpse of the rebel army. "You can't really say that we 'took' [Sisa]," Polay later admitted, "because there was no military resistance. . . . It was more like an 'occupation.'" Polay addressed the townsfolk in the main plaza and invited them to support the insurgency. Roughly thirty young men and women heeded the call, joining the ranks of the rebel army. Polay and his comrades spent the night in town before continuing their march.[14]

■ Back in Lima, legislators criticized the failure of state intelligence to respond to the guerrilla presence in San Martín. Others called for the government to open a political dialogue with the guerrillas and pay closer attention to the demands of the San Martín citizenry.[15] Still others called for a general amnesty to incentivize the Tupac Amaristas to lay down arms.[16] One op-ed writer asked the question that was on everyone's mind: Was San Martín becoming "another Ayacucho?"—a reference to the beleaguered Shining Path stronghold in the south central Andes. All signs pointed to yes.[17]

The government responded by launching its own media blitz. Just five days after the Juanjuí attack, Alan García broadcast a message from the presidential palace. "We must spare Peru more blood and violence," the president remarked in his first-ever televised message directed at the MRTA. "I ask that the group accept the unanimous decision of the people to resolve its problems democratically."[18] He insisted that the guerrillas demilitarize and surrender to a government that "isn't imposed by any foreign power."[19] Interior Minister José Barsallo Burga also went on the offensive, questioning the generous news coverage that the rebels had received in San Martín. In a closed-door meeting with senate leaders, the minister floated the notion that the press was colluding with the MRTA. Senate opposition leaders took the bait, denouncing the accusation before the press.[20] Prime Minister Larco Cox tried a more direct approach. He told reporters that the government had no interest in dialogue and rejected the use of the term "guerrilla" to describe the Tupac Amaristas. Despite being "uniformed, very disciplined and with a friendly attitude toward the population," the Tupac Amaristas were terrorists.[21]

The García administration backed up its rhetoric with a massive counteroffensive in San Martín. On 10 November, just days after the sacking of Juanjuí, García declared a state of emergency in San Martín, issuing a curfew throughout the war zone and suspending civil liberties. In the coming days, helicopter after helicopter arrived in the zone, unloading no fewer than 500 police personnel.[22] Less than a week after the state of emergency declaration, the joint chiefs of the armed forces touched down in Tarapoto to oversee operation "Down with the MRTA." The objective of this counterinsurgency effort was to hunt down and eliminate the MRTA's base of operations in the jungle. By now, Peruvian intelligence had confirmed the identity of rebel leader "Comandante Rolando" as Víctor Polay Campos, and soldiers had explicit orders to capture him "dead or alive."[23]

The counterinsurgency was largely the work of Defense Minister Enrique López Albújar. López Albújar's father had been a famous writer whose works helped found the *indigenista* literary school. Enrique Sr. wrote beautiful stories and poems about Andean life that inspired empathy and compassion. Enrique Jr. had a much different calling. After finishing at the top of his class in the army academy, he received military training in the Panama Canal Zone, Fort Knox, and the United Kingdom. He went on to occupy important posts during the military dictatorship of Morales Bermúdez, serving on the president's executive council. Now, the fifty-seven-year-old served as the nation's first defense minister. He had the stern face of a commander, a man who gave orders and fully expected them to be completed.[24] It was López Albújar who persuaded the president to declare martial law in San Martín in late 1987. He believed that only a scorched-earth campaign would restore law and order to the Amazon and thwart the rebel advancement. He asked the people of San Martín to "put their total trust in the Armed Forces," which would have utmost respect for human rights and the rules of engagement.[25] During his visits, he would walk around in his olive fatigues and cap, a black pistol loosely holstered at the hip.[26]

The general understood the importance of winning the symbolic struggle in the Amazon. In Alto Sisa, the Tupac Amaristas confronted an army patrol in a mid-November battle that produced minor casualties on both sides.[27] Three days later, police captured three presumed rebels as they attempted to dig up the body of one of their fallen comrades and drape the MRTA flag over the tombstone.[28] The security forces took great pride in winning this battle of the flags. In December, a column of Tupac Amaristas was forced to flee at a moment's notice when an army patrol closed in on their camp near San José de Sisa. Although the raid produced no casualties or injuries, the army flew in members of the media to photograph the patrol climbing atop a palm tree to remove the rebel flag.[29] The following day, López Albújar presided over a ceremony in Lima's Flag Plaza, where participants paid homage to the Peruvian triband. The ceremony corresponded to the Day of the Reservists, in honor of the reserve army that helped defend the country against the Chileans during the War of the Pacific, but López Albújar used the occasion to discuss the advances that his troops had made in the Amazon. After the ceremony, he proclaimed that the armed forces had made significant strides in the war against the MRTA, citing the previous day's incursion as an example. He assured reporters that the armed forces would continue to operate effectively against the "terrorists."[30]

■ Since moving into his big sister's home in Tarapoto in late 1987, young Daniel Bravo had accepted the counterinsurgency as the new normal. "I think that was when our childhood was interrupted," he later said.[31] It wasn't uncommon for his pickup soccer games to come to a sudden halt when the propellers of a helicopter roared overhead, or for teams of soldiers to raid his neighbors' homes. In the evenings, Daniel and his friends stopped whatever they were doing to run inside before the six o'clock curfew set in. Anyone caught in the streets after that, no matter how young, was subject to immediate arrest. As he sat in his sister Yasi's house in the evening, he could hear gunshots in the distance. Sometimes, soldiers or police would pound on the door in the middle of the night, demanding to take a census of the household.

The troops had reason to inspect Yasi's home: both she and her husband were in the MRTA. On occasion, they would host meetings with different Tupac Amaristas and, of course, more *tíos* whom Daniel barely knew. "Once again," he remembered, "it was *tío* this, *tío* that," just like the days back on the cooperative. Yasi, a nurse in the local clinic, would take in sick or wounded Tupac Amaristas and treat them in her Tarapoto home. One night, the soldiers ransacked the house when his sister was out of town. Daniel was jolted awake at midnight when the soldiers kicked in his door. The soldiers searched the house up and down, tossing everything about before finally leaving. After that, the home visits became a regular occurrence. During one nighttime raid, a neighbor came to their defense.

"Get out of here!" yelled the neighbor as the soldiers left the house. "Don't you have anything better to do than pick on little kids? Get out of here! Get out!"

The soldiers, Daniel recalled, returned almost weekly, and each time the neighbor gave them a piece of his mind. Sometimes the soldiers would let it go. At other times they would smack the neighbor across the face. But no matter how many times they returned, the same old neighbor kept yelling at them to leave. "There's nothing to see here! Go pick on someone else!" Daniel wasn't sure whether his neighbor knew that Yasi was involved in the movement.

Sometimes Yasi would ask her brother to do small tasks for her, like run guns from San Miguel to Tarapoto. Even with all the military checkpoints, soldiers didn't suspect children of subversive activity at first. Daniel and other boys would simply fill their backpacks with guns and run them past the checkpoints without raising any suspicion. When he got home, he would give the backpack to Yasi and go outside to play, never giving it a second thought.

■ Despite Defense Minister López Albújar's efforts to control the narrative of the war in the jungle, the "Tupac Amaru, Liberator" campaign captured the imagination of the Peruvian people. Much of the buzz centered around the group's militant young commander, Víctor Polay. Polay understood the crucial role that the media could play in political aesthetics, and he used this to his advantage. Shortly before their first actions in Tabalosos and Juanjuí, his men took pictures of themselves preparing for combat. These photographs would make it into Peru's leading newspapers and magazines. He also allowed trusted media sources exclusive access into his conquered towns.

The first to arrive was Channel 5 reporter Alejandro Guerrero. Guerrero's crew arrived the day after the rebels' victories in Juanjuí and San José de Sisa. His television interview, broadcast on national airwaves, presented the MRTA as a formidable and disciplined guerrilla army, shattering the government's narrative that the group was little more than a band of narcotraffickers.[32] In Sinami, a small hamlet of just over 1,200 residents, Polay allowed journalists from different papers to interview him. It was the first time he appeared unmasked before the press—sort of. The reporters found Polay sitting atop a rock in the dirt-floored patio of a local peasant's home. Between his shaded sunglasses and olive green cap, it was difficult to make out his face. He also insisted on being photographed from behind. When asked for his name, he gave only his *nom de guerre*, Rolando.[33]

The reporters took a seat on a wooden bench directly across from Polay, their backs to the row of armed guerrillas guarding the door.

The rebel commander began explaining the significance of the Northeastern Front's actions, reminding his visitors that the Tupac Amaristas had begun their guerrilla campaign in Tabalosos as an act of tribute to the peasants killed by police in 1982.

He also made a point of articulating his movement's nationalist identity. Asked if his guerrillas received any foreign aid, he retorted, "No, the personnel under my command is trained for these actions. There isn't a single foreigner among my men. . . . We're all Peruvians. . . . Our movement is authentically Peruvian. We've only followed the example of others, like the Cubans, the Nicaraguans, whose actions we respect, but I repeat, our guerrilla army is Peruvian."[34] This was only partly true. It may have been the case that no rural guerrillas were foreigners, but the MRTA enlisted plenty of help from the outside, from Chilean Miristas to Bolivian, Colombian, and Ecuadorian rebels. Some of these insurgents even operated inside the country. Polay's misleading comments underscore a recognition on his part of the optics of having foreign fighters on Peruvian soil. If his organization was to stand any chance of winning over hearts and minds, it would need to appear Peruvian in name and composition. Polay also used the opportunity to distinguish his group from Shining Path, whose penchant for violence was by now notorious throughout the country. Unlike the rival guerrilla group, whose vision of the Peruvian reality he described as "mistaken" and "questionable," the MRTA was a true revolutionary movement, one that spoke "the language of the people."[35] Here again, Polay understood the importance of discursively linking his movement to the nation. Unlike the wayward Senderistas, the Tupac Amaristas were salt-of-the-earth Peruvians.

After chatting with the press for roughly three hours, Polay stood up and retired for the evening. There was a festive atmosphere that night, with plenty of music and dancing. The reporters snapped pictures of peasant women dancing the *tunche*, a local dance, with the bearded and mustachioed guerrillas, who never stopped clutching their guns as they danced the night away. These photos, published in the major newspapers the next day, created an image of a guerrilla army that had won the support of the local populace.[36]

It was only a matter of time before government and media sources confirmed Polay's true identity. He might have been counting on it. The speculation cloaked the commander in mystique: Víctor Polay, the Aprista golden boy turned guerrilla fighter; Víctor Polay, the president's former roommate turned archnemesis. The more people knew about Polay's identity, the more incredible his story seemed. The more incredible the story, the more people wanted to know. Peruvians had trouble believing that the son of the ruling party's cofounder would risk his life fighting a guerrilla war in the middle of the Amazon. Yet there he was, giving interviews in San José de Sisa. The sheer implausibility of it all led some to speculate that Polay had only shown up for the photo op before chartering a private plane out of the country. Other papers reported that he had fled the jungle on a drug-loaded jet. "I hate to break it to you," Polay told *Cambio* in an exclusive mid-December interview, "but [rumors of my escape] are nothing more than the wishful thinking or dreams of the Armed Forces and Aprista government."[37]

The MRTA thus wrapped up 1987 at the height of its splendor, having successfully distanced itself from Shining Path in the public eye and enjoying a groundswell of support. While exact numbers are difficult to obtain, it is estimated that the organization had no fewer than 1,000 rebels and several thousand more active supporters by the decade's end.[38] Many of these new recruits had been inspired by the "Tupac Amaru, Liberator" campaign. This was the case with Carlos Peña, a Lima high schooler who hadn't known much about the MRTA before 1987. Carlos devoured newspaper reports of the rebels' "brilliant, victorious campaign" in San Martín. Reading these headlines from streetside magazine stands, he concluded that the MRTA represented "a different option" to Shining Path's campaign of destruction.[39] When he got into San Marcos University the following year, he volunteered for the rebel army. He would be among the dozens of San Marcos students taking oaths of loyalty to the MRTA before a statue of the "heroic guerilla" himself, Che Guevara, that year. "Without a doubt," historian Nelson Manrique observed, "that was the moment in which the [MRTA's] prestige reached its greatest heights."[40] But would it last?

8

Rodrigo's Journey

Rodrigo was the oldest of seven children in the Gálvez household. The Gálvezes lived better than most in 1970s Tarapoto. Rodrigo's father owned an estate and drove a pickup truck. It never quite settled with Rodrigo that the field hands had to work for meager pay while his family lived a life of comfort in the tropical city. Sometimes he would jump in his father's truck and join him to check on the workers. During these visits, the teenager would ask the workers if they had a fair wage and enough to eat. At other times he would pester his dad to pay them overtime when they worked long hours.

As a student at Tarapoto's Colegio Santa Rosa, Rodrigo stayed in school and out of trouble. Franco, his little brother, remembered that Rodrigo always had a stack of books piled high in his bedroom. When Franco asked why he had so many books, Rodrigo said, "You have to learn in order to grow."[1] Rodrigo was always dishing out words of wisdom for his siblings. "When it's time to work, work. When it's time to dance, dance. But never both at the same time," he would say.[2]

By the late 1970s, the department had become a hotbed of social unrest, with students joining peasants and laborers in mass protests. Rodrigo came of age in the midst of this activism. As a student at the Superior Technological Institute, he joined the MIR–Voz Rebelde, a leftist organization with a strong following in San Martín. MIR militants were activists, often at the front lines of regional protests. During one demonstration, the normally even-keeled teen attempted to wrestle a policeman's baton from his hands. Rodrigo failed in the effort and was lucky not to receive a beating—or worse—for his intransigence. Still, the incident, witnessed by many, earned him the respect of his peers.

In 1984, when he was sixteen, Rodrigo joined the navy. By this time, he had already become a Mirista, and it had become common practice for the movement to send its militants into the armed forces so that they could get free combat training. By all accounts, Rodrigo had this in mind when he joined the military. In this sense, joining the military was the first step on a much longer road to revolution, *el viaje*, "the journey," as he called it. Knowing the stakes, and that there would be no turning back once he had embarked on this voyage, Rodrigo tape-recorded a heartfelt farewell address to his family and friends. He spoke in a sweet, almost crystalline voice, slowly and methodically, each word carefully thought out and delivered, as if he were aware that this could be his last recorded message.

"This is a journey that I must take," he said, "even if the destination isn't clear yet, because it's one thing to say what you're going to do, and it's another thing what awaits you." "Everyone," he asserted, audibly breaking up, "is free to choose the kind of social system that one wants to live in, or the means by which to achieve it." For Rodrigo, it was a matter of asking oneself, "Do we like the world we live in, or don't we? Do we like our way of life? Is it good or bad?" Rodrigo had already given the matter a good deal of thought. "It is my conclusion that the life that our people live, their way of life, the hunger and the thirst and everything else, if I'm being honest I'm not in favor of it. This is why I've taken one additional measure, and I hope to achieve it."[3] The additional measure to which he referred seems to have been his decision to join the MIR.

He left some parting words for his parents, his *papacito lindo* and his *mamacita*, whom he knew wouldn't be happy with his decision. "I hope that you follow the path of your choosing, and while I don't know if the path that I've chosen sits well with you, I tell you with a heavy heart that . . . one is free to choose the life he wants to lead, the path he wants to follow, and how he wants to live in this Peruvian nation." For Rodrigo, that path, that journey, would begin through the navy.

He interrupted his farewell by singing songs. "I leave you with these small words," he said, "and the hope of returning one day." With that, he begged his family's pardon, "because I don't know how to sing," and cheered them with songs from Andean folklore.

The sun cast its shadow,
And the Indian was born.
The sun cast its shadow,
And the Indian was born.

Prisoner of the meadows,
Meager Indian slave.
Indian of the shadows,
No sun to light your face.

Yesterday a mountain peak,
Today you are only dust.
Whenever your name I speak,
Your entrails they do thrust.

You will become the mountain again
A sparkle in your eye
You will be happy and grin
And so will I.

Rodrigo was right about one thing: his journey didn't end with the military. True to his word, he returned to San Martín upon completing his basic training and rejoined the MIR. When the group merged with the MRTA the following year, he joined its newly christened Northeastern Front. Given Rodrigo's formal military training and local rapport with the Tarapoto elite and peasantry, it is unsurprising that he would become a leader in the regional guerrilla front. As one MRTA document put it, Rodrigo "is one of those comrades who demonstrates a capacity to learn as well as initiative and dedication."[4] When the MRTA launched its jungle insurgency in late 1987, Rodrigo was among the first to lead, joining Víctor Polay in his assault on Juanjuí and Sisa.[5]

After the campaign, Rodrigo returned to Tarapoto and began coordinating the regional effort there. His parents knew what he was up to. His mother would cry whenever he came around, the thought of something happening to him too much to bear. His father was more understanding. "Do what you have to do," he told Rodrigo, "and be safe."[6] This proved easier said than done. After Defense Minister López Albújar declared martial law in the city, the army captured Rodrigo and detained him for several days. His father called in every favor to secure his son's release from custody. Both the MRTA and Rodrigo's family claimed that he was tortured during his detention.[7] A family photograph taken shortly after his release supports this allegation. The image depicts Rodrigo with his father and little brother,

Franco, standing in front of the family pickup truck. According to Franco, the picture, taken shortly after Rodrigo's release, showed a young man who had lost significant muscle mass. The abuse didn't keep Rodrigo out of the movement for long, and he went right back to his militancy in the MRTA. Now, however, he had to be more careful, as he was on the state's watch list. Next time, his father wouldn't be able to pull strings so easily.

9
Crime and Punishment

Peter Cárdenas was well aware that his cover could be blown at any moment. If he left his safe house even briefly, police could arrest him. "I knew they could nab me at any minute here," he recalled. "It was a sure thing." The unmistakable patch of white beard hair on his lower left chin didn't exactly make him inconspicuous, either. He would have been lying if he said he didn't want to be in the jungle with his comrades Víctor Polay and Néstor Cerpa. What Che-loving revolutionary didn't dream of being part of a guerrilla *foco*? Plus, it would be much harder to fall into the hands of the enemy under the cover of the jungle. As the person in charge of rebel operations in Lima, however, the "Sicilian" could ill-afford to leave the capital for more than a short period of time. "It was my duty" to stay in Lima, he explained. "What else was I supposed to do?"[1]

Imagine Cárdenas's concern when the National Directorate decided to send him and fellow MRTA cofounder Hugo Avallaneda to Mexico City in early 1988 to make contact with an important source there. Just what the Directorate hoped to get out of the meeting is unclear, but it must have been both sensitive and valuable to risk sending two top-ranking members. As with Cárdenas, Avallaneda had been with the MRTA from its inception. Together, they made up two-thirds of the group's original Lima command, with Polay being the third. Avallaneda's instructions were to appear at the cafeteria of the Universidad Nacional Autónoma de México at a predetermined time to meet a new contact. To make sure the man in question was the right person, Avallaneda was to ask, "How's the view in the Plaza of the 3 Cultures?" to which his contact would reply, "Like a mid-summer night's dream."[2] That would be the signal for the meeting to take place.

The Directorate knew that it was taking a big risk sending *El Gringo* and *El Negro* abroad. As a precaution, it fabricated fake Ecuadorian passports to help the two leaders get through customs. When Cárdenas and Avallaneda arrived at Jorge Chávez International Airport on Sunday, 2 February 1988, and prepared to board the Air Panama flight to Mexico City, it was all they could do to remain calm. An alert customs agent noticed their conspicuous behavior and asked to view their passports. Cárdenas and Avallaneda handed over the documents and cautiously answered the agent's questions. Whoever had falsified the passports had done a bang-up job, fooling even the suspicious agent. There was only one problem. If these two travelers were Ecuadorian, why did they speak with Lima accents? When pressed on this, Cárdenas and Avallaneda confessed that they were, in fact, Peruvian, but that due to a family crisis they had needed to flee the country. The agent remained unpersuaded, pegging them for drug smugglers. Airport police promptly intervened, arresting them and transporting them to DINTID, the drug enforcement agency. En route, one of the arrested rebels attempted to throw himself from the vehicle, but to no avail. When that didn't work, Cárdenas and Avallaneda offered to pay the police $6,000 cash if they let them go. The police demurred, delivering them to DINTID authorities. Only after background checks revealed no prior drug-related arrests did police realize they may be insurgents and handed them over to the counterterrorism police. Upon further inspection, the DINCOTE police realized that they had two of the MRTA's top leaders in their control.[3]

The capture of Peter Cárdenas and Hugo Avallaneda was the latest in a string of high-profile arrests of MRTA militants. Less than a month earlier, the army had captured Sístero García, commander of the Northeastern Front in San Martín and former associate of Alberto Gálvez who had helped Víctor Polay and Néstor Cerpa sack Juanjuí and Tabalosos.[4] Since Gálvez had been arrested the previous year, it appeared that, for the first time since the MRTA launched its insurgency in 1984, the counterinsurgency apparatus was closing in on the leadership.

Only Víctor Polay and Néstor Cerpa remained at large. Cerpa had always had a knack for avoiding authorities. It had been months since the interior minister had announced that *El Gordo*'s days were numbered, and the stocky rebel remained as slippery as ever. Polay had since returned to Lima, perming his hair and growing a moustache to throw off his pursuers. One night, he threw caution to the wind and went out with two of his comrades, donning a pair of dark sunglasses in the middle of the night. The three were loitering by a food stand near the national soccer stadium, munching on *anticuchos*, the succulent shish kebab made up of diced cow heart. As they stood eating, Leo, one of Polay's first students in the movement, noticed a sheet of paper plastered to a telephone pole. He leaned in to get a closer look, only to see a sketch of Polay's face underneath the word "Wanted." Below it was the cash award being offered for the rebel leader's capture. Leo subtly elbowed Polay and gestured toward the poster.

"That's you!" Leo whispered.

Polay looked over and confirmed with his own eyes. The only thing he could do was laugh it off.[5] He was safe. For now.

In August 1988, Polay, Cerpa, and the remaining members of the Central Committee convened their second congress from an undisclosed location. The Central Committee chose as its slogan for the meeting, "With Masses, in the revolutionary war, let us advance in the conquest of popular power."[6] Once again, symbolism and historical memory reigned. "Every revolutionary movement," read the meeting's opening article, "is the result of a historical development of the struggle of a people for liberty and justice." The MRTA was simply "the greatest expression of the struggles of the Peruvian people."[7] The conference took place under the symbols of Peru's revolutionary past, from Tupac Amaru and his rebel wife, Micaela Bastidas, to José Carlos Mariátegui and Luis De La Puente Uceda. These figures shared symbolic space with other figures from the Latin American and global left. As always, Che Guevara maintained his seat at the metaphorical table, but so too did Marx, Lenin, and Ho Chi Minh.[8] The meeting began with a reflection of the importance of history, connecting the MRTA's current struggle to Peru's national heritage. The committee members recalled the splendor of Tawantinsuyo, the Inca empire, and gave their revolutionary namesake his due. Unable to resist exoticizing Andeans, the rebels asserted that Tupac Amaru represented "the national indigenous consciousness, which pursued national liberty under indigenous hegemony, but also looked to integrate other races, ethnicities, and nationalities."[9] The committee went on to survey Peruvian history, highlighting the different generational struggles up to the present. In this way, the MRTA presented itself as existing not in a vacuum but, rather, as the embodiment of a historic struggle as old as Peru itself.[10] Only after emphasizing this historical connection did the Central Committee members move on to other matters.

The August 1988 congress presented an opportunity for the MRTA, which now enjoyed unprecedented favorability despite the recent loss of some of its leaders, to renew its commitment to social democracy and diversity and to repudiate Shining Path–style violence. Indeed, the resolutions passed during the congress suggested a willingness by the majority on the Central Committee to do this. These leaders used the occasion to advocate a kind of democratic socialism rather than a top-down, state-led model. Given the reach of imperialism and capitalism in the country, they believed it critical to wage a revolution of a socialist character, but they reiterated that the society they hoped to build would be founded on democratic principles. The Peru of the future would be a "Socialist Democracy," that is, "a democracy predicated on an organized people, on the public welfare, on the freedom of expression, assembly, [and] religion, and on the defense of the people's human rights."[11] The new revolutionary state would be decentralized, "block by block, barrio by barrio, town by town," each official elected from her or his own base.[12] Other articles included the promotion of multiculturalism, in recognition of Peru's racial and cultural diversity, and gender equality "at the workplace and in all areas of human activity, including the responsibilities of the revolutionary works in all levels of the construction of the socialist society."[13] The article went so far as to call for the elimination of "all forms of discrimination and violence against women by combating machismo."[14]

The guerrilla leadership seemed to be hitting all the right notes, advancing a vision for the future that included social democracy, multiculturalism, and the elimination of gender discrimination and misogyny. It was the most inclusive, democratic platform the MRTA had articulated to date, and it represented a tremendous opportunity to begin putting these socially progressive ideals into practice. Unfortunately, none of these aspirational visions ever made its way into the MRTA's day-to-day operations. Instead of taking the congress as a point of departure for rebel culture and conduct, MRTA hard-liners, almost all of them mestizo, heterosexual men, pushed forward a familiar practice of authoritarianism, misogyny, racial discrimination, homophobia, and gratuitous violence that would alienate them from the very population they hoped to win over.

Some of this behavior fit within the confines of "crime and punishment." During the congress, the Central Committee defined what exactly constituted a crime in the eyes of the revolution. In addition to legal crimes like theft, drug use, homicide, and rape, the committee included other infractions such as factionalism, treason, desertion, informing, and the abuse of authority. These infractions could result in expulsion from the party or even death.[15] But if revolutionary crime and punishment made sense from a military discipline standpoint, MRTA hard-liners would interpret the article loosely, often using it as a pretext for committing the very abuses the article was designed to prevent. In the coming years, these hard-liners would use the 1988 statute on crime and punishment to justify some of the most egregious atrocities of the thirteen-year insurgency.

If anything, the article ratified a position that the leadership had already adopted. Earlier that year, the group remotely issued a death sentence for thirty-two-year-old Carmen Rosa Cusquén, a Lambayeque-based attorney who rebel leaders concluded had struck a deal with police. The Central Committee believed that Cusquén's collaboration had led to the death of three Tupac Amaristas, charging her in absentia with "defection and treason."[16] In early 1988, Cusquén began receiving death threats by telephone. In April, two gunmen fired on her as she walked her one-year-old son home from church. Medics rushed Cusquén to Loayza Hospital to perform life-saving surgery. On 1 June, the night before she was cleared for release, two hitmen walked into her hospital room with silencers and finished the job, shooting her in the arm and head.[17]

The rebels also stepped up the unpopular practice of kidnapping for ransom during this period. In the morning hours of 7 July 1988, a MRTA column stormed the CAPSA Battery store and kidnapped owner Héctor Jerí García. As far as the guerrillas were concerned, Jerí embodied everything that was wrong with Peruvian society. His workers had been on strike, demanding higher wages. More important, Jerí was a retired army general, which made him fair game in their eyes. A group of Tupac Amaristas snatched the general, placing him in an undercover cell, or, as they called it, a "People's Prison," for over a month.[18] The negotiations almost broke down in mid-August when Sócrates Porta Solano and Miguel Pasache, the two Tupac Amaristas charged with negotiating Jerí's release, went missing.[19] The rebels' bodies washed ashore in Cañete the next day, each bearing signs of torture and with kill shots to the head. A paramilitary death squad, the Comando Rodrigo Franco, later took credit for the hit.[20] Fortunately, the rebels did not hold this against their hostage. In September, they released a series of photographs and a "proof of life" video as evidence that they were adhering to the Geneva Conventions, but the images of the disheveled, silver-haired general only contributed to mounting skepticism about the group's tactics.[21] Shortly thereafter, the rebels released Jerí.

Elsewhere, the rebels kidnapped industrialists who didn't pay their revolutionary head tax, or *cupos*. *Caretas* ran an article about one of these victims, Carlos Ferreyros. The man identified as Inmate Number 00102 in the People's Prison had been captured by MRTA commandos in December 1988. According to the Tupac Amaristas, Ferreyros represented one of the "12 Apostles," a nickname for the dozen families believed to run the country in the Peruvian oligarchy. Symbolically, the MRTA declared, Ferreyros's kidnapping represented "a major blow to the country's economic power."[22] In reality, Ferreyros had only inherited 7.5 percent of his father's construction fortune, and many of the family's industries were in fact owned by worker collectives. "Carlos Ferreyros Aspíllaga," *Caretas* editorialized, "hardly fits the description of an industrial exploiter." This didn't stop the rebels from attacking six of his family's enterprises in early February.[23] These attacks came only a month after Tupac Amaristas killed another hostage, Armando Lastra, after police attempted to intervene during the money drop.[24] "The ends don't justify the means," lamented another *Caretas* column, noting the irony in the MRTA's insistence that it respected human life. "There's nothing heroic about death and violence."[25]

■ Ever since Víctor Polay launched his guerrilla campaign in San Martín, Defense Minister Enrique López Albújar had made it his mission to eradicate the jungle of all remaining MRTA forces. For over a year, López Albújar's military had swept the department, taking the fight to the Tupac Amaristas and sending them on the run. López Albújar's scorched-earth tactics had paid off, inflicting heavy rebel casualties and securing a number of rebel weapons and bases. In January 1988, travelers in the valley of Sisa found the decomposing bodies of fifty Tupac Amaristas who had been wounded after skirmishes with the army. The camouflaged rebels had succumbed to their wounds in the coming days. Only after travelers noticed large flocks of buzzards swarming did they discover what had taken place there.[26] By now, the defense minister had become a thorn in the MRTA's side, and he showed no signs of relenting. If anything, he was just getting started.

In early 1989, López Albújar traveled to San Martín to inspect the counterinsurgency operations in the emergency zone. After visiting with authorities in Tocache and Pucallpa, he considered expanding martial law to encompass more of the department. Now, however, he also had to deal with recent rebel activity in other parts of the country. If his tactics in San Martín had succeeded in keeping the Tupac Amaristas at bay, why shouldn't they do the same in places like Junín, where both Shining Path and the MRTA had been active in recent weeks? With this in mind, the mustachioed defense minister planned a trip to Huancayo, a bustling highland city in the south-central Andean department of Junín.[27]

Junín had become a major base of operations for the insurgents, with Tupac Amaristas operating in the city of Huancayo as well as in the surrounding hills. In February 1989, the MRTA regional committee decided to hold a meeting there to discuss the expansion of its guerrilla operations. Polay had been holed up for more than a month in a safe house in Codiva, which made it difficult for him to stay in the loop. The Huancayo meeting was going to be an important one, however, determining the future of the guerrilla campaign. Time was of the essence, as Shining Path was quickly encroaching on MRTA terrain, having recently assassinated a Tupac Amarista leader who had been organizing peasant self-defense militias, the famed *rondas campesinas*.[28]

When his comrades requested that he attend the next day's meeting in person, Polay, who had always been a risk-taker, took the overnight bus to the mountain city. He had a believable cover, traveling with Rosa Luz Padilla Baca, a twenty-six-year-old San Marcos student who had recently gotten involved with the movement.[29] Padilla and Polay posed as young lovers on a weekend getaway to the countryside. The couple made it onto the Mariscal Cáceres bus line without raising any suspicion. The bus bounced along the highway, tossing the passengers to and fro as it weaved up the steep Andean mountain range. Polay and Padilla disembarked a little after six in the morning, tired and dreary from the nauseating climb. According to Polay, his comrade left the tourist hotel to pass the time while he remained behind to take a long-overdue nap.[30]

Their visit coincided with that of Defense Minister López Albújar, who, as luck would have it, decided to lodge at the tourist hotel. The general didn't take any chances with security, sending an army patrol to sweep the premises. When Padilla returned to the hotel around noon, it was swarming with soldiers who were searching everyone entering. When Captain Gamaniel Ortiz Herrera found a firearm and a grenade inside Padilla's backpack, he detained her and called in the arrest. By the time commander Miguel Amoretti arrived on the scene, intelligence personnel had already begun interrogating Padilla. For more than an hour the agents tried to get her to talk, but to no avail.[31] Amoretti approached a housekeeper and asked if he had any information about the young woman. The employee recalled that she had recently checked into a room on the second floor. Amoretti went to the front desk and flipped through the registration book for the list of guests who had checked in on the second floor that day. The only guest not accounted for was one Eudoxio Rosales del Campo, who had checked into room 22 earlier that morning and never left.[32]

Amoretti called his commanders and requested permission to raid the room in question. He put together a small team made up of five army, police, and intelligence operatives to enter the room, with another fifteen combat soldiers standing by. After clearing the area of civilians, the soldiers fanned out into two teams and headed up the stairs. On Amoretti's signal, one of the soldiers kicked in the door, catching the Tupac Amarista leader off guard. Polay didn't put up a fight as the soldiers ordered him to surrender, submitting to the first group as the second cleared the room. Among other things, the soldiers found a pistol and two grenades under the bed. As they searched the room, Polay demanded to speak with the man in charge. When Amoretti stepped forward, the rebel chieftain identified himself and offered to pay the captain $5,000 if he let him go. Amoretti refused, ordering one of his captains to take Polay back to headquarters for processing. Padilla would be transported separately.[33]

Alan García was on his way home from a trip to Caracas when he learned of the capture of his former roommate. Back in Lima, he held an impromptu press conference in the Chavín room of the presidential palace. He boasted that the state had dealt a "decisive blow" to the insurgency. The president reiterated his confidence in the police and armed forces in defending democracy against those who had "resorted to crime to destroy the institutions in which all Peruvians believe."[34] The following day, he had even harsher words for the rebels, labeling Polay a *capo* in one breath while dismissing him as a "petty delinquent" the next.[35] The president wasn't the only one who shared in this triumph. General López Albújar, the defense minister whose serendipitous hotel stay led to Polay's arrest, echoed his commander in chief's praise. The optimistic defense minister contended that Polay's capture could potentially "neutralize" the rebel group's actions in the region.[36]

Authorities took every precaution to transfer Polay to DINCOTE headquarters back in Lima. They placed their prisoner in a bulletproof vest and gave him a police escort throughout the 570-kilometer trek to the coast. Five hours and fifteen minutes later, the caravan pulled up to the green high-rise on Lima's España Avenue. The streets surrounding the building had been dotted with armored vehicles in anticipation of the press conference.[37]

Marco Miyashiro, the major in charge of the counterterrorism police's MRTA unit, would normally have been among the first to interrogate the prisoner. Miyashiro hadn't seen Polay since his Boy Scout days, and he still harbored fond memories of beaches and bonfires when it came to his former Alligator Troop leader. These were memories he preferred to keep. He opted to send another official to do the questioning. Before sending the official off, Miyashiro made a simple request: "Tell him that I said 'hi.'"

Upon receiving the message, Polay smiled, thinking back on the days of old, singing around a campfire with the "affable, smiling young" boy from Alligator Troup.[38]

"Tell him," Polay said, "that I remember him well, and that there are no hard feelings."[39]

This warm-up act of genuine humanity was immediately followed by a farce of a headliner. Two agents in short-sleeved, collared shirts and thin neckties, their guns holstered to their vests, led Polay by the biceps to the sixth-floor patio, where a dozen officers in bulletproof vests faced 200 journalists. Polay, hands cuffed behind his back, clean-shaven and sporting a blue nylon windbreaker, didn't even wait for his escorts to stop walking before breaking the silence.

"We reject the insults of Mr. Alan García, who lacks the moral authority to label us petty delinquents. We are combatants, revolutionary guerrillas!"[40]

The police immediately shut down the press conference. As Polay's stern-faced custodians pulled him away, he cried, "Tupac Amaru Lives and Will Prevail! Long Live the Tupac Amaru Revolutionary Movement!"[41] The whole episode lasted about twenty seconds, and the confused reporters scratched their heads at what had just transpired.[42] Once again, Polay had proved himself the more savvy media manipulator, reappropriating the García regime's public relations stunt for the MRTA.

The arrest of Víctor Polay was the most high-profile capture of 1989, but it wasn't the last. Two months later, police arrested Tupac Amarista leader Miguel Rincón Rincón at a routine traffic stop in Lima. The thirty-eight-year-old UNI graduate had been transporting José Luis Francisco Gutiérrez, a member of the Colombian M-19 guerrilla group. Officials believed that the MRTA had been coordinating efforts across national borders with the Colombian rebels to secure weapons and tactical training.[43] Rincón was just the latest in a growing list of MRTA leaders in police custody: Polay, Gálvez, Rincón, Avallaneda, García, Cárdenas. By April 1989, there were serious concerns as to whether the Tupac Amaristas could withstand this much loss of leadership. Indeed, the only high-profile leader who remained at large was Néstor Cerpa. It was up to the stocky commander to right the ship.

10

El Gordo Returns

The fatigue-wearing guerrillas sat in silence, shoulder to shoulder inside two rickety cargo trucks as they bounced up and down the windy Andean highway. Most of them were college students from cities like Lima, Huancayo, and Chiclayo. They had joined the ranks of the MRTA Central Front. Roughly half had spent the previous months fighting in the jungle; the rest had been assigned to the highlands. Now they all joined forces to finish the job they had failed to do in Cuzco five years earlier: unleash a guerrilla army in the heart of the Andes.[1]

Two veterans of left-wing militancy commanded the guerrillas. At age twenty-eight, Chiclayo native Miguel Córdova was already a seasoned fighter. The man whose chin whiskers had earned him the nickname *El Gallito*, the "Little Rooster," had been in the MIR before joining the MRTA. Now a member of the Central Committee, Córdova had fought alongside Víctor Polay in Juanjuí during the "Tupac Amaru, Liberator" campaign of 1987. A year before that he had been part of the América Batallion, working with guerrillas in Colombia.[2] Antonio Meza, the co-commander, had been born to humble beginnings. A peasant farmer, Meza was a union leader in his native Satipo who had fought with the MIR guerrillas back in 1965. Meza had been with the MRTA from its inception, participating in its failed guerrilla front in Cuzco in 1984. For Meza, setting up a new Central Front in the Andes was the fulfillment of a pledge long in the making.[3]

It was still pitch-black in the early hours of 28 April 1989. At that altitude, less than five kilometers from the valley of Jauja, the dry mountain air penetrates the bones, rendering it difficult to breathe without moaning. They would be in Jauja soon, but their real target was the city of Tarma. There, the MRTA Central Front hoped to launch the most spectacular occupation since the seizure of Juanjuí two years earlier. To numb their bodies and their minds, the Tupac Amaristas sipped on bottles of *zacazaca*, a local brew of cane liquor.[4]

At half past four, the trucks stopped. The guerrillas remained still as they overheard the conversation between Miguel Aquino, the driver of the leading truck, and military personnel. Aquino was not a member of the MRTA. A day earlier, the twenty-two-year-old trucker had been sitting in the plaza of Cucimarca when sixty-five masked rebels hijacked his truck and him along with it. The rebels let Aquino's brother join him as copilot for the misadventure. After filling up the truck with gas, the rebels led the Aquino brothers to a nearby town, where they took another trucker hostage as well.

When they got to the outskirts of the town of Molinos, the rebels ordered Aquino to stop the truck so they could rest. It was then that he met the driver of the other truck, Adril Hinostroza. The drivers compared notes, wondering what fate had in store for them. Hinostroza said he understood the guerillas were going to occupy the town of Jauja. Finally, around three in the morning, the rebels instructed Aquino to continue on his route. An hour and a half later he stumbled into the army checkpoint.[5]

Aquino nervously handed over the paperwork from his green Ford. It all checked out. The soldier let him pass.

If the Tupac Amaristas thought they were out of the woods, they were mistaken. Four hundred meters down the road, they reached yet another checkpoint.

"Documents," barked Johnny Morales, the lieutenant operating the checkpoint. Aquino handed over the paperwork without uttering a word.

"Where are you headed?" Morales asked.

"To Concepción, lieutenant," replied the Tupac Amarista in the passenger seat.

"What are you carrying?"

"Potatoes."

Morales studied the passengers' faces.

"Alright," he said. "Let's have a look."

The rebels in the back of the truck readied their automatic rifles as Morales and four other soldiers approached. As soon as the soldiers opened the hatch, the Tupac Amaristas opened fire, unloading a barrage of bullets and killing them instantly.[6]

Aquino hightailed it for the surrounding mountains. He was lucky. Before the guerrillas inside the truck could even get out, bullets rained down upon them. Alerted to their presence in the area beforehand, the army had placed a 100-man column on each side of the narrow road. The soldiers had been lurking in the dark, waiting to ambush the unsuspecting guerrillas. The rebels in the first truck never stood a chance. They were like sitting ducks, each one of them falling under the spray of bullets. None of them survived.[7]

The guerrillas in the trailing truck fared only slightly better. A handful jumped out of the vehicle, only to face an assault of gunfire and hand grenades. Some made it past the crossfire, only to be tracked down and killed alongside the road.[8] According to the MRTA, only ten managed to escape into the darkness, taking refuge in the homes of local villagers. The firefight continued as the sun crept up over the mountains. An army communiqué filed that day reported that the battle had left sixty-two Tupac Amaristas killed in addition to Lieutenant Johnny Morales and four of his colleagues.[9]

The MRTA never accepted the army's version of the battle. The guerrilla group issued an official communiqué of its own, charging that the rebels, outmatched and outnumbered, had "heroically" fought off the enemy "for several hours," killing thirteen unlucky soldiers and wounding thirty-four more. According to the statement, only forty-two rebels had been killed in the battle; the remaining twenty casualties had been innocent bystanders. The "uniformed hyenas," the statement alleged, had gone on a veritable killing spree in the nearby villages, murdering women, children, and elderly people in cold blood in their search for more victims.[10] The MRTA victims fared no better; many of them had been "murdered in cold blood after the battle." This massacre only exposed the "increasingly genocidal character of the reactionary army."[11] The MRTA pledged to turn this defeat into a revolutionary rally cry.

Today, we raise our flags to our fallen comrades, and before their heroic example, we pledge to fight until we prevail.
April 28, example of the Heroic Tupac Amarista Combatant
Honor and Glory to the Fallen Guerrillas!
With Masses and Arms, Country or Death, We Will Prevail![12]

No matter which way they spun it, the Central Committee members rec-ognized the severity of the Molinos defeat. "We don't deny that these events represent a major military setback," they conceded.[13] With many of their key leaders already behind bars, the guerrillas lacked both the command struc-ture and, now, the numbers to combat the forces of the state. This is to say nothing of the heavy blow to morale within the guerrilla ranks.

The MRTA held one man responsible for the Molinos massacre: Enrique López Albújar. The defense minister was an easy scapegoat. He had long been a thorn in the side of the guerrillas. He was the one, after all, who had overseen the counterinsurgency effort in San Martín. That campaign had led to the death, detainment, and torture of a number of rebels and civil-ians. Now, López Albújar was expanding the military intervention to include the central Andes. Nor was the arrest of Víctor Polay lost on the rebels. Had it not been for the general's impromptu visit to the tourist hotel in Huancayo, the rebel leader would still be free. For some hard-liners in the Directorate, the Molinos debacle was the final straw. It was more than just a military defeat; it was a massacre. They believed the army had been under orders to give no quarter to the rebels. What else could explain why so many had died in the skirmish? The rebels also had it on good authority that many of their comrades had been killed after the initial encounter, captured alive and killed in cold blood. And even though the defense minister was not the one who made the call, the MRTA leaders believed the buck stopped with him.

■ Rodrigo Gálvez, the young militant who had switched from the MIR to the MRTA after completing his basic training in the Peruvian navy, had long since recovered from his 1987 detention and torture at the hands of the army. After the arrest of Sístero García, the Directorate named Rodrigo commander of the Northeastern Front. Within two months of the Molinos debacle, Rodrigo led a column of thirty Tupac Amaristas down a narrow road into the town of Pacaizapa and began lobbing grenades at the police station.

Juan Francisco Polanco was one of the policemen inside the station. Polanco was no stranger to rebel activity. He had cut his teeth in Ayacucho at the height of the counterinsurgency against Shining Path. In February 1987, the Maoists attacked his police station in a pitched battle that left two Sen-deristas dead and a number of police wounded. That the Senderistas were "bloodthirsty," Polanco had no doubt, but he knew the military wasn't much better. When soldiers arrived at his base in Puquio, they came wearing ski masks, and they tortured civilians without due process and forced them to confess to things they hadn't done. The soldiers would leave corpses in the streets for their victims' family members to retrieve.

Once Polanco had even dared to denounce the abuses to the local military commander.

"Oh," said the commander, "you must be one of them." Polanco knew the insinuation. "One of them" meant "a terrorist." It was a veiled threat, a way of letting him know that if he kept nosing around, he might end up accused of terrorism himself.

Polanco wanted to get as far from the war as possible. After a brief stint in Lima, he requested a transfer to Iquitos, a region that had been relatively calm during the political violence. He got his transfer, but not to Iquitos. Instead, he wound up in the Civil Guard of Moyobamba, the capital of San Martín. Now he faced a different enemy in the MRTA. After two of his colleagues fell during the firefight, he knew that it was a lost cause. He and the remaining officers retreated through the back door, dashing toward the hills while Rodrigo Gálvez's troops advanced on the station. When the rebels came into the station, they found it completely empty. They attempted to chase Polanco and his men down, but they were already well into the mountains. The policeman who had escaped death at the hands of rebels just two years earlier had done it again.

Rodrigo Gálvez's troops stuck around in the station long after Polanco and his men had retreated. At five in the morning, they left town carrying five comrades who had fallen in the battle.[14] Half an hour later, Rodrigo came across the truck of the businessman and general secretary of APRA's San Martín operations, Demetrio Tafur Ruíz. Tafur Ruíz happened to be returning to Tarapoto following a trip to Trujillo. As his comrades recalled, Rodrigo "quickly adapts to the central tenets that characterize the MRTA, like initiative, audacity, and aggressiveness to carry out his tasks." This was no exception. When Rodrigo came across Tafur Ruíz's vehicle, he commandeered it, taking the Aprista leader hostage before ditching him by an old bridge after receiving a ransom payment. Before leaving town, Rodrigo ordered his troops to attack the police station with explosives, causing fatalities on the inside. After dynamiting local buildings and graffitiing the walls, he brought the townspeople together and repeated the entire spectacle.[15]

During his visits to Tarapoto, Rodrigo would hold meetings in young Daniel Bravo's home. For the past two years, Daniel's sister Yasi had been operating as a Tupac Amarista along with her husband, and they had now converted their home into a regional safe house, complete with hidden weapons and a two-way radio to communicate with different troops. "This is a safe house," Yasi would remind Daniel. "You can never bring your friends here." Daniel understood, even though he had a hard time explaining to his friends why they weren't welcome inside his home.

"Nah," Daniel would say, "my sister's mean. She doesn't like people coming over."

Rodrigo often included Daniel in his plans, making the young teenager feel important.

"If the army comes," he told Daniel, "if there's a raid, we're going to blow out the wall and head to the field."[16]

Daniel always helped set up the house for these secret meetings, affixing a different color wrapping paper to the walls each week so that the visitors couldn't identify the interior. Whenever Rodrigo pulled up in his car with a blindfolded guest, Daniel knew to turn off all the lights in the house. But when the meetings began, Daniel would leave the room. He didn't listen, didn't witness. It was his sister's way of protecting him.

"You know nothing," Yasi said. "You're never going to prison because you know nothing."

That wasn't entirely true. The more her own profile grew in the MRTA, the more Yasi asked of her kid brother. He was now too old to get away with smuggling arms in his backpack, but he could still lend a hand to the cause.

"You know what?" Yasi casually told him one day in 1989. "I need you to go to the port to pick up a person and take him to San Miguel."

Daniel hopped on his Botazo 185 motorcycle and zipped over to the meeting spot along the riverbank. He went inside El Zambito, the lonely port restaurant, carrying a comb in his hand as per Yasi's instructions. He was to look for a man with construction paper in his right hand and a cigarette in the other. Much to his surprise, the old watering hole was bustling with patrons, almost all of them smoking cigarettes. Daniel walked up and down the aisles. When he came upon a pot-bellied man holding a piece of paper in his hand, he immediately began having doubts. "This can't be the guy," he thought. "He looks like a trucker!"

He decided to use the secret passcode.

"Do you need a ruler for your construction paper?"

The fat man looked up at the teenager and replied, "No, I need a comb for my hair."

That was it. Daniel handed the tubby man his comb and walked outside alone. He waited by his motorcycle for a few moments until the man came out and hopped on the back.

"I hope this motorcycle can take the weight of this fat *tío*," Daniel thought. He gave the throttle a thrust and took off, the back seat scraping the dirt as they peeled off.

"Where did you learn to ride?" the man yelled nervously into the wind.

"In Tarapoto!"

"Take it easy. Just take it nice and slow. We wouldn't want you to roll it!"

"Don't worry!" Daniel called back, amused.

They must have been quite the sight: the skinny fifteen-year-old on one end and the overweight, middle-aged man with the goatee sitting behind him. They rode until they arrived at the safe house. A bunch of Tupac Amaristas dressed in all black had gathered inside. Daniel walked up to one of the rebels.

"I brought you an old fatso," he quipped.

"You better watch your mouth, boy," said the militant, firmly. "He's the boss."

Daniel could hardly contain his embarrassment. He had just given a lift to Néstor Cerpa, commander of the rebel army.[17]

Cerpa had taken over command since the fall of Víctor Polay the previous year. Unlike Shining Path's overweight chieftain, Abimael Guzmán, who never saw a day of battle during twelve years of clandestinity, Cerpa was a man of action. Within two months of Víctor Polay's arrest, Cerpa led an amphibious attack on Contamana, a small town of about 5,000 inhabitants on the shore of the Ucayali River. Once the police surrendered their station, Cerpa gathered the townspeople in the main square and urged them to support the movement. He explained that the MRTA had already effectively taken over the zone. The rebels had forces everywhere, had already carried out successful actions in Tarapoto, and were about to carry out another in Pucallpa. Despite setbacks, in other words, the rebels were not going anywhere.

Shortly thereafter, Cerpa led the townspeople to the local rice mill.

"Go on, take it," he told the locals. His troops robbed the banks as the townspeople made off with more than 500 tons of rice.[18]

11

The General's Station Wagon

The Molinos massacre marked a major turning point for the MRTA. If the early years of the rebellion had been characterized by actions of heavy symbolic import and a general avoidance of civilian casualties, the Molinos affair ushered in a darker, dirtier period of fighting. In addition to depleting the rebel ranks and bringing morale to an all-time low, Molinos stripped the insurgency of all romantic pretense. No longer could the Tupac Amaristas ignore that they were at war, a real war with real, human stakes. And while the guerrillas never entirely abandoned their symbolic war, the months following the Molinos massacre were among the most violent in the insurgency. The Tupac Amaristas never bought the army's version of what went down in Molinos, claiming instead that dozens of their comrades had been executed in cold blood after surrendering. This only fed calls for retaliation and vengeance from the most hard-line rebels. With much of the leadership behind bars, there was little stopping the group's extremists from carrying out their own agendas. This further contributed to the guerrillas' negative image in the court of public opinion. By mid-1990, much of the public and the media had turned on the Tupac Amaristas, and there was little reason to believe that the guerrillas would rebound.

■ The beleaguered guerrillas attempted to establish a front in the jungle of Oxapampa, a province in the department of Pasco. Unlike the mostly Spanish-speaking peasantry of San Martín, the communities of Puerto Bermúdez, Oxapampa, were made up of Asháninka natives.[1] The Asháninka had a long history of autonomy that dated back to the colonial period. It was there that Juan Santos Atahualpa led his famous rebellion against the Spaniards in 1742.[2] Although the Asháninka did not live in isolation, many were skeptical of any plans to alter their way of life. When Shining Path and MRTA guerrillas entered the zone in the late 1980s, some indigenous leaders were understandably reticent. The MRTA leaders exhibited little regard for this history, if they knew it at all. Just as they had done in highland Cuzco in 1984, the rebels made no effort to learn the indigenous customs, language, history, or political system. Instead, they believed that the Asháninka would support them simply because they were on the side of people.

At first, it seemed as if this tactic might work. The Tupac Amaristas gathered the villagers to discuss their problems and hear their grievances. The guerrillas played soccer with the natives and swore to protect them against Shining Path incursions.[3] In each village they passed through, the Tupac Amaristas recruited youngsters into their ranks, youngsters like Juan. Juan had found the prospects of the guerrilla war appealing, but he quickly found himself relegated to menial tasks. He realized that he was only useful to the guerrillas as an auxiliary and that they never really considered him an equal. "They kept me under close watch," Juan later told reporters, "and they made me cook for them. After a few weeks I told them I wanted to be a guerrilla like them." The Tupac Amaristas indulged Juan's request, giving him military and political training but never promoting him past the rank of camp cook. "They kept putting me off," Juan explained, "and they never put me in the field of battle. I was always just in charge of cooking."[4]

Juan was not the only Asháninka who felt this way. Other villagers also complained that the guerrillas only used them for their resources and knowledge of the local terrain. The Asháninka could serve as guides and cooks, but they were not welcome to join the ranks of the armed combatants. "They treated us like dirt," one villager said. This treatment betrayed the mestizo commanders' racial bias toward Peru's indigenous population. It didn't matter that the Central Committee had only one year earlier approved a resolution endorsing multiculturalism. To the mestizo commanders in Oxapampa, the Asháninka were second-class citizens, not worthy of their respect.

Given the disregard that local commanders had for them, it should come as no surprise that the Asháninka decided not to have anything to do with the rebellion. Alejandro Calderón, president of Puerto Bermúdez, was among the Asháninka leaders to question the motives of the Tupac Amaristas. When the rebels first arrived to the area in mid-1989, Calderón had initially been receptive, inviting them to stay in the community for a time and listening to their proposals.[5] In time, however, he grew intolerant, no doubt turned off by their disdain for the local populace. Under Calderón's leadership, the Asháninka of Puerto Bermúdez formed their own *ronda campesina* to expel the rebels from the region. The Tupac Amaristas retaliated by kidnapping Calderón and two other local leaders and holding them hostage at their jungle camp in December 1989.

Tigre was one of the rebels who attended to Calderón during his captivity. The previous year, a stray police bullet had struck Tigre's mother in the heart during a teachers' rally in his native Pucallpa, killing her instantly. Tigre was only fourteen at the time and knew very little about socialism or insurgency, but he felt compelled to do something to avenge his mother's death. "I wanted to take out all my hatred on the police, you know?" he said later.[6] He sought out some local members he knew from the MRTA's Western Front and asked if he could join. Now, a year later, he found himself in the middle of the jungle, surrounded by Asháninka natives and trigger-happy commanders.

Tigre was a light-skinned mestizo himself, but his commanders' treatment of the indigenous population in Oxapampa never settled well with him. What struck him the most was the ease with which his commanders justified killing Calderón. In addition to his recalcitrance when it came to accepting the presence of the MRTA, Calderón had an enmity with the rebels that went way back. The commanders said that Calderón had butted heads with them back when they were with the MIR. Calderón, they said, had turned over Máximo Velando, one of the original 1965 guerrillas, nearly twenty-five years earlier. As some of the Tupac Amaristas had been involved in the MIR campaign, they had never let that episode go.[7] This was their time for revenge.

It was Franco, Tigre's commander, who ordered the execution of Calderón.

"Let's kill this Judas who traded Máximo Velando for a couple of roof tiles," Franco suggested.

The guerrillas obeyed, coldly putting a bullet in the Asháninka leader's head. According to Tigre, the execution of an indigenous authority did not appear to weigh on the conscience of Franco or the other unit leaders. "They walked around the camp all proud of themselves, as if they had just achieved some magnificent triumph."[8] Franco's apparent comfort with ordering the assassination of an Asháninka leader demonstrates the contempt that some Tupac Amaristas had for indigenous customs and political practices. That Calderón had the political and cultural legitimacy of his community didn't seem to weigh on the mestizo commander, nor did he concern himself with the reason why the Asháninka rejected the rebels in the first place.

This attitude did not reflect that of all rebels, of course. Tigre was one of several rank-and-file guerrillas who objected. Together, they demanded that they decamp at once.

"No, we're fine right where we are," said Franco, again underestimating his indigenous hosts.

Tigre and his comrades felt compelled to obey the orders of their commander, spending the night in the camp. It was 5:30 the next morning when the crackling voice of a rebel lookout came over the radio.

"They're coming!"

Neither Tigre nor his comrades could quite make out the cry.

"Come in! Come in! Come in, over!" they said, but there was no reply on the other end of the walkie-talkie.

"It's nothing, it's nothing," Franco said. "Carry on."

Half an hour later, a plane flew overhead, but it turned out to be a small private jet. One nervous Tupac Amarista fired a single shot anyway.

The shot caught the attention of a nearby army column, which had apparently been alerted to the rebels' presence by the Asháninka following Calderón's execution. The army ambush came swiftly. Tigre threw himself on the ground. "It was a total debacle," he recalled. "It was madness." There were explosions all around. He decided to make a run for it, seeking cover in the foliage. As he was running, the first bullet struck him in the buttocks, and a second struck him in the shoulder. And then he fell. He knew he was hurt, but at fifteen, didn't think he could actually die.

"Comrade," Tigre cried, flagging down a Bolivian in his ranks, "I'm hit!"

"Get up, *carajo*, dammit!" the Bolivian ordered. "I'm looking for Jenny! I'm looking for Jenny!" The guerrilla was looking for a light-skinned comrade with whom he had fallen desperately in love.

That was enough for Tigre to snap to. He picked himself up and ran for cover in the brush, reuniting with three of his comrades in the jungle. That night, he could hardly sleep. In addition to the two bullets still lodged in his body, crawling jungle ants feasted on his open wounds. Later Tigre and his four comrades caught up with some others in their column. The commanders told them not to worry, assuring them that they would be taken to Cuba to receive the best medical attention the world had to offer.

"We never went, though," Tigre said amusedly years later. Instead, it was Franco who deserted, leaving his subordinates to fend for themselves.[9]

Juan, the Asháninka cook, was attending to the food when the army attacked the camp. He took advantage of the confusion to desert to his village. The execution of Calderón disturbed him, and he told his fellow villagers what had happened to their leader. Upon learning of the death of his father, Alcides Calderón dropped his studies in Lima's Federico Villarreal University to take over as leader of Puerto Bermúdez. As the new spiritual leader, Alcides made it his first order of business to organize a local militia to track down his father's killers and bring them to justice. On 26 December 1989, the fifty-three Asháninka communities of the Pichis valley named Alcides the new *Pinkatzari*, or spiritual-political leader, pledging their allegiance to him and vowing to avenge his father's death. As a condition of his reemergence into the community after having joined ranks with the Tupac Amaristas, Juan agreed to help identify members of the MRTA.[10]

In their racial hubris, the rebel commanders had awoken a sleeping giant. Within weeks of the killing of Alejandro Calderón, his son Alcides had amassed an army of 4,000 natives to comb the jungle in search of fleeing guerrillas. Men and women armed with machetes, spears, and bows and poison-tipped arrows combed the region. They came up with their own secret signals to communicate with one another, imitating the whistles of local birds. On the walls of huts and buildings, villagers painted over MRTA slogans with phrases like "ACE's Revenge" (La Venganza de ACE, Alejandro Calderón Espinoza), and "War to the Death against the MRTA" (Guerra a Muerte al MRTA).[11]

"We have the whole valley under control," Alcides told some visiting reporters from Lima; "we're sweeping palm to palm."[12]

During one mid-January 1990 sweep, the militia fighters, or *ronderos*, intercepted a pickup truck transporting three unidentified subjects. The *ronderos* promptly rounded them up and transported them by motorboat down the river to their camp.

At nightfall, the *ronderos*, their faces painted in red war paint and carrying spears, bows, and arrows, marched the three shirtless suspects, hands tied behind their backs, into an old fuel storage room and shoved them to the floor. Juan, his face wrapped in white cloth underneath a baseball cap to protect his anonymity, stepped forward. He identified the three subjects immediately as Tupac Amaristas. Later that night, Alcides held court there in the storage room. An Asháninka chief served as judge for the trial.

"I know you three," Juan said, pointing to the one closest to the wall. "You're Huamán, leader of the Victoria camp." Turning to the next one, he said, "You're Sergio, another MRTA from Victoria. And you're Jaime, the worst of them all. The three of you are from the MRTA and you're responsible for the kidnapping and detainment of Alejandro Calderón, you might even be part of the squadron that shot him, and now you will pay for your crime."[13]

The man identified as Huamán began to protest, his eyes swelling with tears. "I'm not a terrorist, I'm a field laborer. I've brought my savings here to buy a farm and move here, next to my brother-in-law's property. My name is Francisco Huamán and no matter what you say, you've got me confused with someone else. I have no idea what you're talking about. I'm a father of eight children and I want to move here to work."

"Don't play dumb, crybaby," Juan said. "Are you really going to tell me that you're not a terrorist? Don't you remember all the times you insulted the cook. Well, guess what? I was that cook. Don't come around here with those lies about your children and your little farm, I know you well."

"For the love of God," cried Huamán. "Let me prove to you that I'm not from the MRTA, that group that harms everyone, that only steals and lives high on the hog, I'm not one of those who joins the guerrillas to get rich, I'm a humble man who wants to work in the fields. For the love of God, I beg you to bring me before the PIP, I have friends there who know me and know I'm a field hand."

Juan's accusations continued despite the suspects' denials. Once Juan had finished his interrogations, Huamán looked up at the journalists, who had witnessed the entire exchange.

"Señores journalists," he pleaded. "I want you to know that something terrible is about to happen to us. I don't think they should dispose of our lives due to the accusations of one mad man. You are all about to witnesses a murder."

The journalists concurred, urging Alcides to turn the suspects over to the authorities.

"The Bible tells us," Alcides replied, "that you reap what you sow and that's what we're doing here. If these men killed our leader and with all the people they've killed, why can't we, who've declared war, take the same measures against them? Still, we'll bring them back to camp and continue the investigation and if they're innocent, we'll let them go, and if they're guilty, we'll submit them to Asháninka justice."

With that, Alcides ordered the men into a canoe as the torrential rains poured down over the valley.[14] In all likelihood, they were killed, along with twenty-four other suspects whom the Asháninka had rounded up in recent days.

"The assassination of our father and chief has rocked us to the core," Alcides told reporters the following day. "Our decision is singular and final. We are at war."[15]

When word got out that the *rondas campesinas* were hunting down guerrillas, the rebels in Tigre's camp retreated from Asháninka territory. Ricardo, the new second-in-command after Franco's desertion, went to check on Tigre, who was still in bad shape after receiving two bullet wounds during the army raid. Ricardo offered take him to a proper house where he would get the medical treatment he needed.

"No, comrade," Tigre replied. "I'm staying. I'd rather die beside you all."

A comrade who was working as a medic cured him with whatever herbal remedies she could muster, but one bullet remained lodged in his shoulder. Although he would never part with the bullet, Tigre recovered enough strength to move on his own. By late January, Ricardo, hoping to avoid an all-out war with the Asháninka, ordered a full-scale retreat toward Ucayali.

■ Rodrigo Gálvez continued to command the Northeastern Front, engaging in numerous altercations with the police and, mostly, the armed forces, which by now were at full force in San Martín. To play it safe, the twenty-six-year-old went around with an armed bodyguard named Charly. Charly had gotten his hands on a police uniform for an upcoming operation, but his comrades, mistaking him for a cop, pelted him with bullets, killing him instantly. Now Rodrigo was left without his usual armed escort.

Around 8:00 P.M. on 9 February 1990, Rodrigo led a column of 350 Tupac Amaristas to attack the town of Picota. As always, they targeted the police station. As luck would have it, Juan Francisco Polanco, the policeman who had escaped Rodrigo's troops by the skin of his teeth the previous year, was now posted there. Polanco knew the drill. First came the grenade blasts. Then the gunshots. Fortunately, his men were better equipped than the last time. They had plenty of ammo, so they were prepared for the long haul. They exchanged fire, holding down the fort for several hours amid the onslaught. Finally, around two in the morning, there was a break in the action. Polanco could overhear the Tupac Amaristas calling for one another outside. He abandoned his post and stood up to peek outside. At that precise moment, three Tupac Amaristas charged toward the outer wall of the station. Spotting Polanco, one of the guerrillas lobbed a hand grenade. The grenade exploded in midair, and the debris caught Polanco's face and knocked him to the floor. As he lay there, his left eye permanently blinded, his colleagues realized that they had lost the battle and abandoned the station.

Still injured but conscious, Polanco played dead and discreetly pulled out his hand grenade as three rebel commanders entered the station. He could hear them calling each other by name—Charl, Alipio, and a third whose name didn't register. That third commander was, in all likelihood, Rodrigo.

When the comrades weren't paying attention, Polanco threw his grenade at them. It exploded, killing the two identifiable victims and injuring the third, who quickly abandoned the post.

At that moment, Polanco's colleagues came out of hiding and retreated from the station. They took him and the other wounded to the hospital. Polanco, now partially blind, was one of the lucky ones. Another of his colleagues had lost an arm, and another a leg, but there were no casualties on the side of the police.[16]

Rodrigo ordered his troops to leave the town before daybreak. One of his men had been injured in the shootout with police, and Rodrigo put him on a motorcycle and rode him out of town. What he didn't realize was that the army had been alerted to the shootout. The soldiers ambushed him as he left town on the bike. He tried to escape into the hills, but he took several bullets to the body. He was wounded but still living, and he couldn't advance as the soldiers approached. One of the soldiers was an old schoolmate of Rodrigo's named Jari. Apparently, their prior relationship didn't earn Rodrigo any sympathy. Rodrigo's comrades, who witnessed the capture from the surrounding hills, would tell his family that it was Jari, the very soldier who had once run the same halls as Rodrigo, who pulled the fatal trigger before lighting a match and tossing it at his former classmate's feet.[17]

Rodrigo had always accepted his fate. He knew there was a strong chance he wouldn't live to see the rebellion prevail, but he felt he couldn't sit around while Peru burned. Before embarking on his journey six years earlier, he had left his parents with a sad song and "the hope of returning one day." Now there would be no hope of return. The green hills claimed his ashes like the indigenous protagonist of his song:

You Will Become the Mountain Again
A Sparkle in Your Eye
You Will Be Happy and Grin
And So Will I.

■ Roger Pinchi Vásquez had a life-or-death decision to make. His whole life, he had been struggling to come to terms with his homosexuality. "I tried to hide it," he later explained, "for the sake of my mom, my dad, my studies." Now, as an adult teaching in Tocache in 1990, he wanted nothing more than to come out of the closet, but there was another factor to consider. The MRTA controlled this town in San Martín, and the regional commanders made their homophobia clear.

A year earlier, the Northeastern command had sent out communiqués indicating that the rebels would serve as a kind of moral authority in Tarapoto, targeting anyone who was openly gay. It was a loose interpretation of the "crime and punishment" clause passed during the 1989 congress, designed to curb thievery, drug trafficking, and drug addiction. Regional commanders, however, added homosexuality to the list of revolutionary crimes, equating it with these other immoral behaviors. True to their word, a band of Tupac Amaristas raided the city's nightclubs and brothels on the night of 31 May 1989, pulling out individuals believed to be homosexual drug addicts. The rebels took the suspects to the 9 de Diciembre neighborhood and forced them to line up. The guerrillas separated eight of them and shot them one by one.[18]

Actions such as these struck terror in the hearts of men like Pinchi. It was hard enough being gay in Peru in 1990. This added a new cause for concern. Pinchi wasn't alone. His brother, François, was also gay and transgender. François owned a popular hair salon in Tarapoto and, according to Pinchi, was adored by his clients. But he also knew how difficult it could be to come out. When Pinchi confided in his brother one day, telling him that he too was gay, François urged him to tread carefully.

"It's not easy being gay," François said. "It's a rough and terrible life. Think long and hard before you go down that road."

"I've thought long and hard and I'm ready to go down that road," Pinchi said.

But Pinchi changed his mind when the MRTA began targeting homosexuals. When he moved to Tocache and realized it was crawling with Tupac Amaristas, he found himself at a crossroads. "If I come out," he thought, "they'll kill me." He decided to keep up the charade, getting a girlfriend and attempting to fly under the radar.

Pinchi might have gotten away with the ruse were it not for an unfortunate case of mistaken identity. During his time teaching in Tocache in 1990, the local Tupac Amaristas abducted him and held him captive in their camp. For the next eight days, the guerrillas took turns beating, name-calling, and finally raping him. It wasn't until the commander walked into the camp and lifted the badly beaten Pinchi's head that he realized he had captured the wrong person, mistaking him for his brother, François. After this, the commander let Pinchi go.

Pinchi immediately sought out his brother in Tarapoto to warn him that he had been blacklisted by the rebels. François couldn't believe it.

"I pay my war tax," he said, "I give money. I give everything. Why would they kill me?" Despite Pinchi's pleading, François resolved to continue working in his salon.

Just as Pinchi feared, the Tupac Amaristas abducted François and took him to an old farm in Morales district known as La Chacra. There, the guerrillas put François into a pigsty and gave him five shots to the head.[19]

The Pinchi brothers were two of several LGBTQ people subjected to MRTA hate crimes during the early 1990s. Their stories serve as a chilling reminder of the dangers that await when a political movement succumbs to the whims of its most belligerent, intolerant wing. Notwithstanding the Central Committee's 1988 statute promoting gender equality and denouncing machismo, some regional commanders used the rebellion as an opportunity to instill fear in the LGBTQ community. This homophobia was by no means unique to the MRTA or even the Peruvian left but was a disturbing symptom of Cold War hypermasculinity. Whether in Stalin's Soviet Union or Castro's Cuba, systematic discrimination and violence against members of the LGBTQ community made up part of a broader culture of machismo and gender intolerance among the very men who advocated a more just and egalitarian world order. To be sure, the left was not alone in this regard, as crimes by right-wing groups and state security forces against the LGBTQ community were also heinous and often more systematic during this period. Moreover, the left has made far more progress with respect to LGBTQ rights in the twenty-first century than have its adversaries on the right. Nevertheless, it is worth noting that homophobia among both the left and the right during the Cold War was pervasive, toxic, and at times, deadly.

■ In May 1989, less than a month after the Molinos incident and a month before his sixtieth birthday, Enrique López Albújar stepped down as defense minister. After an illustrious military and political career, the general decided that it was time to enjoy civilian life. He would still remain active, taking over as president of El Sol Chemicals, a company for which he had been a board member.[20] The general took his position seriously. He would show up to the company headquarters three days a week at 9:15 A.M. sharp. The only problem was that, as a retired general and diplomat, he had to rely on his security detail to get him to work on time. When that security detail didn't arrive to pick him up from his home in Higuereta on the morning of 9 January 1990, he was more than a little peeved.

"I'm tired of waiting for the driver!" López Albújar declared to his wife, Maruja, pacing between his living room and front door. "When he gets here, tell him he's fired! I don't want to see him around here anymore." The general huffed out of his home.

The general's station wagon was hardly secure. Unlike his driver's car, which came equipped with tinted, bulletproof windows and two body-guards, his white Nissan was an unremarkable vehicle, easily blending in with the VW bugs and other station wagons that roamed the streets of the capital. López Albújar's security detail also tended to take every precaution, traveling the most secure routes. None of that mattered on this morning, however. López Albújar just wanted to get to his meeting on time.[21]

When the station wagon pulled up to the big financial building on Paseo de la República, the general seemed to have calmed down. He made a U-turn into the parking lot, and the security guard noted that the general was all smiles.[22] López Albújar was in such a hurry to park that he probably didn't notice the white man who pulled out a sports bag and rested it on top of a car across the way. The man then removed a machine gun from the bag and started firing on the general's Nissan. As the bullets peppered the station wagon, López Albújar lost control and crashed into two parked cars while two other gunmen began firing on the car. After a momentary pause, the first shooter raced toward the car and peered inside.

"He's still alive!" shouted the Tupac Amarista gunman. At that moment, one of the other hitmen ran close to the general and unloaded his weapon for good measure. Afterward, the three gunmen, joined by two other look-outs, ran back into a Toyota and sped down the avenue toward Aramburú. Bystanders immediately called in the incident. Shortly after reaching the hospital, López Albújar, who had been shot with seventeen bullets, perished.[23]

The MRTA promptly claimed credit for the assassination, citing it as retribution for the Molinos massacre. Although he would vehemently deny it, Peter Cárdenas, the MRTA's Lima commander, appears to have been the mastermind behind the hit. *El Gringo* had been arrested in 1988 and even spent some time in Canto Grande prison, but he had been released the following year after what some of his comrades suspected was a secret plea bargain with prosecuters.[24] Although these suspicions led Cárdenas to cede command of Lima, he maintained the trust of the most important Tupac Amarista of all, Víctor Polay. This trust enabled Cárdenas to run special, high-risk operations even after Polay's arrest. DINCOTE intelligence placed the "Sicilian" on the same block of the López Albújar assassination days before the attack, evidently scoping out the scene. Moreover, the description that witnesses gave to police about one of the attackers matched that of Cárdenas. Who else had Swedish features with a white patch on his beard? Finally, the style of the attack, which involved removing a machine gun from a bag atop a car and firing it on a target across the street, was a signature

Peter Cárdenas hit. No matter how much evidence DINCOTE agents had linking Cárdenas to the crime, however, he still slipped away undetected.[25]

The assassination of López Albújar showed that the MRTA's bellicose wing had taken control of the movement. For many on the left and in the media who had fancied the MRTA a kind of Robin Hood guerrilla group, the assassination was a bridge too far. In fact, the killing was so uncharacteristically cruel that, in the days following the hit, most media outlets assumed it was the work of Shining Path.[26] Now it was clear that this was the work of an out-of-touch insurgency. Had the guerrillas lost the moral high ground? The recent wave of targeted assassinations certainly seemed to suggest that this was the case: the hate crimes against homosexuals and transgender people, the kidnappings and killings of hostages, the execution of an indigenous leader, and now, the assassination of a retired general. Nelson Manrique's warnings of the "Senderization of the MRTA" seemed to be coming to pass. Others agreed. "If the image that the MRTA hoped to make of itself is that it is 'better' than Shining Path," wrote *Caretas*, "the Robin Hood syndrome will soon be forgotten."[27]

What was left of the MRTA leadership understood that it needed to repair the self-inflicted damage that it had incurred in the realm of public relations. Even the most sympathetic leftists were beginning to turn on the Tupac Amaristas, dismissing them as just another bloodthirsty terrorist organization. Even Néstor Cerpa, who had always been among the hard-liners, understood the need to dial it back. He and the remaining members of the Directorate concluded that a grandiose, attention-grabbing action of nonviolence might just win back the hearts and minds of the left and the equally important favor of the press. With his back to the wall, Cerpa started hatching a plan.

12
Freedom Tunnel

Víctor Polay sat in his cell on the third floor of Cellblock 2-A in Canto Grande maximum-security prison. Prison officials had separated the guerrilla leader from the other MRTA inmates, placing him in one of the two lone cells on the third floor. In the other sat Osmán Morote, then considered number 2 in the Shining Path hierarchy and the highest-ranking Senderista behind bars. The L-shaped cell came equipped with a bed, a kitchenette, a small desk, and a modest shelf of books and magazines; it even had a small music box and a TV. On top of the shelf sat a framed drawing of Tupac Amaru, his bulging biceps raised and his fists clenched, emerging triumphantly from the masses. Underneath the image was the phrase, *Tupac Amaru Lives and Will Prevail!*[1]

Polay examined the tiny stamp of Santa Sarita Colonia that a group of mothers of the Tupac Amarista prisoners had given him during visitation hours earlier that day.

"She's a miracle-worker and will protect you," one of the mothers had said. "She's the people's saint and she's on our side."

Polay appreciated the gesture. After two years inside Miguel Castro Castro Maximum Security Prison, he would take all the help he could get.[2]

■ Miguel Castro Castro Prison, commonly known as Canto Grande, The Big Stone, was inaugurated on 15 January 1986, at the height of the civil war. A modern facility for modern times, it housed the nation's most dangerous prisoners: drug traffickers, mafia kingpins, and of course, terrorists. The facility had an octagonal shape with guard towers on every corner peering down on the common area and a high-tech security system offering twenty-four-hour video surveillance of every floor—a Foucauldian panopticon if ever there was one.[3] Immediately upon Canto Grande's inauguration, the national penitentiary system transported all of the MRTA and Shining Path prisoners to the new facility.[4]

That Canto Grande was touted as escape-proof didn't stop prisoners from trying. The Tupac Amaristas had been planning an escape route almost from the prison's inception. At the time, Víctor Polay was still running operations in Lima. "We knew that over the course of the internal armed conflict it was inevitable that more and more comrades would fall, so we were always researching different ways to free them," he wrote.[5] As a child in Callao, Polay had sat mesmerized while his father's Aprista comrades enchanted him with tales of daring prison escapes. The escapees had become folk heroes among the persecuted left, earning superhero status, like the Invisible Man, who walked out the front door of El Frontón undetected by authorities. Now the MRTA's Inmate Number 1, Polay could become a living legend in his own right if he could only elude his watchful jailers.

Polay turned to his group's transnational leftist network for advice. Earlier in the war, he had managed a sit-down with Raúl Sendic, the leader of Uruguay's like-named Tupamaro guerrillas. Sendic had made international headlines in 1971 when he and a group of more than 100 Tupamaro inmates escaped Montevideo's Punto Carretas prison.[6] During their brief encounter, Sendic told Polay how his Uruguayan comrades had pulled off the stunt, down to the last detail. Of course, escaping from Canto Grande would be a much harder task, isolated as it was from the street by more distance and with more modern surveillance technology. For Polay, however, the only takeaway from the story of Sendic's escape was that it could be done. That ray of hope was all the Tupac Amarista leader needed.[7]

The Directorate began devising a plan to bust their imprisoned comrades out of jail. The prisoners realized that the sewage ducts of the prison connected all the cellblocks, and they began roaming the ducts to start digging a one-man tunnel.[8] On 17 July 1987, prison guards discovered trails of dirt on the floor of the underground sewage ducts. After telling their supervisors, the guards performed an all-out inspection of the facility, uncovering a twenty-meter-long tunnel. Although prison authorities didn't immediately suspect the MRTA, the discovery brought all plans for an escape to a halt.[9]

The MRTA commanders went back to the drawing board. "We needed to start thinking outside the box," Polay later wrote, "breaking with the tradition of tunnels that we've seen so many times re-created in Hollywood." That's when he realized that "it had to be from the outside-in." The rebel organization had a pipeline of creative geniuses from Peru's finest engineering university, La UNI, who could provide technical, creative, and logistical support.[10] They also had an in with the National Miners Federation, "experts," Polay knew, "in building tunnels." "We concluded that we had the theory, the technique, and the experience to construct the track that would lead our combatants to freedom."

Polay was arrested before the construction got under way, but he did his best to help it along from the inside. He turned his isolation into his greatest advantage. From his small wooden desk far from the gaze of the guards, he drew up blueprints and notes on the guards' vulnerabilities. During visitation hours, loyal allies would smuggle these messages and blueprints out of the prison for Peter Cárdenas and Néstor Cerpa to scrutinize with their best engineers.[11] The Directorate found a couple of young sympathizers, Víctor and Rosa Vargas, to pose as a newlywed couple and purchase a lot just 300 meters from the MRTA cellblock. After purchasing the lot, the Vargases built a small home. At first blush, it looked like any other startup home, but with one exception: the bedroom had a false bookcase blocking a trap door to a secret underground tunnel.[12]

The couple was unenthusiastic about the plan, but they were good sports at first. Every day, Víctor Vargas, who went by the nickname "the Goth," presumably due to his punk look, would leave before daylight in his powder blue Dodge 300, supposedly heading to work at the market. He came home every day at one in the afternoon, the Peruvian lunch hour, and returned again in the evening in his truck, parking it in the garage overnight. It was a classic Peruvian workshift; the neighbors never suspected that the truck was hauling two loads of dirt a day.[13]

When he learned that his new life of confinement could last more than a year, the Goth started looking for an exit strategy. He and Rosa began sabotaging the operation in the hopes of getting released from their duties. One night, they hosted a dinner party while the diggers were still working below. The diggers had no choice but to sweat it out in the hot, stuffy tunnel, waiting for the guests to leave. It was after midnight when the Goth finally let them surface, not having bothered to prepare them a meal. On another occasion, the Goth and Rosa left town without warning, leaving the workers totally exposed. This prompted a meeting between the Goth and Néstor Cerpa at a Lima restaurant.

Cerpa reminded the Goth that his sudden departure was tantamount to desertion. Didn't he know what the MRTA did to traitors?

"I don't give a damn," the Goth said.

"If you don't behave correctly, we will have to take other, stronger measures with you," Cerpa said.

The Goth was unshaken. "I've made a decision, and if anything happens to me, there are people who are prepared to do something about it."[14]

The Goth explained that he had made arrangements to blow the rebels' cover should anything happen to him or Rosa. If Cerpa let them walk, however, he wouldn't tell a soul.[15]

"Look," Cerpa said, "that doesn't bother us. Naturally, we want you to carry out your job. But you must understand one thing clearly: this project must not be betrayed."

The Goth held firm. He said that he would not be going back to the safe house under any circumstances, but he offered a compromise. "Bring in another couple, and I'll introduce them to the neighbors as relatives of mine."[16]

Cerpa must have felt as if he had little choice in the matter. He had said it himself: the mission was too important to compromise. He accepted the Goth's ultimatum on the spot. The Goth lived up to his end of the bargain, introducing another couple, Richard and Sonia, to his neighbors as his nephew and nephew's wife, who were moving in with him for a while. After that, Víctor and Rosa Vargas left, never to return.[17]

The change of plans put the operation on hold until the new couple settled in. Richard and Sonia proved to be much better collaborators, blasting the radio all day and bringing in dogs and chickens to muffle the sound of digging.[18] During the day, Sonia, an attractive young woman by all accounts, would walk over to the outer gates of the prison to chat up the guards. Feigning flirtation and interest, she would casually inquire about their daily routine, which the attention-craved sentries happily delivered. Evidently, they had no idea that miners were slowly chipping away the earth beneath their feet.[19]

The tunnel was an engineering feat. At 1.5 meters high by 1 meter wide, it was big enough for two grown men to pass each other and wide enough for mine cars to pass through with loads of dirt. Wooden supporting beams lined the ceiling every 1 to 3 meters, and there was even a small shower so the workers could wash up before surfacing. For light, they siphoned off electricity from the prison.

The diggers advanced slowly, methodically, every day. Teams of four took shifts, surgical masks plastered to their faces, from eight in the morning until five in the evening. Depending on the conditions of the soil, the workers could only advance 30 to 40 centimeters a day at first, chiseling away at a cloth-covered wedge of pointed hardwood with a sledgehammer. At 20 degrees Celsius, the men had to endure infections, headaches, intestinal problems, and other afflictions caused by the suffocating heat and dirt.[20]

By November 1989, the diggers had only advanced 35 meters, with over 265 meters to go. If they wanted to break ground in the next year, they would need to kick it into high gear. To speed things along, Cerpa approved a plan allowing for three teams of three to work at a time. After that, they began advancing by an average of 3 meters a day, slowly making their way underneath the prison walls.[21]

■ Víctor Polay and Alberto Gálvez were two of a handful of prisoners with knowledge of the operation. The risk of discovery was simply too great to allow others in on the plan. One day, Polay woke up to the sound of tractors in the prison yard. He got up and peered outside. Sure enough, a bulldozer was digging up dirt next to the outer wall. Were the prison authorities onto them?

"What's happening out there?" Polay asked unassumingly. "Are they finally putting in that water reservoir?"

"No," the guard replied. "They're looking for a tunnel. Last night the guards in the tower heard digging noises. They think it's coming from Pavilion 6-A, and now they're trying to uncover it."[22]

Canto Grande was set up like a Peruvian cake. Unlike Americans, who simply cut the round dessert into equal slices, Peruvians carve out a circle in the middle of the cake first. The tips of the equally proportioned slices never touch, instead abutting the round center. Canto Grande had a similar design, with each cellblock, or pavilion, abutting the round prison yard. The only main difference between the Peruvian pastry and the maximum-security prison was the narrow gap between the walls of each cellblock, designed to keep each cellblock physically isolated. These narrow alleyways, accessible only to prisoners out in the yard, were known collectively as No Man's Land.

Polay knew that his diggers had been working under Pavilion 2-A, several slices away from where the guards were looking. Still, this was too close for comfort. The guards had deduced that the prisoners in 2-A, who ranked among the country's most notorious drug traffickers, were tunneling out from the pavilion. They had no idea that the digging had come from the outside-in, much less from a different cellblock. Polay was happy to indulge the guards' theory.

Down below, the MRTA diggers huddled in complete silence as the backhoes dug their trenches, brushing clouds of earth onto their heads.

"They've found us," whispered Jaime, one of the diggers.

"They've heard us," corrected Armando, his fellow digger, "but they haven't found us yet. Stop the digging, and let's get back to the base."[23] The diggers quietly shuffled back the length of the tunnel to the safe house. They determined that they were still safe. Their tunnel was a full 15 meters beneath the surface, beyond the contemplation of the guards. There was no way, Armando argued, that the guards would dig 15 meters deep to look for tunnels, especially if they thought the prisoners were escaping from the inside. No, Armando said. They would wait it out until the search stopped and continue their work.[24]

Meanwhile, Polay tried to bide his time and avoid raising suspicion. One day, the prison commandant came by his cellblock.

"What do you think we're doing out there, Señor Polay," he asked.

"I imagine you're putting in a water reservoir."

"No, we're hunting for a tunnel that the narcos are digging."

"If you're so worried about tunnels," Polay offered, "why don't you dig a moat five meters deep running all the way around the outer wall?"

"You know, that's not such a bad idea."[25]

It wouldn't be the last time Polay had to throw his jailers off the scent. A short while later, he was chatting up a couple of guards when one of them commented on his sudden weight loss.

"You aren't looking well, Mr. Polay. You're losing weight. What's wrong? Aren't your comrades feeding you properly?"

"No," Polay joked, gesturing toward the trench that the guards had bulldozed. "I'm dieting to lose weight so I can escape through your tunnel over there."

The two guards shared a hearty chuckle.

"It's true," Polay said. "I read about the tunnel escape in Chile several years ago, and there was a fat man who got stuck halfway through. He deserved it, of course, but the worst part was that all the prisoners behind him were prevented from completing their escape. So I'm taking no chances."

The guards laughed again. "It never entered their minds that it might be true," Polay later said.[26]

After two days of digging a trench 5 meters deep and 25 meters long, the prison guards finally called off the search. The project was back on. By June 1990, the MRTA operation was in full swing, with eighteen diggers taking two shifts of nine workers each and another four on standby inside the safe house.[27] They were now underneath the prison yard. The only thing that remained was a final stretch of about 65 meters, a gradual incline that would slope up the final 15 meters to the surface. Never ones to miss an opportunity to invoke historical memory, the diggers christened this final leg "Tupac Amaru, Liberator."[28]

While the diggers worked their way toward the surface, Polay continued business as usual. His terrorism trial had already begun, and he appeared at the court on Thursday, 5 July, to face prosecutor Juan Cabello. Cabello had introduced a handgun to the judge as evidence and asked Polay to examine it.

"Do you recognize this gun as yours?" Cabello asked.

"I don't know. Could be," Polay said.

"Show the tribunal how it's used."

Polay, all smiles in his leather jacket, took the weapon in both hands, held it up and cocked it with an air of familiarity before handing it back to his interrogator. Polay's smugness was lost on no one, but everyone missed the reason why. It didn't matter if the judge threw the book at him. If everything went according to plan, he wouldn't be around long enough to hear the verdict.[29]

■ On Sunday, 9 July, the whole world tuned in to the World Cup soccer final, a championship rematch that would see Diego Maradona's Argentine squad surrender the title to West Germany. At 4:00 P.M. that day, a Tupac Amarista digger named Antonio took his shift. He knew he was close, as he could hear footsteps and music above him. Two and a half hours later, the ground above him began to cave in. He leaped back, worried he would be buried alive. Much to his surprise, very little dirt fell. Confused under the darkness and dirt, he fixed his eyes on a small circle of light. He shone his flashlight on it, turning it off immediately when he realized he was looking at the sky above the prison yard: the light at the end of the tunnel.[30]

The diggers weren't supposed to reach the surface for another two days. That was the day for which Néstor Cerpa, Peter Cárdenas, and the Directorate had arranged for a team of getaway cars. What's more, the diggers were supposed to surface inside Pavilion 2-A, the MRTA men's cellblock. Due to the cave-in, however, they ended up in the narrow alleyway adjacent to the pavilion; they were in No Man's Land. This meant that the hole could be discovered by any of the common prisoners or, worse still, a guard.

Tucked away between the towering walls of the neighboring cellblocks, No Man's Land was as good a spot as any for mischievous prisoners to escape the guards' supervision for a spell. Sure enough, two common prisoners ducked into the narrow path that day and rolled up a joint. They hadn't been smoking long before one of them spotted the hole in the ground.

"Son-of-a-bitch!" he said. "It's a goddam tunnel!"

"Yeah," replied his companion, "and it's gotta be the MRTA gang next door that's digging it."[31]

The man draped his jacket over the hole. The fewer people who knew about this, the more leverage the potheads would have. The only problem was that the pair of them were too baked to make any lucid decisions. They would have to tell Pichirulo.

Every cellblock had a prisoner who ran things, a kind of boss who called the shots, got a cut from every illegal transaction, and approved all major decisions. Pichirulo was that man. The smokers found Pichirulo and told him of their discovery. They asked if he had any bright ideas. He did.[32]

The three gentlemen—the two smokers and Pichirulo—found Fernando Valladares, Lucero Cumpa's husband, and showed him the hole. Valladares, who by all accounts was not in on the escape plot yet, played it cool. "I told them they would be well rewarded for keeping their mouths shut," he recalled, "and I gave them some money to buy liquor, cigarettes, cocaine paste, whatever. All three of them, including Pichirulo, were convinced they'd struck gold and were already looking forward to months of black-mailing the organization in return for their silence while we dug our way out of Canto Grande."[33]

The three common prisoners left satisfied. Once they had turned the corner, Valladares knelt down and pressed his mouth to the tiny hole.

"*Patria o muerte!*" he hissed, waiting for the reply. "Fatherland or death!"

"*Venceremos!*" came the call from down below. "We will prevail!"

Valladares covered the hole again with the jacket and went to find Alberto Gálvez, the top-ranking rebel leader in the cellblock.

"They found it," Valladares said. "We have to go now because the tunnel has already caved in. We have to go!"[34]

"Hold on," Gálvez said, confused. "Let's assess the situation first."

He arranged for a private meeting with Pichirulo, cellblock boss to cell-block boss.

"Who else knows about this?" Gálvez asked.

"The only ones who know are the three of us. Those two [smokers] and me," Pichirulo said.

Gálvez nodded. He explained the truth about the tunnel, that it was already finished and that the Tupac Amaristas would be escaping that night under the cover of darkness. And then he made Pichirulo a proposition.

"If you can keep those guys quiet and distracted, you can come with us."

Pichirulo was more than happy to comply. He said he could buy the two potheads off with about fifty U.S. dollars, enough money to keep them high for a very long time. Gálvez handed over the cash, and Pichirulo took it from there.[35]

There was no time to waste. Gálvez knew they would have to leave that night to avoid anyone else discovering the hole. He put Valladares in charge of informing his wife and the isolated Polay about the plan.

Polay was surprised to see Valladares bring him his dinner that evening. Usually, it was Gálvez who did so. Valladares handed the commander his tray along with a bespectacled teddy bear.

"Here's your radio, Comandante," Valladares whispered as he handed Polay the stuffed animal. "You should get in touch with Rodrigo [the code name for Gálvez] immediately, because some common prisoners have discovered the tunnel."

Polay was at a loss. Valladares wasn't even supposed to know about the tunnel.

"Thanks, that's fine," was all he could muster. He waited until he was alone in his cell and pulled the walkie-talkie out of the teddy bear to radio Valladares.

Was the car ready at the safe house, he asked? Valladares replied that there was none. That settled it. They would wait. The original plan was to start leaving at 2:00 A.M., after the night watch took its shift. The night watch was always more relaxed than the day shift, with guards often drifting off in the damp winter cold.

"First of all," Polay said, "we have to control the people who found the tunnel and all the common prisoners in 2-A so they don't suspect what's going on. Have all three teams ready to go, but let's try to hold out until tomorrow morning as planned. It's important that we all get away cleanly."

Before long, Antonio radioed in from the safe house. Polay asked to speak with someone from the National Directorate to coordinate the escape. He preferred to talk to his longtime comrade and trusted friend, Peter Cárdenas. The "Sicilian" had been coordinating the logistics of the escape the whole time, and he'd thought of everything: getaway cars, drivers, changes of clothes, fake IDs, first aid, anything the rebels could possibly need during their great escape. The only problem was that, as Cárdenas had not expected to put the plan into action that night, he had already gone dark for the evening, a precaution to avoid detection by authorities. Antonio said he would arrange for transport from the safe house. Polay would have to accept this for now.[36]

Meanwhile, Alberto Gálvez went over to the other comrades to fill them in. He explained that there was a tunnel.

"It's not how we planned," he said, but it would have to do. The good news was that the police "had no idea." He stressed that no one needed to leave who didn't want to. Those who did, however, would need to leave "in an orderly fashion." At least one man remained behind.[37]

As Gálvez made arrangements with the men, Valladares headed to the women's cellblock and looked for his wife, Lucero Cumpa. He handed her a walkie-talkie and a pistol and told her they were escaping that night.

"What?" she thought, incredulously. "It can't be!"

The more her husband talked, the more she believed him. There would be three teams. The first, code-named "Tiger 1," would be the prisoners from the men's cellblock. They would be the first go down the tunnel. The second, "Tiger 2," would be responsible for rescuing Polay from his isolated cellblock. They would leave second. The women would leave third.

"And what's our code name?" Cumpa asked.

"Cupid."

"What?" Cumpa frowned. "Not Tiger?"

"Cupid."[38]

Even in their haste to coordinate an escape, the men couldn't resist relegating their women comrades to a secondary status, assigning them an effeminate, emotion-based code name and leaving them to escape last.

■ Valladares and Gálvez watched the changing of the guard at 3:00 A.M. A short while later, Gálvez led the first group of twenty prisoners into position.

"The first shipment is on the way," Valladares radioed. The guard on duty had his head buried in a newspaper and his back turned to the escapees, who shuffled down the stairs in single file. It was down to Gálvez, as leader of the group, to enter the hole first. He slid down feet-first, landing on the dirt floor below as the diggers received him and ushered him down the dimly lit tunnel. As he scuttled forward, it was everything he could do to breathe. The heat was smoldering, suffocating. He could feel sweat dripping down his forehead, soaking his chest. The tunnel seemed to go on forever, but adrenaline kept him going. Finally, he reached the end of the tunnel and climbed up into the safe house. His body was dripping with sweat, as if someone

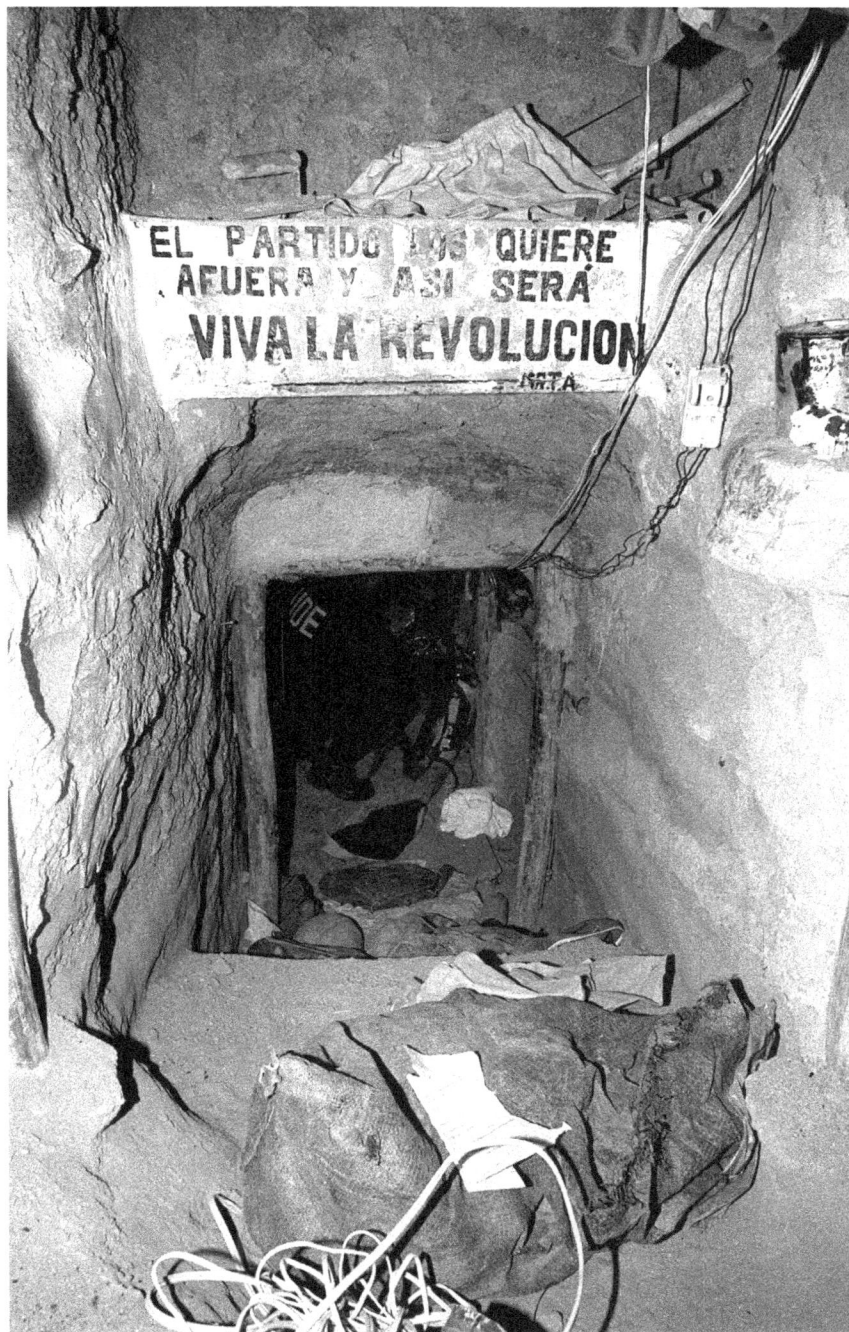

Tunnel built by MRTA for Canto Grande prison escape, 1990
(photo by Oscar Medrano, *Caretas*, with kind permission)

had poured buckets of water on him. "I must have lost two pounds" of water weight, he surmised. A small price to pay for his freedom.[39]

Once the twentieth man had cleared, Valladares radioed Polay.

"Alpha is coming your way. Over."

"Roger and out," Polay replied. Valladares led a team of five prisoners, armed and dressed in black, through the sewage ducts to retrieve their leader from his top-floor cell.

Polay had already changed into all-black clothes and was waiting anxiously as the rescue team made its way toward the third floor. "The time ticked by and nothing happened," Polay recalled. "I imagined the worst, of course: that something had gone wrong and they had been intercepted."

After twenty minutes, Valladares radioed in. "A is waiting for you."

Polay sprang into action. He had the keys to the first and second barred doors. He climbed up on his cell room chair and pushed the skylight open, pulling himself onto the roof and crawling across it toward the ramp leading to Pavilion 6-B. He found the rope and tied it around his waist so that the team could pull him up the ramp to the roof of 6-B. Once he was in place, they went down the two flights, right under the guards' noses. "We had to cling to the shadows," Polay remembered, "and slip across the lighted area one by one." Finally, they made it through the door and into the ducts, each one holding onto the shoulder of the man ahead. "We went through the mess hall window," Polay wrote, "and there was the freedom tunnel, a rabbit hole about 1 meter in diameter. What a wonderful sensation!"

Another comrade entered the hole first, followed by Polay.

"The comandante is on his way," radioed one of the men. Polay followed his rescuers down the stuffy tunnel, hunched over and choking on the heat through his scarf and cap, his body dripping sweat. Still he tried to take in the wonderful engineering work that had gone into the construction. "It looked like it had no end," one escapee said of the tunnel.[40]

Ten minutes later, Polay had reached the end of the 332-meter tunnel and climbed the ladder out of the hole in the safe house. The mothers had been right. Santa Sarita Colonia, the patron saint on the little stamp they had given him earlier that day, had indeed been looking after him. And she had pulled off a miracle. "At long last," Polay said, "we were free!"[41]

■ Only the women remained. Lucero Cumpa had been charged with leading their escape. Earlier that afternoon, she had informed the others about the existence of the tunnel.[42] Their flight, she knew, would be complicated. Yolanda, one of the prisoners, had recently given birth and was suffering from a uterine infection. Another, Valentina, had sustained a back injury.

Cumpa doubted their ability to travel down the tunnel without assistance. When she radioed her husband to tell him the situation, he told her not to worry; their comrades would be waiting for them with mining carts to roll them to freedom.

The women's first order of business would be to subdue the two common prisoners with whom they shared a cellblock. María Bautista and Milagros Herrera were on friendly enough terms with their fellow inmates, but telling them about the tunnel was too risky. Cumpa had some of the other women slip sleeping pills into their sodas, but only María drank hers. Milagros remained wide-eyed, watching the commotion inside the cell, hardly touching her dinner. She seemed to be onto them.

Around 3:00 A.M., Cumpa watched the changing of the guard and Polay's ascent to the rooftop forty-five minutes later. Only then did she wake María and approach the bright-eyed Milagros to fill them in.

"We have to tie you up," Cumpa explained. "It's for your own good." That way, María and Milagros wouldn't be suspected of aiding and abetting their escape.

The two women said they understood, wishing their cellmates Godspeed and allowing themselves to be bound and gagged. Before leaving the cell, Cumpa bent over and gave them each a gentle kiss on the forehead.[43]

Cumpa gathered all eight MRTA women in the cell.

"Does anyone want to stay behind?" she asked. "This is your last chance."

No one said a word.

With that, Cumpa held up her pistol in one hand and her walkie-talkie in the other and led the women to the barred stairway. The others were armed with nothing but glass bottles. Their instructions were to wait until team "Tiger 2" was in place downstairs, outside their cellblock, to retrieve them. Cumpa would then use a car jack that they had smuggled in to pry open the bars leading to the stairway.

She waited. Time seemed move in slow motion; 3:30 turned to 4:00 A.M., 4:00 to 4:45. "Still nothing," she remembered those tense moments waiting by the stairs. Finally, at 4:50, a crackle came over the radio.

"We're on our way."

She grabbed the car jack, slid it between the iron bars, and began turning the crank. The bars began spreading apart. Between the nerves, the pressure, the cranking, and her sweaty palms, the jack slipped from her grasp, crashing to the ground as the noise reverberated off the concrete walls. "And then . . . boots," Cumpa recalled. The guards were quickstepping up the staircase.[44]

"Plan B!" she hissed.

One of the women readied her empty soda bottle and hid by the side of the gate. When the first guard came up and the iron gate swung open, she broke the bottle over his head. The guard cried out and fell over, then got back up and ran down the stairs. Cumpa and the other women followed him down. When they reached the bottom, they found two guards standing next to their injured colleague. Cumpa waved her pistol at them and told them to back away slowly. No one needed to get hurt. The guards raised their hands and slowly stepped away as she and the others headed outside.

Now it would be a matter of time before the guards sounded the alarm. Cumpa found Tito Cruz Sánchez, a young fighter from the San Martín guerrilla front, standing beside the chain-link fence in front of the yard with a small team. They helped the women jump the fence and led them to the open space next to Pavilion 2-A. No sooner had Cumpa peered into the hole than Tito grabbed her and tossed her inside. She instinctively got to her knees and started crawling.[45]

"On your feet, comrade," one of the diggers said. She stood up. Only then did she appreciate the size of the tunnel. She told the men about the injured women, but these women insisted on proceeding on foot, no doubt wanting to prove to the men that they could endure the pain and escape on their own. Cumpa hunched over for the first leg, and when the tunnel got bigger, she stood and began sprinting so hard that she crashed head-first into the tunnel wall. The hit knocked her flat on her back. Shaking it off, she got back to her feet and tried again, only to run into the wall a second time. "After that," she recalled, "I was more careful."[46]

Cumpa finally made it to the end of the tunnel and into the safe house. She waited to make sure the other eight women came out. She was surprised to see that Yolanda and Valentina, the two enfeebled women, had made it without assistance. Once Valentina climbed up into the house, however, the adrenaline wore off and she passed out. It didn't matter; she had come out on her own. Valentina's comrades produced some smelling salts to revive her.[47]

Peter Cárdenas had arranged to have a caravan of *combis*, shuttles, escort the prisoners from the safe house. The only problem was that he had made those arrangements for two days later, when the escape was originally supposed to take place. Now the "Sicilian" was nowhere to be found, and the guerrillas in the safe house were frantically working on the escape plan. The fugitives had to wait for ten minutes for the first getaway car to arrive. It was an old clunker of a truck with a bad motor, but it would have to do. Víctor Polay, Alberto Gálvez, and Lucero Cumpa all hunkered down in the bed and on the floorboard while the truck pulled out of the garage, taking advantage of the last precious moments of darkness. The truck was so decrepit that it broke down on the outskirts of Lima. The three cellblock leaders had no choice but to get separate cars. Cumpa joined a truckload of fugitive women and men while Polay and Gálvez caught their own ride. It was at that time that someone snapped a photo. Cumpa, Rosa Luz Padilla (the woman who had been captured alongside Polay in Huancayo), and the other escapees were all smiles; some of them put up their pointer and middle fingers, emulating a peace sign. For the MRTA, this stood for something else: V for Victory. As the morning sun peeked over the hills, kissing the lonely road out of Lurigancho, the cars split off into the labyrinth of the capital toward their respective hideaways.[48]

As a child, Polay had always marveled at the stories of Apristas who vanished from inside the penitentiary. Now, as his rickety truck disappeared into the menagerie of the waking metropolis, Víctor Polay Campos became his own rebel action figure. He had become the Invisible Man.

"Polay's Tunnel," as it became known, was 332 meters long. Experts estimated that the diggers had removed some 950 tons of dirt over the course of the one-year project.[49] The escape of the forty-eight Tupac Amaristas was a shot in the arm for the floundering movement. The MRTA had now recovered all of its forces and leadership, pulling off an attention-grabbing stunt with no casualties. The event made headlines in all major media outlets for days and even months to come. Most of the coverage focused on the amazing, unprecedented feat and on the total incompetence—perhaps even collusion—of the outgoing García administration. At long last, the public relations gods seemed to be smiling once again on the Tupac Amaru Revolutionary Movement.

Part 3

13
Fujishock

The Canto Grande prison escape was a public relations coup for the Tupac Amaru Revolutionary Movement. Not even the stronger, more lethal Shining Path had achieved something so epic. To do so without the loss of a single life added a touch of romanticism to the narrative. "It generated an enormous sympathy and respect within the population," wrote Polay, "and many identified with the action, which punished and mocked a government that had allowed for all the plagues of Egypt to fall on its people. . . . It also gave us an image of an MRTA that broke its shackles and chains and re-created itself resurging victoriously over its enemies."[1] As the remaining days of the García administration dwindled, so did its hold on the media narrative. Officials accused prison authorities of assisting the prisoners, while critics accused the president of colluding with the rebels. García and Polay had been close once, after all. Had the president, with one foot out the door, given his old roommate a final parting gift? The timing and circumstances of the escape only fueled the conspiracy theory.[2]

The fact that no one knew Polay's whereabouts thickened the plot. "Is Polay Back in the Jungle?" asked *La República* three days after his escape.[3] No one knew for sure. A lightning assault on the jungle town of Yurimaguas less than three weeks after his flight added to the speculation.[4] When asked if Polay had spearheaded the attack, Interior Minister Agustín Mantilla gave an unreassuring answer: "I can't say whether Polay or any of the Canto Grande escapees were there, as the information I have at the moment is very sketchy."[5]

This proved to be a turning point for the rebels. In one fell swoop, the MRTA had replenished most of its army and support base, exposed the incompetence of the state, and captured the attention of the media and the public. Never before had the group held such political leverage. Some in the rebel leadership, including Víctor Polay and Alberto Gálvez, believed this to be their best opportunity to negotiate an end to the armed conflict and a dignified entry into the legal political sphere. They hoped that president-elect Alberto Fujimori, a political neophyte, would welcome the opportunity to disarm one of the country's fiercest guerrilla organizations. Fujimori had been a long-shot candidate. The former La Molina University rector had run against acclaimed writer and neoliberal Mario Vargas Llosa. Vargas Llosa had been favored to win until the run-off elections, at which point the diminutive Fujimori began gaining momentum in the polls. Popularly known as *El Chino*, the Chinaman, despite his purely Japanese heritage, Fujimori tapped into popular dissatisfaction with the status quo. His campaign slogan, *Un presidente como tú*, "A president like you," hit home on this populist message. In electing Fujimori, the Peruvians had doubled down on democratic populism after a disappointing experiment with Aprismo. "Víctor and I had reached the conclusion that the time had come to enter negotiations" with the incoming administration, Alberto Gálvez recalled.[6]

Not everyone agreed. Néstor Cerpa and Miguel Rincón, two hard-liners who had taken the reins in Polay's and Gálvez's absence, felt that a negotiated settlement would compromise their ideological purity. "The two of them were completely opposed" to a truce, Gálvez said. "They didn't want to be like the M-19," the Colombian guerrilla group whose 1985 cease-fire ended in a hostage crisis and an army massacre. Cerpa and Rincón's hard-line faction believed that the only way out of the conflict was through military triumph.[7]

Polay and Gálvez convened a meeting of the Central Committee in August 1990 to settle the matter. As soon as the meeting was under way, Fujimori, just weeks into his presidency, announced that he was implementing economic austerity measures to control hyperinflation. The plan, popularly dubbed the "Fujishock," brought the entire economy to a standstill. Although the plan did help bring long-term stabilization to the national economy, everyday Peruvians felt immediate and, in some cases, lasting pain. The fact that Fujimori had specifically run against this neoliberal policy on the campaign trail contributed to the sense of collective shock.

Given this curveball, Polay tabled the truce proposal, effectively placating the hard-liners who advocated continuing the armed struggle. It was a politically fatal decision, for the rebels would never again hold such political leverage.

Nor would the MRTA leadership ever be so collectivist in makeup or practice. Polay used the August conference to reassert his personal authority following a long absence, stacking the Central Committee with loyalist hard-liners like Peter Cárdenas.[8] Despite orchestrating the prison escape from the outside, the blue-eyed special operations commander had been on the outs with interim leaders who believed he had cut a deal with prosecutors in exchange for a reduced prison sentence. Still, Polay trusted Cárdenas and believed him to be personally loyal, a quality that he would need if he were to regain control of the rebel command structure. Rather than reinstate Cárdenas directly into the Central Committee, Polay chose a tactic of gradual ascent, relying on him increasingly for Lima operations. Polay also introduced another name to the Central Committee: Lucero Cumpa. Before her arrest, Cumpa had worked under Cárdenas as a Lima cell leader. Now the young Comas militant found herself, temporarily at least, outranking her former commander. Cumpa had demonstrated remarkable leadership during the prison escape and, Polay and Gálvez agreed, had earned a seat at the table. That Peter Cárdenas could vouch for Cumpa's personal loyalty also helped.

While Polay loyalists were on the ascent, his detractors found themselves on the outs. These included Sístero García, commander of the Northeastern Front before and after Rodrigo Gálvez's death, and Orestes Dávila Torres, chief of military operations in Lima. Polay moved swiftly to strip these men of authority. He claimed to be getting rid of bad seeds and reclaiming the moral high ground in the war. According to Polay, it was García who had overseen the firing squads against homosexuals and other petty criminals. Polay would have no more of it. "And from that moment forward," he wrote, "the practice stopped."[9] García and Dávila had their own explanation for Polay's sudden move. It was a power grab, simple and plain, an act of Caudillismo designed to consolidate his authority and silence his most vocal critics.[10]

Polay's actions at the conference did little to assuage these concerns. One of his first orders of business was to reconstitute the National Directorate, the most elite body within the rebel hierarchy, outranking the broader Central Committee. According to the initial alliance, the Directorate should consist of three MRTA members and three MIR members. The newly constituted Directorate would now consist of four members from the original

MRTA (Polay, Néstor Cerpa, Miguel Rincón, and Américo Gilvonio) and only two Miristas (Alberto Gálvez and Rodolfo Klien).[11] This would ensure Polay's influence over operations going forward, and it also put the MRTA hard-liners in the majority. Now Gálvez found himself a lonely voice for unconditional peace in the Directorate. Although Polay still favored entering talks with the government, he adopted a position that the party's most militant wing could accept: they would enter peace negotiations by forcing the government's hand militarily. "We could go home and be hunted down like sitting ducks, crying about how we shouldn't have taken up arms," he later explained, "or we could look for a political exit fighting." He considered the second option "the most dignified and consequential."[12]

To achieve these ends, the rebels turned to a familiar tactic: kidnapping. This time, they would capture Gerardo López, a young congressman in the president's political party, Cambio 90. The rebels hoped that López would bring the president to the negotiating table. The twenty-eight-year-old congressman fancied himself a man of the people despite his conservative leanings. He still lived with his mother in a ramshackle house in Villa El Salvador, one of Lima's oldest shantytowns, and he took the bus home every day after working in downtown Lima. The Tupac Amaristas from Villa knew López well and believed, as Polay recalled, that he was "a democratic person."[13] This October evening in 1990 was a Sunday, so López hadn't gone to work that day. He had just plopped down to rest when someone came to the door. His cousin, Luis Quirós, opened the door to a gentleman who said he needed to talk to the congressman. From the next room, López asked his cousin to confirm on whose behalf the man was calling.

"I'm from CUAVE," the gentleman replied, referring to the neighborhood association with which López was affiliated. The answer was satisfactory enough, and so López got up and threw on a jacket. He found his mother and family watching their new color TV in the living room and sat down for a spell. After a moment, he announced, "I'm taking off," and went to the door.

Outside, he met the gentleman and shook his hand.

"Hi," replied the stranger, "You know me."

This unsettled López, who recoiled slightly.

"Don't worry, shorty," said the gentleman, resting his hand on the congressman's shoulder, "nothing's going to happen to you."

At that moment, another man stepped out of the shadows and placed his hand on López's other shoulder.

"Nothing's going to happen to you," repeated the second man. The Tupac Amaristas were joined by a third, and they quietly escorted López toward the street.[14]

"I was scared," López later reported. "I thought I was going to die."[15]

The rebels explained that they were members of the MRTA and that their leaders wanted to have a word with him. They took the congressman to an undisclosed location, where he met with several hooded rebels who claimed to be leaders of the movement.

Was Polay one of those masked men? López couldn't say for sure. "Still," he admitted, "I can't rule out that Polay Campos was one of my interrogators."

Whoever they were, they wanted the president's attention. As López was a congressman from Fujimori's political party, the masked rebels hoped that he could make that happen. They told him to deliver a message to the president: they were open to talks with the government, but they weren't ready to lay down arms.[16] After holding López for several days, they delivered him to Guido Lombardi, a journalist from the TV news program *Panorama*, to relay their message to both the president and the Peruvian public. López headed straight to the station on Alejandro Tirado Street, where he conducted an interview. It was another public relations win, as police weren't even aware that López had been released until he appeared on-screen.[17] When López arrived at the presidential palace the following day, however, Fujimori refused to see him.[18] Speaking before the National Congress of Private Enterprise several days later, the president reaffirmed his decision not to play the MRTA's game. "Why," Fujimori asked, "would I dialogue with an armed group that resorts to violence, murder and confrontation with our armed forces, tries to subvert democratic order and the rule of law?" Even if he were to open talks with the rebels, Fujimori added, he wouldn't do it through López. Any true democratic government, he explained, "doesn't need middle men or spontaneity to dialogue."[19]

It seemed for the first time as if the Tupac Amaristas had met their match. Fujimori had a knack for public relations, and he understood the importance of winning the news cycle. For the first time, the MRTA's media blitz had backfired. Rather than reconsider the use of force as a negotiating tactic, however, the rebels concluded that it hadn't been extreme enough. "It became clear to us that any hopes of dialogue or accord would only be possible if we made it happen through political-military force," Polay wrote.[20] On that, they were sorely mistaken. "What we didn't realize was that Fujimori didn't have the slightest interest in doing it."[21]

■ Lucero Cumpa had come a long way since her days painting subversive graffiti on walls. She was now a Central Committee member with an expanding list of responsibilities.[22] She took on the new mantle reluctantly at first. She had always wanted to join the rural insurgency as a guerrilla fighter, and she hoped that this might be her opportunity to do it. Besides, she knew that remaining in Lima was dangerous. "The city is really risky," she later testified, "because we're always being looked for and my photo had appeared as one of the escapees."[23] Moreover, she feared what would happen to her family. She was a single mother now. Her husband, Valladares, had been killed in action in Cuzco shortly after the prison escape. Her two-year-old daughter, Karina, was being raised by another woman in the movement, but she knew the counterinsurgency forces would stop at nothing to get to her. "They would arrest you and bring in your family as collaborators."[24] She also knew that Karina was her Achilles' heel. "The person who they looked for the most was my daughter because they [knew] that she is the thing I love the most in this world. They knew that if they got her it would be unbearable."[25]

One day, she called home to check in on her mother. María always had a way of reassuring her, and today was no exception.

"Daughter," she said, "I'm getting old. You're young, and you have to keep fighting. If I'm arrested, I forbid you to turn yourself in. Do you understand?"

A lump formed in Cumpa's throat as she listened to María's words. "Yes, mother," was all she could get out.

"And if I die," María continued, "you are not to come to my funeral."

At that, Cumpa began to weep, knowing this was goodbye.

She continued to oversee operations in Lima. Many of these were by now familiar. The rebels continued their symbolic war against imperialism, bombing the U.S. Embassy. The United States was in the midst of Operation Desert Storm, an act of aggression that the Tupac Amaristas decried as more Yankee meddling in foreign affairs. But just as Cumpa feared, her days as a free woman were numbered.

One day in February 1991, she went to the marketplace in Magdalena to do some shopping. The idea was to run to the store before meeting up with a contact, so she had in her purse a sheet with all the day's appointments and the code names of each contact. At the home of one of these contacts was her daughter, Karina, and the sheet included the code name and directions where Cumpa could find her.[26] As she waited for her contact in the park, DINCOTE agents pulled up and grabbed her. She quickly snatched the sheet with Karina's whereabouts from her purse and stuffed it into her mouth before the agents could react. The agents attempted to pry the wad from her mouth, but she clenched her jaw. According to Cumpa, the agents flipped her upside down, pinched her nose, and punched her in the gut to force her mouth open. She tried to focus, to produce as much saliva as she could to lubricate her throat so that the wad of paper would slide down. Finally, she swallowed, opened her mouth, and gasped for air. The infuriated detectives took her back to DINCOTE headquarters.[27]

Cumpa spent the next fifteen days in police custody. There, she claimed to have been tortured yet again.[28] Still she didn't give any information. "The one thing that has sustained me throughout my life has been my clean conscience," she later said, "and my dignity."[29] For her, remaining steadfast in her refusal to talk to her captors was an example of both. When it became clear that she wouldn't talk, DINCOTE officials tried a different tactic. After several days, the colonel in charge of the unit summoned her to his office.

Playing the role of the good cop, the colonel asked Cumpa how she was doing. She remained silent. He asked even more questions, but she didn't say anything. She didn't even stir in her chair or move a muscle. She just stared ahead with a blank expression, pretending the colonel wasn't there. "I didn't say A or B or C," Cumpa said of the encounter. "I didn't give him a thing." Annoyed, the colonel sent her back to her cell.

Cumpa was in good spirits when authorities transferred her and five other women prisoners from the temporary detention center in Magdalena to the Palace of Justice in downtown Lima for processing on the morning of 9 March 1991. She chitchatted with the guards and, according to the other transferees, even "flirted" with them. As the armored vehicle approached the corner of Junín and Brasil Avenues, a white Toyota bolted in front of the vehicle, cutting it off and forcing driver Lizandro Guzmán to slam on the brakes. At that moment, a man and a woman who had been dining at a restaurant on the corner stood and began firing on the police vehicle as they approached on foot, killing Guzmán instantly and mortally wounding his copilot, Javier Ramos.

Inside the police vehicle, the prisoners began to scream.

"Hit the floor, *carajo*!" Cumpa cried as the bullets hemmed the vehicle. "Save yourselves!"

Six more assailants jumped out of a brown Bronco truck that had been stationed on the side of the road and began firing on the police truck while two more subjects from the Toyota approached the back door. One of the guards, Arce Ramírez, fired back but was wounded in the shootout. The other officer mounted one of the prisoners to prevent her from moving. When the attackers reached the car, Cumpa recognized them as fellow Tupac Amaristas. She jumped out of the truck and boarded the Toyota with two of her rescuers. The car sped away before anyone could sound the alarm.[30]

Cumpa insisted that she had no knowledge of the rescue beforehand. "I was just as surprised as everyone else in the car," she said.[31] The operation, it turned out, had been the work of Peter Cárdenas, her former Lima commander and Polay's right-hand man. According to Cumpa, Cárdenas had proposed the rescue mission to his comrades in the Central Committee "without my permission!"[32] Cárdenas personally oversaw the operation from start to finish, and police believed he had even driven the getaway car while Alberto Gálvez wheeled the Bronco.[33] Cárdenas had no trouble recruiting operatives for the mission. One of the first to volunteer was Liliana, a longtime friend from her early days of militancy whom Cumpa esteemed like a sister. It had been years since the two women had seen each other. Now Liliana, no longer a teenager, had come to her rescue in this risky mission. Before jumping into the Toyota, Cumpa gave her friend "an ever so brief" hug. When they got to the safe house, the two met again. This time, the long-awaited embrace took place, and they both broke into tears in each other's arms.[34]

"The rescue changed my life completely," Cumpa said.[35] She became an overnight media sensation. Who was this woman rebel that the MRTA would go through such lengths to rescue? The press offered unsurprisingly gendered speculation: she was pregnant; she was Néstor Cerpa's lover; she was pregnant and Néstor Cerpa was the father.[36] No one considered that Lucero Cumpa may have been rescued because she was a critical member of the rebel leadership. Seizing on the media attention, the Directorate conceded to a series of interviews with their new poster child. "There were few recognizable faces in the MRTA," Cumpa recalled, "and none of them were women."[37] The Directorate reasoned that showing off one of its strong, independent women could do the movement some good. Víctor Polay personally asked Cumpa if she would be the new "face" of the MRTA. Although she had her reservations about allowing "personalism or individualism" to get in the way of the collective identity of the movement, she accepted the mantle.[38]

Her first mainstream interview was with *Caretas* journalist Arbilio Arroyo. Arroyo would be the only man involved in the encounter. Everyone else, from the militant who picked him up at the prearranged meeting spot to Cumpa's two gun-wielding bodyguards, were women. The interview took place in a carefully staged setting in which the twenty-eight-year-old rebel appeared, weapon in hand before a MRTA flag, in her beret and olive fatigues. After removing the tape from Arroyo's eyes, the women led him to a table where the interview would take place. As the reporter asked his questions, Cumpa, appearing relaxed and confident, answered thoughtfully while the two women guards, their faces covered in bandanas with sun-

Lucero Cumpa poses for a photo following escape from police custody, 1991
(photo by Arbilio Arroyo, *Caretas*, with kind permission)

glasses over their eyes, stood by menacingly. Arroyo covered a range of topics, from the Canto Grande escape to the reported strife within the party. He also asked the question that was on many a reporter's mind.

"Is it true that when you were captured in 1987, you were with Néstor Serpa [*sic*] Cartolini's child?"[39]

"It's true that I was pregnant in 1987," Cumpa chuckled, "but what I share with comrade Serpa [*sic*] is a political-military unity. There's no sentimental relationship there."[40]

Cumpa allowed Arroyo to take several pictures before they parted ways. There she stood, before the flag of the MRTA, flanked by two other armed women, poised to take over Peru. These highly staged photos and interviews gave the impression that women held a much higher position in the MRTA than they really did. This performed gender empowerment was little more than that, however. Yes, Lucero Cumpa had achieved some authority and celebrity in the movement, but she was very much the exception. Instead, the Directorate used Cumpa in order to appear more feminist than it actually was. This contradiction is evident in the clothes that Cumpa wore in her *Caretas* photos. In practice, only members of the guerrilla army, which operated exclusively in the countryside, wore olive fatigues; urban militants like Cumpa wore civilian clothes. Yet, as Cumpa well knew, the Directorate, with few exceptions, barred women from joining the guerrilla army. This means that the Directorate, desperate as it was to appear feminist, dressed Cumpa like a soldier in an all-male army that she couldn't even join.

■ The Directorate still hoped to leverage the MRTA's media attention vis-à-vis the government. While Peter Cárdenas planned Lucero Cumpa's rescue operation, Polay and Cerpa sent word in San Martín that they were still willing to negotiate a truce from a position of military force.[41] Two months later, following a hostile takeover of Rioja, Cerpa's guerrilla column took nine policemen as hostages. *El Gordo* requested that the government send in members of the Red Cross to negotiate a dialogue with the government. Armin Kobel, the Red Cross's Peruvian representative, indicated that his organization was willing to do whatever it could to keep the peace, but that such a move would require, by law, the consent of the government. Once again, the Fujimori administration rebuffed the offer. "We can't adhere to conditions placed on us by subversive delinquents," Defense Minister Jorge Torres Aciego said.[42]

Cerpa next turned to the church. He brought the nine policemen back to an undisclosed camp in the jungle and allowed them to clean up for a photo. In the picture, which the Tupac Amaristas promptly released to the press, the policemen appeared clean-cut, most of them wearing white T-shirts. They squatted in front of the MRTA flag like a soccer team before a World Cup match. They were all smiling and did not show the slightest sign of distress. "The police hostages," according to one *Caretas* article, "look like they're enjoying a picnic in Chaclacayo [a district known for its agreeable weather and pleasant landscape]."[43] Cerpa also allowed the hostages to make radio addresses, broadcast throughout the region, indicating that their captors had adhered to the Geneva Conventions and afforded them the treatment due prisoners of war.[44]

On the afternoon of 6 June 1991, Cerpa brought together ten handpicked Peruvian and foreign journalists to witness the handover of the hostages to the bishop of Moyobamba, Venancio Orbe Uriarte. Cerpa, who had shed a few pounds living in the jungle, wore fatigues, a beret, and a red-and-white MRTA handkerchief pulled beneath the eyes. He requested, on the bishop's honor, that the Catholic Church step up its condemnation of human rights abuses at the hands of the Peruvian security forces in San Martín. The bishop promised that he would do his part. The following evening, the rebels released the police hostages unharmed along the mouth of the Boca de Yantaló River.[45]

That may have been the last time the MRTA appeared united. In the coming weeks, the rebel group would be plagued by infighting, a crisis of leadership, and more high-profile arrests. The first to fall, as was the case the last time, was Alberto Gálvez. Gálvez had never fully bought into the idea of the rebels fighting their way out of the conflict. That he had fallen in love with Rosa Luz Padilla, the rebel who had been captured alongside Víctor Polay in Huancayo two years earlier, didn't help. Apparently, Padilla and Polay had a falling out after their capture. While neither has gone on record about the source of the rift, it was serious enough to result in Padilla's withdrawal, voluntarily or by force, from the MRTA. After this split, Gálvez and Padilla became romantically involved, and although Padilla was no longer a member of the subversive group, she elected to flee with her former comrades during their July 1990 prison escape. By 1991, she and Gálvez were sharing an apartment in Marbella, at the edge of the beach in Magdalena del Mar. Eager to live the straight and narrow, she enrolled in English classes at the Peruvian British Institute, took up karate, and even opened a corner video store in San Isidro. Gálvez, who despite his reservations had no intention of leaving the MRTA, knew that Padilla would never be able to return to normalcy as long as she was with him. He tried to persuade her to leave the country and start a new life for herself oversees. Maybe she could even live in Italy, sipping cappuccinos along the canals of Venice.

"Look," Gálvez said, "I can pull together a small amount—not much, maybe three or four thousand dollars—but enough to get you started, enough to build you a new life."[46]

Padilla said she would think about it. She didn't want to leave her beloved Peru, and she certainly didn't want to leave Gálvez; but she also knew that she couldn't live a normal life as long as she was dating one of the country's most wanted subversives. The two had already altered their appearances. Gálvez, now thirty-seven, had lost the goatee and glasses and cropped his hair short. Padilla had traded in her wavy black mane for a blonde boy cut. They were constantly looking over their shoulders, waiting for the authorities to storm in any moment. No matter how much Padilla hated to admit it, she knew that something had to give. Perhaps Italy wasn't such a bad idea after all.[47]

One afternoon in early June 1991, Padilla left Gálvez a note under the door: "My love, I won't be long. I'll be back, at the latest, at 6:30. I'm in [karate] class. Kisses. I love you."[48]

Gálvez would never get the note. Before he returned that day, Marco Miyashiro's DINCOTE agents arrested him at a restaurant in Jesús María while he was dining with a comrade.[49]

Facing the same captor for the second time in four years, Gálvez was struck with an uncanny sense of déjà vu.

"Don't you have anyone else to arrest?" he asked the detective.[50]

Padilla returned that evening. Sensing something was amiss, or perhaps reading a distress signal that Gálvez had left for her, she stopped short before walking into the apartment complex and turned around to leave; but the agents intercepted her. They brought her up to the apartment, where Gálvez and Miyashiro were already waiting. Miyashiro allowed the couple one final embrace before hauling them off to DINCOTE headquarters.[51]

Eleven months. That was the extent of Gálvez's and Padilla's liberty. Neither of them would taste it again until the next century. It was the first high-profile bust of Tupac Amaristas since their escape the previous year. The capture also exposed some of the rifts that were beginning to fracture the movement from within. In July 1991, Orestes Dávila Torres, head of Lima operations and one of the Tupac Amaristas whose role had been diminished since Polay's return to power, publicly accused Polay of tipping off police as to Gálvez's whereabouts. The rebel chieftain had already set up Sístero García, the leader of the Northeastern Front in San Martín, Dávila Torres alleged—all part of his new "authoritarian" rulership over the MRTA.[52]

Whether or not Polay had actually been behind the arrests, the new hardline Directorate clearly did not approve of one of its own airing these grievances publicly. The following month, a MRTA hit squad gunned Dávila Torres down in broad daylight as he crossed the Universitaria and Argentina intersection. According to eyewitnesses, a man matching the description of Peter "the Sicilian" Cárdenas had pulled his car alongside Dávila Torres, got out, and shot him in the leg as he tried to hide between two kiosks. Dávila fell to his knees, at which point an armed woman approached from the side and finished him off. The assassins returned to their vehicles and sped away before anyone could react.[53] If true, this report indicates that Dávila Torres was gunned down by the very man Polay had handpicked to replace him in the Lima command. Regardless, the hit showed the lengths to which the newly constituted Directorate was willing to go to silence detractors. To most observers, the MRTA was looking more like Shining Path than its leaders cared to admit.

14

Where the Potatoes Are Cooking

Lucero Cumpa was the new MRTA poster child: young, beautiful, and mestiza. As she knew, "there weren't many recognizable faces in the MRTA." Until then, Víctor Polay and Néstor Cerpa had been the most famous Tupac Amaristas. Cumpa felt ambivalent about her new celebrity. "I was honored that the Directorate trusted me with such an important task, but at the same time it changed my life, because my life was suddenly public and I had to accept that new role." It was a bitter pill to swallow. She had always believed that a true revolutionary should be "discreet, with integrity, without seeking fame."[1] That was no longer an option. Whether she liked it or not, she had become a spokeswoman for the movement. This meant that her role would be more public relations than combat. Her likeness appeared everywhere in the press. The police were constantly raiding her house and harassing her family members, including her most distant relatives. "I was the most wanted person [in the MRTA] and my picture was everywhere in the press," she said. "I mean, I was being looked for at every corner, and I had to spend months on end holed up."[2]

She could see her chances of joining the rural guerrilla front dwindling. She still asked to be moved to the countryside, arguing that she could blend in more easily in the jungle. "I always wanted to be where the potatoes are cooking," she said, a colloquial expression referring to being where the action is.[3] But the Directorate had other plans for their new celebrity. She was their spokeswoman now, and her best role would be as an ambassador to the world. That meant leaving Peru. "They told me they had to send me overseas to proselytize for the MRTA and get my feet wet," Cumpa recalled. "At first I didn't want to because it was always a matter of personal conscience to stick with the people through thick and thin." To suddenly leave her comrades in the middle of war felt wrong. How could she live abroad while her people were tortured, starving, and desperate? But orders were orders, and Cumpa, the dutiful soldier, accepted them without complaint.[4]

Cumpa's first stop was in Europe. Germany was still fresh off its own democratization process, and the rubble of the Berlin Wall—to which Cumpa helped herself a piece—was still fresh. There, she attempted to make contacts with potential allies and raise awareness about the Peruvian cause and conflict. She attended various meetings and conferences of the left, hoping to raise awareness about the MRTA and make some contacts in the international solidarity movement. She even gave public lectures on "The Peruvian Reality" and what the MRTA hoped to achieve with its revolution.[5] "I was the only one speaking on behalf of the MRTA," she recalled. Wherever she went, people wanted know how it was that Peru had descended into violence, and why the MRTA believed that more violence, even of a revolutionary sort, would redress these problems. "That was a really hard question to answer," she later admitted, "more so for outsiders who didn't live in that reality." She tried to explain that the MRTA didn't start the fire, that it had grown after centuries of oppression.[6]

The year 1992 was difficult for Cumpa. Walking the streets of Paris with a map and not speaking the language, she felt like a fish out of water. The worst of it was that she felt completely cut off from her homeland. In the pre-internet days of the early 1990s, news from Peru was hard to come by. She didn't even know how the insurgency was going, much less other news from the Andean nation. "After I left I was virtually cut off from the most dramatic news from the country," she said. "I couldn't even have an organic life. I didn't even know about La Cantuta, Barrios Altos, Tarata, the assassination of María Elena Moyano [all flashpoints in the Shining Path war]. I didn't know any of it." It was as if she were in a bubble in which the war continued in Peru but time stood still for her.[7]

The only time she learned anything about the rebellion was when she checked in with Peter Cárdenas by pay phone. Sometimes, however, she would have preferred not knowing. During one of these check-ins, she asked about Liliana, her longtime friend who had rescued her from police custody in 1991 and who operated in Cárdenas's special forces squadron. Liliana was dead, Cárdenas said. Tears filled Cumpa's eyes as the Swedish Peruvian recounted the story. Liliana's team had engaged in a high-stakes attack on Radio Patrulla, a police station on Grau Avenue. The police had repelled the assault, chasing Liliana and her two comrades down the street until they surrendered. Once they had caught up to the suspects, Cárdenas said, the police killed each of them, Liliana included, with a single shot to the head. Cumpa couldn't contain her emotions. Liliana was like a little sister, and Cumpa hadn't been there to protect her.

"For this," she swore, tears streaming down her cheek, "I'll never forgive you."[8]

Peter Cárdenas had much bigger problems to deal with. Víctor Polay had left the country earlier that year, entrusting him with running operations in an increasingly hostile capital. In April 1992, Fujimori had dissolved congress, suspended constitutional guarantees, and purged the press in an unprecedented self-coup. The president assumed dictatorial powers, instituting martial law and suspending due process for suspected insurgents. Cárdenas feared it would be a matter of time before he fell into government hands.[9]

The "Sicilian" had been living in a safe house with his twenty-three-year-old girlfriend, Clara. A San Marcos student, Clara had joined a solidarity campaign to bring food, clothing, books, and other essential items to the political prisoners during Cárdenas's brief 1989 incarceration. When Cárdenas got out of prison later that year, the two kept in touch, and the "Sicilian" leaned on the innocent-looking mestiza to carry out minor tasks for the movement. Eventually, the two became romantically involved, and Clara took on a more active role in the insurgency.[10] Then, in early 1992, Cárdenas asked Clara if she would be willing to run a safe house with him. The two would pose as a middle-class couple, with Clara serving as the public face to the neighbors and Cárdenas keeping a low profile. Clara accepted the invitation on the spot.[11]

While Clara kept up appearances and operated the MRTA printing press, Cárdenas continued to oversee operations in the metropolitan area. He had always been cavalier in his disregard for clandestinity, appearing in broad daylight to meet up with contacts and, at times, to lead military operations. "It was so dumb," Clara said of their lackluster security measures. "How could we have been so . . . reckless?"[12]

One night in April 1992, within days of Fujimori's self-coup, the couple awoke to a disconcerting knock at the door. Still in her pajamas, Clara ran over to the bedroom window and peeked outside. The apartment building was swarming with police, as many as forty of them, and they had the place surrounded. Seconds later, Cárdenas appeared beside her.

"What do we do?" he asked.

"Go, go!" Clara cried. She might be able to stall the agents while he escaped through the secret hatch. When Cárdenas grabbed his revolver and cracked the trap door, he saw a team of agents barreling down on him. He quickly ran into the living room and found Clara standing with a revolver in one hand and a grenade in the other. Cárdenas peered out the window.

"If we throw the grenade at the cop car, we can take them all out!" he cried.

Clara looked at Cárdenas as if he'd lost his mind. "If we do that, we'll kill everyone who lives in this building! Besides, it still won't guarantee our escape."

"Well, I'm not going out like this!"

"It's over," Clara said.

"Okay," Cárdenas conceded. "Okay."

The agents burst into the room. The first to arrive grabbed Cárdenas from behind and put him in an immobilizing headlock with his hands behind his back as the commander walked in.

"Ah, you're that damned guy!" the commander said.[13]

In the excitement over capturing one of the MRTA leaders, none of the agents noticed Clara, still standing with grenade in hand. Infuriated by the harsh treatment of her comrade and partner, Clara flung her arm around the neck of the agent closest to her and held up the grenade threateningly.

"Let him go!" she ordered.

Another agent pointed his gun and shot at the floor, grazing Clara's foot.

"Grab that crazy woman!" he cried.

Clara couldn't even feel the hole in her foot as she pointed her gun at the oncoming agents. Now it was Cárdenas's turn to play it cool.

"Clara," he said in a calming tone. "Easy."

Cárdenas never used Clara's real name. Even when they were alone, he called her by her *nom de guerre*. Hearing him talk to her in that familiar way was enough to make Clara lower her weapon. After that, the police apprehended them both and brought them to DINCOTE.[14]

Cárdenas tried to downplay the significance of his arrest. "People fall," he told one interviewer following his capture. "It's inevitable. We're at war, in an internal conflict. In every war we're going to hit the enemy, but the enemy is also going to hit us. We just have to adjust accordingly."[15] In truth, his arrest couldn't have come at a worse time for the MRTA. Most of the

Directorate members had fled to the countryside to avoid detection following Fujimori's self-coup. Others, like Lucero Cumpa and Víctor Polay, were out of the country trying to build solidarity overseas. This created a crisis of leadership in Lima, the MRTA's main base of operations. Nervous about losing control of the insurgency and of flagging morale, Polay, ever the gambler, decided to risk all and return to Lima.[16] He changed his appearance, donning a thin moustache, perming his hair, and growing out a potbelly. He entered Peru with a fake ID, passing himself off as Oscar Fausto Wilson Trujillo.[17] Looking back, he admitted that this decision may have been ill-advised, driven as much by a sense of "Leninist machismo" as anything else. When he arrived, he found the situation more dire than he had feared. "Many of the structures of military work and service were loose and there was a lot of mistrust, due to the captures," he wrote.[18]

Always concerned with winning the media war, he went to work on a plan to rescue Cárdenas from custody. "We knew that due to his public importance, the government wouldn't be able to downplay this victory, as it had been doing in our other actions."[19] Polay put Rafael Salgado, an urban commander, in charge of the rescue operation while he made plans to join Néstor Cerpa in the rural guerrilla front.[20]

A little before 10:00 P.M. on the night of 9 June 1992, Polay laced up his sneakers, threw on his beige jacket, and headed over to Joy's Grill, a café in San Borja, to meet up with some colleagues to discuss the transition. Once inside, he took a seat and ordered a coffee while waiting for Salgado to arrive. As he sipped his coffee, a gentleman walked up to the table.

"Hey *Chino*," the man said in a familiar tone, "what are you doing here?"

Polay looked up at the man. He had never seen him before in his life.

"DINCOTE," Polay sighed. "Well, I'm fucked."[21]

Polay kept calm, speaking in an amicable tone with the DINCOTE commander as the other agents surrounded him. He offered no resistance as they led him out of the building and into the squad car. He even asked by name about some of the agents who had been involved in his first arrest back in 1989.[22] He remained cocky when his captors brought him out for a photo two days later.

"The causes of man are invincible!" he cried, fully aware that the cameras were rolling. "The people will prevail! *Viva* the MRTA!"[23]

For all his posturing, however, Polay must have known that this time would be different. Fujimori's Peru was a veritable police state, with steadfast curfews and military tribunals with hooded judges. Now, paramilitary hit squads massacred civilians in broad daylight. This time, there would be

Víctor Polay following arrest, 1992 (photo by José Vilca, *Caretas*, with kind permission)

no tunnels or heroic prison breaks, no sympathetic media coverage or prison cells with televisions sets. This time, Polay's confinement would be solitary, absolute. This time, there would be no light at the end of the tunnel.[24]

■ Lucero Cumpa felt helpless in Europe. She was too far away from the action to be of any use to the cause. One by one, her comrades were falling, and she couldn't do a thing about it. She pleaded with her commanders to let her back into Peru, but they demurred. Instead, they sent her in late 1992 to Central America, where the FMLN guerrillas were in negotiations with the Salvadoran government over a peace agreement. In addition to getting important training from their Central American brethren, the MRTA hoped to get advice and solidarity about how they could reach their own accord with the Fujimori administration. Cumpa was happy to get out of Europe and return to Latin America, even if it was still thousands of miles away from the Andes. During the trip, she attended a conference of the Latin American left in Managua. Nicaragua was the only Latin American country since the Cuban Revolution in which the armed left toppled the regime, and even though the conservative opposition now controlled the central government, the Sandinistas still held plenty of sway in the country and could operate politically without fear of the kind of reprisals that took place elsewhere in the hemisphere.

During one of the session breaks, a conference delegate named Moyano, from Peru's own Patria Roja party, approached Cumpa and began chatting her up.

"Hello," Moyano said. "Are you from Peru?"

"Yes. Name's Lucero Cumpa Miranda."

Moyano nearly fell over. Cumpa had indeed become a celebrity, and her reputation preceded her. Nor was she known only in Peru. The two began talking, and before long, delegates from guerrilla groups across Latin America were approaching to meet the famed rebel. Although the encounter helped put the MRTA on the map within Latin American revolutionary circles, it only reinforced the perception within the Directorate that Cumpa was too high-profile a figure to return to Peru in the current climate. That didn't keep her from trying, however.[25]

Cumpa's persistence paid off. Before the year's end, she received word that her request had finally been granted. Not only was the Directorate finally allowing her to return to Peru, but she would do so as commander of San Martín's newly minted Rodrigo Gálvez Guerrilla Front, named after the fallen guerrilla commander.[26]

Cumpa could hardly contain her excitement. She attended the remainder of the conference in a state of anxious anticipation. The day before the conference came to a close, the consul told her that the Cuban representative wanted to meet her. Cumpa had been an admirer of the Cuban Revolution since her days as a UNI student. And now the delegate from Cuba wanted to meet her? When at last she met the Cuban delegate, he cut to the chase.

"I've arranged for your passage to Cuba."

Cumpa couldn't believe her ears. For as long as she could remember, she had dreamed of going to the island that started it all, the wellspring of the Latin American revolution. Now she was being invited to the country as an honored guest. She was so flattered that she nearly accepted, before remembering that she had just been granted return to Peru.

"I can't," she said, disappointed. "I have another commitment."

"I understand," the consul replied. "Consider it an open invitation."

Cumpa thanked the consul for his understanding and was on her way. She told herself that she would make it to Cuba one day, after the Peruvian conflict had ended and she lived as a free woman. But it was never to be. A much crueler fate awaited her in the Amazon.

15

In the Wolf's Mouth

When Inocencio didn't arrive home from his aunt's house one night in 1991, Daniel Bravo began to worry. He called his aunt, but she said Inocencio never arrived the night before. According to Daniel, his twenty-one-year-old brother had never been affiliated with the MRTA. "He never had anything to do with it, he never got involved in anything like that."[1] Daniel feared that having Yasi for a sister had led to Inocencio's disappearance.

"Shoot," thought Daniel, "that means they can come in the middle of the night and kidnap me, too!"

Inocencio never did show. Instead, he would join the long list of the war's disappeared, the *desaparecidos*. As with most *desaparecido* families, Daniel wouldn't rest until he learned what had happened to his brother. On his sister's urging, he joined the army. For Daniel, the decision to join the military was twofold. First, it was a matter of survival. He knew that, given Yasi's subversive activity, he too could end up on the list of missing persons. Joining the army would be a means of avoiding that fate. Second, he hoped, perhaps naively as a boy of sixteen, that he could search for clues as to where his brother was buried. For Yasi, however, Daniel's enrollment in the military could be of use to the rebellion. He could serve as a kind of spy, collecting important information about the enemy.

Daniel completed his basic training in late 1991 and returned to the military base in Tabalosos, not far from his hometown. The following year, the army captured two young women suspected of guerrilla activity and brought them back to the base. Daniel was standing guard outside the interrogation room when the women came by. He caught a glimpse of them before quickly lowering his head. He had seen them before in his sister's safe house. Had they recognized him? And if so, would they talk?

He tried to use his position as guard to dissuade the other soldiers from raping and torturing the two suspects. When his colleagues came up to have a go at the women, he refused to let them pass. He did this to save his own neck as well as out of concern for the women. Eventually, however, he was replaced and sent on a brief assignment to Moyobamba, the jungle capital. When he returned four days later, he learned that the soldiers had tortured and raped the women incessantly. Now the women were willing to talk. The words sent Daniel into a mild panic. He returned to the dormitory not knowing if he had been identified.

Around six in the evening, a lieutenant and sublieutenant came to the dormitory and pulled him aside. Daniel looked down and noticed that the sublieutenant was carrying a pistol in his hand.

"Hand in your weapon," ordered the official.

"Why?" Daniel asked.

"Hand in your weapon, *cholo*."

"No, I'm not doing that."

At that moment, eight other soldiers—four of them in ski masks—came out from different rooms and surrounded him. Before he could react, the soldiers forced him into a chair and tied his hands behind his back.

"You motherfucker!" cried one of the soldiers. "You knew about the ambush the other day!"

"Who sent you?" another demanded. "Are you with Shining Path? Are you with the MIR? Who sent you?"

"No one sent me!" Daniel cried. "I joined of my own volition."

"You volunteered, didn't you?" asked one interrogator.

"Yes."

"Why?"

"Because I didn't have papers."

The soldiers left Daniel alone in the room, still sitting in the chair. After a while, a lieutenant known as Brando came in to speak with Daniel. Brando had a well-deserved reputation for gratuitous violence. "The guy was a friggin' criminal," said Daniel, who had personally witnessed him hack a man to death with a machete.

Brando seemed to delight in torturing the teen. After a while, another captain came in, assuming the role of the "good cop."

"Look, son," he said softly, "I'm not going to hit you. You know I don't hit people. All I need from you is to give me three bases in Tarapoto. Just three safe houses."

Daniel, of course, knew that his sister was still operating a safe house in the city. But he continued his strategy of denial. "I don't know anything, captain."

"We'll transfer you to Lima. You'll study there for a year and then we'll send you to a military academy and make you an officer. You'll be a career soldier. All you have to do is tell us who sent you and give me three safe houses in Tarapoto."

"Gee," said Daniel, "it's just that I don't know anyone."

"Just tell us where your sister is."

That confirmed it. They knew about Yasi. What else did they already know?

"I don't know."

"Your sister, Yasi."

Daniel continued to deny any knowledge.

Finally, the captain relented. "Look," he said before leaving the room, "if you want to talk at all tonight, just send for me. If you don't, you know what's going to happen. They're going to beat you. They're going to torture you. Brando is going to make you suffer, but I won't. So whenever you're ready to talk—even if it's in the middle of the night—just send for me." And with that, the captain left the room and Brando returned.

Brando dragged Daniel over to the bathroom. There was a bathtub filled with water and a rope hanging from a ceiling beam. Music blared from the speakers as Brando tied Daniel's hands behind his back and pulled the rope, lifting him by his hands. Daniel hung in the air, the weight of his body nearly dislocating his shoulders, as Brando delivered a series of powerful body punches. "When you're hanging there you feel like your body is going to rip off and your arms are going to just stay there dangling," Daniel said as he relived the experience years later. After several rounds of this, Brando put Daniel's head and shoulders on a board, dropped him upside down over the tub, and waterboarded him. "Shoot," Daniel recalled, "you know when they do that the water gets in your nose and it feels like it's going to burst out of your head, you know?"

The torture continued for six days straight, but no matter how much Brando beat, waterboarded, hung, or humiliated him, Daniel refused to give up his sister's whereabouts. Brando threatened to kill him and dump his body in the Rioja River, but he maintained his innocence.

On the sixth day, Daniel heard the door creak open. Still blindfolded, he stiffened his body, preparing for the coming onslaught of kicks and punches. "When I would hear that door open, shoot, I would stiffen up . . . because you knew they weren't coming to cuddle!" Instead of receiving the usual bodyshots, he heard a familiar voice. It was Fredy, one of his fellow enlistees. Fredy had come into the bathroom under the pretense of interrogating him. Once inside, Fredy got in close and lowered his voice.

"All that stuff about taking you to Rioja is a lie. You just have to hold out a little longer and they're going to have no choice [but to let you go]."

Daniel nodded. "Can you loosen up my rope a little?"

Fredy did so hurriedly. "We're running drills today," he whispered knowingly. "Exercise drills, at around 5 or 5:30. Calisthenics." And with that, Fredy left the room.

That evening, Daniel listened closely for the sound of the training outside. He waited until the routine was well under way. Fredy had loosened his bands just enough to where he could untie them completely. He remembered the shoe-tying riddle from his childhood days: "A knot in the wolf's mouth, make it a loop and it comes right out." Even with his hands behind his back, the trick worked. Hands free, he ripped off the blindfold and looked up. Like many rural schools, this one was built on the cheap, which meant that the wooden beams on the ceiling weren't nailed down. He brought the chair over to the wall, stood on top of it, lifted himself on top of the wall, and moved the ceiling beams. If he could just make it to the other side of the wall, it was a fifty-meter shot to the mountainous rainforest. As he slowly climbed along the side of the wall, he could see the guard seated below with his back turned. Daniel dropped down onto the guard, rendering him unconscious—or at least dazed—and made a mad dash for the forest. As he ran, he could hear a voice from the watchtower.

"He's getting away!"

He didn't look back. He could see the mountain as machine gun fire dotted the ground around him. "I just kept running," he recalled. "I just ran and ran and thought, 'If they hit you, they hit you,' you know?" As soon as he made it to the mountain, he found a prickly bush and jumped inside.

"He got away!" he overheard the guards saying as they entered the forest.

"He must have gone down that way!"

Daniel crouched in the bushes, trying not to make a sound. "In those moments, one can only think of God, you know?"

"Please, God, please God," he prayed, asking the Lord to get him out of there alive.

Then, whether it was divine intervention, the tropical climate, or the revisionist narrative of a trauma survivor, it began, Daniel claimed, to rain.

"Let's go back and get some ponchos," a soldier offered. The others agreed.

Daniel waited until the soldiers' voices had disappeared before he emerged from the bushes. He stumbled forward all night until he happened upon a small hut early the following morning. There was a woman inside, not very old, perhaps in her thirties.

"Where are you going, young man?" she asked, looking him up and down. He still had on his soldier's T-shirt and fatigue pants, but he was shoeless.

"They're looking for me, *señora*," he admitted.

"Who's looking for you?"

"The soldiers."

"You're the one!" she exclaimed. "You're the comrade who escaped from the holding cell." "*Ñañito*," she said, referring to him in the regional term of endearment. "The soldiers already came through here last night. They said they were looking for a colleague who had escaped from the military base. They went uphill. They should be returning any time now. You shouldn't go by the road. Go into the mountains."

Daniel thanked the woman for her time and continued on his way. Fearing that he would only get lost in the jungle, he ignored her advice and continued to walk alongside the road. As he rounded one hill, he saw a lone soldier standing along the bend.

"There he is!" cried the soldier, firing his weapon.

The bullet missed Daniel as he ran. He was running on pure adrenaline now. "When you're scared, you are capable of scaling a palm tree!"

He dived directly off the road, sliding down the side of the mountain toward the river. Up above, the soldiers peered over, shooting at him as he slid down. After what felt like an eighty-meter drop, but was likely much shorter, Daniel finally landed on a tree trunk. "If it weren't for that trunk, the fall would have surely killed me."

As it was still early morning, the soldiers couldn't see where Daniel had landed. They finally gave up, no doubt thinking that the river had claimed him. Once they had left the scene, Daniel climbed back up to the top of the mountain. His ankle had swollen to the size of a baseball from the fall, but he was alive. When he got up, another peasant woman found him and took him in to attend to his ankle.

"It's not broken. It's just a sprain," she assured him as she rubbed a warm substance on the puffy skin. She broke off a stick and braced his ankle for good measure. Turning to her young boy of seven or eight years, she said, "Take your *tío* uproad and leave him on the path to San Miguel."

It wasn't too long ago that Daniel was the little boy, attending to MIR rebels—his *tíos*—in his jungle cooperative. Now he was the uncle.

The boy led Daniel to a spot from which he could walk to San Miguel.

"Alright, *tío*," the boy said, pointing forward. "There's the valley. Head in that direction."

Daniel thanked the boy and went on his way. He remained in town for three days, resting his ankle before continuing along his path. This time, he went to the rebel camp to find his sister.

Yasi was not happy to see her little brother hanging around the encampment.

"You can't stay here in the camp. You have to go to Lima."

"No," Daniel said. "I'm staying."

Yasi called her commander over to settle the matter. Moments later, a pudgy man with a goatee walked up. Daniel had seen him before. He had given the man a lift on his motorcycle.

"You're the kid who picked me up that time, aren't you?" Néstor Cerpa said.

"Yeah, that's me."

Cerpa looked the scrawny teenager up and down. "You can't stay here. You should go to Lima and get an education, but you can't stay here."

"Well, I'm not going anywhere. I'm staying right here."

Cerpa tried one more time to order Daniel to leave, and once more Daniel insisted on staying.

"Fine," Cerpa conceded. "You can stay here for three days to think about it. But then you're out of here."

And so it was that Daniel Bravo became a MRTA guerrilla. He had gone from the wolf's mouth to the fox's hole.

16

The Internal Revolution

Esperanza Tapia was just sixteen when the MRTA launched its insurgency in 1984. Those days she was more interested in the dreamy presidential candidate, Alan García, than in armed insurgency. Tall, dark, and handsome with a boyish grin and wavy black hair, the thirty-five-year-old Aprista addressed adoring crowds with soaring rhetoric and a message of economic nationalism that made capitalists shudder. APRA party headquarters happened to be visible from the window of Esperanza's downtown classroom. Every day, she would stare out the window, hoping to catch a glimpse of the presidential hopeful as he ducked into his office.[1]

Those fleeting glances at Peru's future president were the highlights of the curly-haired teenager's day. When class dismissed, she would embark on the two-hour public transit trip back to Villa El Salvador, the poor shantytown that had been the location of the MRTA's first armed action. As the bus headed down Via Expresa in fits and starts, she caught glimpses of the letter V graffitied in black along the highway underpass.

Esperanza had never heard of the MRTA. She was much more familiar with Shining Path. At night, the Senderistas would knock over power lines, blacking out the entire barrio before torching the hills to light up the night sky with a giant, sparkling sickle and hammer. Sometimes, the rebels would hang dead dogs on lampposts throughout the neighborhood in a political reference to China's "running dog" Deng Xiaoping, which, like the lamp-post dogs, went way over her head. Once, the Senderistas gunned down a Villa leader in front of his wife and infant child. "What's that about?" Esperanza wondered as she listened to the talk on the street. "I don't like it." The rebels claimed to be fighting for the people, but, as she figured, "we are the people, and they are only harming us."[2]

It was simply the latest in a series of political references that Esperanza didn't fully understand, like the time a young man came onto the bus peddling copies of Lenin's *What Is to Be Done?* She reached into her purse and purchased the pamphlet for a handful of coins, thinking it a self-help book. When she realized she had purchased leftist literature, she still finished it, but she didn't comprehend much.

Her proclivities always leaned toward creative writing, anyway. Poetry, in particular, appealed to her. When she read Nicaraguan poet Yaconda Veré's "The Man I Loved" earlier that year, it touched her on a profoundly personal level. "That's the kind of man I want!" she thought. If she couldn't find a man who would treat her with dignity and respect, she simply wouldn't have one.

Life wasn't easy as a lower-class girl from Villa, where food was scarce and money was tight. It seemed, through her sixteen-year-old eyes, that her parents were always fighting and her two older brothers kept picking on her. No one, she felt, truly understood her. She kept a diary where she would spill her guts every day, divulging her loftiest dreams, her innermost desires, her most vexing anxieties. Writing was her only cathartic escape in an unapologetically mundane world.

It was Antonio, the boyfriend of her best friend, Tania, who first introduced her to the MRTA. Antonio was a student at San Marcos who saw something in Esperanza.

"I've got something I think you're going to like," he whispered one day when Tania wasn't around. "Read it discreetly and let's talk."

The text turned out to be MRTA propaganda, an early work describing the group's ideology and platform. The words seemed to pop right off the page; it was the first piece of political literature that really resonated with her. She looked for Antonio at a party later and asked him to dance.

"So," she said, lowering her voice. "I read the book. I loved it. Is that the kind of stuff you read in college?"

"Yes, you've got to come to San Marcos!"

Esperanza had always dreamed of going to Peru's flagship public university. It had a reputation for academic excellence and political radicalism. Her elementary school teacher, who had introduced her to Mariátegui and encouraged her creative writing, had also been a San Marcos alum, so she felt as if it were a good fit for her. She was less certain about joining a revolutionary movement. "When I commit to something, I jump in with both feet," she explained years later. She wasn't about to take this decision lightly.

"I do want to get involved in politics," she told Antonio one day, "but I want to know all that's out there before committing to a specific party."

Antonio gave her space to explore her options. When she got accepted into San Marcos in 1988, Antonio fronted her the money to offset the costs. There, she found herself swimming in a sea of possibility. It seemed as if every political orientation had an interest group on campus. There were Apristas and Communists, Socialists and United Leftists. But Shining Path and the MRTA had the most visible presence. Revolutionary paintings and posters adorned the windows and walls of the buildings, another symbolic battleground in which neither side ceded an inch. When she entered her psychology classrooms, there would be one blackboard chalked in MRTA slogans and symbols and another one for Shining Path. Sometimes, militants in ski masks from one or another group would barge into the classroom unannounced, pass out flyers, and deliver impromptu speeches in support of their respective rebellions while the professors, either too afraid or tacitly supportive, stood by.

Esperanza maintained contact with Antonio. He plied her with readings and talked politics whenever she pleased. She agreed that there was much wrong with Peruvian society—one walk through Villa was testament to that. But was armed revolution the answer? Antonio told her that she need look no further than 1973 Chile. She had been a child when Pinochet staged a coup ousting democratically elected socialist Salvador Allende from power. Allende had committed suicide while Pinochet's troops bombarded the presidential palace. Fifteen years later, many still believed—mistakenly, it turned out—that the plotters had assassinated the sitting president. This was all the proof Antonio needed that true social change would never take place democratically. It would take armed insurrection, as the Cuban and Nicaraguan revolutions had shown.

Esperanza found Antonio's argument compelling, and it ultimately led to her decision to join the MRTA. The only question was how. It wasn't as if she could just audition for a group that most Peruvians considered a terrorist organization. Usually, the rebels hand-selected their recruits after weeks—even months—of careful vetting. Patience, however, was never one of Esperanza's virtues. "I don't wait around," she described herself. "I just ask."

She found Antonio one day and came right out with it: "Tell your friends I want to join."

He told her that there was already a secret meeting scheduled for the following Sunday. She could attend, he said, "no strings attached." She was to wear dark clothes and wait on the corner of the university at a predetermined time. "It was all so mysterious," Esperanza remembered. She liked that.

When Sunday came around, Esperanza nonchalantly made her way to the front door of her Villa house.

"Why are you dressed like that?" her mother asked.

"I'm going to do some fieldwork."

She went directly to the main avenue outside the university and waited. A while later, a young man approached and told her to keep walking. He walked alongside her until they got to the safe house. Esperanza knocked on the door ever so gently. It cracked open, and an outstretched hand held out two hoods. She took one, discreetly put it over her head, and ducked inside. Twenty hooded recruits were sitting in rows of chairs. On the wall hung the obligatory Tupac Amaru flag with the V that she had seen during her bus rides home from school. She couldn't help but feel enamored as she pulled up a chair. In the front, facing the chairs, sat a panel of hooded Tupac Amaristas. She didn't even realize they were armed until they began talking.

"You all have been handpicked," announced one of the hooded leaders. He waxed passionate about the cause before asking anyone interested to pledge allegiance to the Tupac Amaru Revolutionary Movement. The others were shown the door.

Esperanza was hooked. It was all so mysterious, so romantic, that she couldn't help but take the loyalty oath. "I'm a big dreamer," she later allowed.

She spent the next year as a party militant, carrying out low-risk tasks for the insurgency. She would go to the marketplace and pass around flyers for the party. Now she was the one painting the V on the underpass. Even while carrying out these tasks, though, she continued to question her superiors' wisdom and judgment. "Why paint this wall and not that one?" "Why do only the men get to carry weapons?" The typical answer—because orders were orders—never satisfied her. She believed that, as educated people, they should be making educated decisions. If the orders made sense, they should be followed. If not, the rebels, as educated people, had a responsibility to question them. This attitude never settled right with her mostly male superiors.

As was the case with Lucero Cumpa and so many other Tupac Amarista women, the first obstacle to insurgent life was an overbearing, patriarchal homefront. Like many Limeño families at the time, Esperanza's had been *bien carcelera*, "very imprisoning," with their only daughter. Even as a child, her mother forbade her from playing soccer in the streets with her brothers. "You look like a tomboy," her mother would say, forcing her to put down the ball and get inside. Now, as a teenager, Esperanza had to come up with a litany of socially acceptable excuses for leaving the house at night—going to the library, staying at a friend's house, traveling on a field trip—but her family always met these with suspicion. She wasn't alone. Veronica, a woman who joined the MRTA in the early 1990s, recalled inventing an excuse about a girls' beach trip in order to attend the military training school. When Veronica returned, her mother demanded to know how she had managed to get paler after a week in the sun. Years later, the former rebel could laugh off her lame, on-the-fly excuse about cloud cover, which only intensified her family's scrutiny.[3]

Esperanza found no such humor in her own situation. For her training, she made up an excuse about doing field research for a college project. When she returned, her mother stopped her in the doorway. Why did she look so pale if she had been outside all week? And why did she have blisters on her feet? Her brothers chimed in, adding that she looked "very strange." Esperanza tried to play it off as if they were the ones acting strangely. Eventually, her older brothers discovered the true nature of her activities. They forbade her to join the MRTA, even though they themselves were leftists who had engaged in their share of clandestine action. Bruno, the oldest, tried beating her into submission, to no avail.

As time went on, Esperanza got more involved in the movement, and her studies suffered. She realized she could no longer sustain this double life. Tired of all the excuses, the beatings, the watchful scorn, she packed up her suitcase and left the house when no one was looking, moved into a safe house, and commenced her life as a clandestine rebel. She still tried to keep contact with her family, but it was hard. Bruno continued to beat her. Her father wasn't much better.

"You're an embarrassment," he told her over the phone one day. "You've sullied the family name!"

Esperanza could only cry on the other end of the line. When she was a tubby little girl, no matter how much trouble she got herself into, her father could never stay mad at her, even as he tore her brothers new hides. Now he wanted nothing to do with her.[4]

It wasn't much easier inside the rebellion. Most Cold War Latin American insurgencies were dominated by men, with women making up between 5 and 30 percent of all combatants.[5] These numbers paled in comparison with Peru's Shining Path, where women made up as much as half of the guerrillas and held positions of power up and down the rebel hierarchy. The MRTA displayed no such parity, with gender distribution at different stages of the rebellion fitting within range of its hemispheric counterparts. Esperanza learned this firsthand when she realized that she was not just the only woman in her cell, but the only woman operative in all of Lima when she joined the rebellion. One of the first things her cell leader told her was not to get pregnant.

"Well of course I'm not going to get pregnant!" she retorted, resenting the insinuation.

Esperanza passed every waking hour with the same group of young men. "We went through it all together," she recollected, "the good, the bad, the ugly, the beautiful." She described her daily life inside the MRTA as a kind of "internal revolution" for equal treatment and dignity. Women remained secluded in safe houses all day while the men, even the more recognizable ones, were free to come and go as they pleased. Even though MRTA policy divided the household chores equally among all residents, this was difficult to enforce in a world where few of the men had ever performed these tasks before joining the insurgency.

Esperanza insisted that Paco, her roommate, share equally in the chores. When he complained about having to perform a particularly onerous task, Esperanza held firm.

"You don't like it? Tell me, *papi*, what do you like?" She would gladly swap out chores with him, but she wouldn't let him off the hook. As she put it, "I refused to let them take my poncho."

During one lunchtime conversation, the other men teased Paco for ironing the clothes and doing the dishes.

"You're henpecked!" they joked. Esperanza stood in the next room, fuming.

All she really wanted was to be taken seriously. In order to earn that respect, she felt as if she couldn't let the slightest slight go unnoticed. This, too, exposed her to gendered criticisms about her supposed oversensitivity. For instance, when she confronted one of her comrades for calling her a "fucking idiot," he said, "Don't be so delicate. That's how we guys talk."

"If you have something to say to me, say it," Esperanza said, "but do it with respect." He never spoke to her like that again.

If gender was an obstacle to equal treatment in the organization, it could be an asset in carrying out operations. Men in Peru's police force had difficulty getting past their own stereotypes of women to take them seriously as a subversive threat. This was often a class bias, as lower-class women like Esperanza were far more suspect in the eyes of law enforcement than the upper-class *pitucas*. However, Esperanza found that if she dabbed on some makeup, styled her hair, and donned tight-fitting designer clothes, she could enjoy greater freedom of movement, walking right past a policeman on the way to an armed action without raising suspicion. For this working-class woman from Villa El Salvador, the hardest part was learning to run in high heels.

She realized that the charade worked best if she was hanging on the arm of a man. She was more than happy to play the part of the doting girlfriend for the sake of the mission, but her companions sometimes confused this playacting with the real thing. During one operation, she had to check into a hotel room with Coco, a fellow comrade in her cell, posing as a young couple. The two shared a bed that evening, awaiting further instructions. As she lay in the darkness, she could feel the palm of Coco's hand sliding up her inner thigh. Startled, she sat up and asked what he was doing.

"What, don't you like it?" Coco asked.

"Listen, we are here on business and nothing more."

Coco plopped back on his pillow, frustrated. "What a waste of money!" he said, reminding her that he had footed the bill for the room.

"I'll pay you back if you want," she said, but there was no way she was going to sleep with him.

Encounters like these were common in the MRTA and other late-twentieth-century guerrilla movements. Rebel men intentionally blurred the boundaries between role-playing for public consumption and actual intimacy, taking advantage of private spaces and unequal power relations to sexually harass, assault, and rape women comrades. This speaks to a larger power dynamic within the rebellion, as men felt entitled to rebel women's bodies. For women like Esperanza, part of the internal revolution they found themselves waging daily involved educating their comrades and superiors about professionalization, mutual respect, and sexual restraint. In doing so, they sought to make the MRTA itself more inclusive and responsive to gender equity.

This was no easy task, given the MRTA's rigid patriarchy. Some women who complained about sexual harrassment and rape found themselves demoted or even banished from the rebel ranks. Almost without exception, men held positions of authority, from cell leaders all the way up to the National Directorate. While some of these men were sympathetic, most believed that sexual harrassment was not a problem worth addressing; some of them were the ones committing the assaults. For example, when Esperanza stowed away inside a Lima movie theater with Pedro, her unit commander, one day in 1993, he took advantage of the darkness to stroke her arm and shove his tongue down her throat.

"What are you doing?" Esperanza hissed, fending him off with her hands. "You have a wife!"

"We have to act like we're a couple," Pedro replied, half serious.

This made no sense, as the theater was dark and nearly empty. Esperanza felt used and horrified. She began second-guessing herself, wondering if she had sent mixed signals or overreacted. After replaying the incident over and over in her head, she concluded that Pedro had indeed behaved inappropriately. She complained to Pedro's commander, who was sympathetic and reprimanded him, but the exigencies of clandestinity made it impossible to reassign him to another cell. Now Esperanza was stuck having to face her attacker every day.

Sure enough, Pedro cornered her one day and demanded, "Why'd you have to go and cause a scandal?"

Esperanza refused to be intimidated. "Because what you did was wrong!"

Sometimes complaining to superiors resulted in change, but usually it didn't. Still, women like Esperanza felt that if they didn't complain, if they didn't confront the culture of harassment and misogyny head-on, it would prevail in the end. These women had waged a war to change society for the better, and they saw gender equality as part of that imagined society.

■ By 1993, the MRTA faced yet another crisis, as its numbers had dwindled to the low hundreds. Predictably, the more Tupac Amarista men ended up dead, deserting, or behind bars, the more leverage women had within the movement. It was this shortage of manpower—in a literal sense—that led the Directorate to reconsider its ban on women joining the guerrilla front as well as its inequities in the rebel command structure.

Lucero Cumpa was one of the women who benefited from both of these changes. Desperate for more quality fighters and, for that matter, leaders, the leadership allowed Cumpa back into the country, not as a returning member of the Central Committee but as commander of the Northeastern Front and member of the National Directorate. She would be the first and only woman to command a guerrilla front over the course of the thirteen-year insurgency. She knew that all eyes would be on her, judging her every move, questioning whether a woman could command a guerrilla front. When she accepted the challenge, she did so for all women rebels. "I wanted to show them that a woman could be not just a guerrilla fighter, but a commander."[6]

Cumpa took the *nom de guerre* Liliana, after her late friend who had been killed in action the previous year. Arriving in Lima by land, she headed straight for Tarapoto, where she met up with fellow Directorate members

Néstor Cerpa and Miguel Rincón.[7] Their first order of business would be to take the city of Moyobamba.[8] In nearly six years of fighting in the jungle, the rebels had never taken the departmental capital. If they did so now, they could regain some of the control they had surrendered in recent months.

Cumpa had never been to the Amazon, and although she considered herself fit, no amount of training could prepare her for the harsh conditions and countless hours of hiking through the brush. Her vertigo, from which she had suffered since her first torture session at the hands of police, caused her to lose her balance at the most inopportune moments. She had trouble breathing in the humid tropical air, and the jungle bugs had a feeding frenzy off her fresh blood. To make matters worse, she contracted leishmaniasis, a rare parasitic infection spread by tiny tropical mosquitoes that causes skin sores and, when untreated, can damage internal organs. Cumpa had to stop periodically to receive an injection that would keep the disease at bay. Needless to say, her romantic dreams of running through the jungle like Che Guevara quickly yielded to the harsh realities of life in the hostile Amazon. She knew that all the rebels, men and women alike, were watching her every move to see if she was really up to the task. At times, she doubted whether she was. "But I held my own," she later said with a smile.

Between the vertigo, the sweltering heat, and the backpack that felt as if it weighed more than her, Cumpa struggled to keep her balance. One day, the column was crossing a river on a fallen tree trunk when she felt the world spin around her. The vertigo knocked her off her feet and into the river, and the current swept her downstream. She could feel herself going under, the weight of her backpack and boots pulling her down. Panicked, she removed her backpack and let it drift away. She spotted a rock in the current and tried to swim for it. At that moment, something grabbed her and pulled her toward the rock. Once she caught her breath, she could see that two teenaged rebels had jumped in after her. Those two boys were Daniel Bravo and Tigre. Tigre had joined the Northeastern Front since fleeing the Asháninka militia in Oxapampa in 1989. Daniel had defied his sister's wishes and remained in the MRTA since escaping the army the previous year. Now both country boys found themselves under the command of this Limeña woman, and they awaited her orders.

17

The Stripe-Painted Dog

The rebels hung their hopes on taking Moyobamba, the capital of San Martín. Unlike the other towns they had captured over the course of the insurgency, Moyobamba was a bustling tropical city with a full political and security apparatus. It wouldn't be easy, but the Directorate, still dominated by hard-liners Néstor Cerpa and Miguel Rincón and which now included Lucero Cumpa, believed that taking the town would be an important symbolic and military win at a time when the press and popular opinion had turned on the rebellion. The commanders still hung on to the unrealistic hope that an impressive display of military force could persuade Fujimori to enter peace talks.

With so much on the line, the Directorate left nothing to chance. The commanders gathered their entire Northeastern army and brought in forces from other fronts to help. In January 1993, they had amassed an army of 300 guerrillas for the attack. After completing their training, Cumpa, Rincón, and Cerpa rented an apartment in Tomanguillo, a district just outside the city, and hunkered down to draw up the attack. By now, years of living and running around in the jungle had finally paid off for *El Gordo*. One day, when Cerpa was suiting up for a visit to the rebel camp, he fastened his belt tight around his now-slender waist. Taking notice, Cumpa looked up at her comrade incredulously. Usually, he wore no belt or left it unfastened.

Cerpa held his index finger to his lips with a wink, as if imploring her not to share his secret.[1]

The Directorate relegated the boots-on-the-ground task to other commanders. One of the leaders was Tito Cruz Sánchez, the young man who had helped Cumpa and the other Tupac Amarista women hop the fence during their escape from Canto Grande two and a half years earlier. Daniel Bravo was among the rebels in Tito's twenty-eight-person column. The column spent the night before the 11 January attack camping out on the outskirts of Moyobamba. Around 7:00 P.M. Néstor Cerpa, who had secured a location along the main plaza, radioed Tito to inform him that there was a problem securing the trucks for the attack. Tito turned to his unit and told them they were going to march into the city on foot.

Onlookers munched on fried plantain chips, gawking at the camouflaged guerrillas as they marched through the dusty streets at the edge of the district. Out of the corner of his eye, Daniel noticed a policeman poke his head out of a local watering hole, only to duck back inside when he saw them coming. Had he noticed? Was he sounding the alarm? It was too late to find out.

Night fell. When Daniel got within three blocks of the Moyobamba plaza, his submachine gun began weighing him down. "I've never really thought about death," he explained later. "I always figure that when it's my turn, it's my turn." In that moment, however, he was nervous, the fatigue from the march setting in. They had pulled within several blocks of the plaza when an unsettling communication came over Tito's walkie-talkie. Police had detected their presence. If ever there was a time to call off the attack, this was it. The entire operation hinged on the Tupac Amaristas maintaining the element of surprise, and now they had lost that strategic advantage. Still, the hard-liners in the command center held firm.

"Everyone get to high ground and shoot anything that moves!" the voice radioed.

"Quickstep to the command post!" Tito ordered, referring to the police station.

"If you're getting scared, paint stripes on your dog and make it a tiger!" radioed the voice. Daniel knew what that meant: fake it until you make it.

The breathless guerrillas hadn't even reached the square when the first shots rang out. The police had taken up positions throughout the streets and were firing from all sides. As soon as the shootout began, the new recruits dropped their weapons and deserted. Daniel, Tito, and the others ducked down and pushed forward toward the center of the plaza.

Daniel had always been a sure shot. His steady hand under fire had persuaded Cerpa to allow him to join the rebel army despite his youth. But the explosions from the RPG-7s that were bursting through the walls around him made concentration difficult. He continued his slow advance, with bullets and explosives seeming to come from every direction. Not only had the police secured the station. They were also inside the bank, the church, and all other major buildings along the plaza, taking potshots at the advancing Tupac Amaristas in the well-lit street. Amid the onslaught, Tito sent a runner to knock down the power line.

"When is the power outage coming already?" Daniel thought, his ears ringing from the explosions. Finally, his team took aim at the streetlights to give themselves a fighting chance in the dark. He scuttled over to the front of the police station, hiding behind one of the benches along the plaza. Machine gun blasts rained down from the lookout tower. Tito, who had taken cover beside him, ordered him to fire the RPG-7 to neutralize the tower. Daniel locked and loaded and sent the projectiles toward the windows where the police had taken cover. His ears rang with each deafening blast. "It feels like at any moment your ears are going to bleed," he remembered. After he fired four projectiles, the sound faded, and everything was muffled, as if he were a spectator to a silent movie all around him. He had blasted holes in the sides of the building, but the police had put up sandbags for additional cover and continued to fire down on them. Through the ringing, Daniel thought he heard the policemen suggesting a retreat, but the captains told them to hold firm. The opposing forces remained at loggerheads even as the sun rose over the tropical city. Finally, after daybreak, a contingent of army reinforcements descended on the plaza, leaving Tito no choice but to order a full retreat.

The failed siege of Moyobamba was a major setback for the MRTA. The rebels had hung their hopes on taking the Amazonian capital, and now they were left without an exit strategy. After routing the Tupac Amaristas, government forces went on the counteroffensive, sending the rebels on the run.

■ The Central Committee assigned Esperanza Tapia, the young woman from Villa El Salvador who had struggled for gender equity since joining the insurgency, to take charge of transporting one of the wounded Tupac Amaristas to the hospital. Dolores, the young woman she was supposed to escort, had been shot in the back during the failed Moyobamba raid and was in desperate need of medical attention. Esperanza and a small team of rebels secured a small private plane to transport Dolores to a hospital in Chiclayo.

What followed was not for the squeamish. When Esperanza got to the airport, she took one look at Dolores and knew that her outlook was grim.

The bullet had gone through her lower back and exited through her stomach. Dolores, Esperanza recalled, "stunk to high heaven" when she got on the plane. The stench, a combination of feces and blood and other fluids not intended to leave the human body, was nauseating. When the plane touched down, she lifted Dolores onto a wheelchair, trying her level best not to throw up all over the enfeebled woman. Dolores was barely conscious and completely limp, so Esperanza and her mates found some ropes to tether her floppy head and torso to the wheelchair. For good measure, they tossed a baseball cap and sunglasses on her and caked makeup on her green face. They slid Dolores into a clean pair of blue jeans and plopped a backpack in her lap, as much to prop her up as to cover the blood she was still secreting. Esperanza had never seen blood that color before. It wasn't red, but black, "like shit." "She was like a puppet," she recalled.

Esperanza held her breath and wheeled this moribund stranger through the airport. Much to her surprise, the disguise worked, and no one stopped her as she rolled Dolores to the car. Her orders were to drop Dolores at the hospital door and leave posthaste to avoid detection. The nurses and doctors would take it from there. But when they arrived at the hospital, Dolores started talking.

"Don't leave me!"

Esperanza looked down at the poor young woman. It seemed inhumane to dump and dash. These may well be Dolores's last moments alive. The least Esperanza could do was be by her side when she went into the operating room. And so Esperanza, never one to obey a senseless order, wheeled the patient inside. The doctors told Esperanza they would need to operate right away. This being a provincial hospital, they didn't have all the medications they needed for the procedure. One of the doctors gave Esperanza a list of prescriptions and told her to go to the pharmacy to pick them up herself.

"If not, we won't be able to operate."

Esperanza took the list and went to her local superiors to fill them in. They didn't exactly want to let her go back to the hospital, but she wasn't exactly asking. She explained that this was a life-or-death situation. They finally relented, telling her to leave the medications at the reception desk and depart immediately; they would leave it to others to see to Dolores's recovery.

Medications in hand, Esperanza returned to the hospital fully expecting to follow her orders. Once she got there, however, she decided to hand-deliver the medications to ensure they made it to the doctors. After doing this, she went into the intensive care unit to check on her comrade. Dolores already looked better, and she seemed to be more conscious of her surroundings. Esperanza walked up and squeezed her hand.

"You're going to get arrested," Dolores struggled to say. "Get out of here."

"Don't worry about me. You just worry about getting better."

"I won't forget you," Dolores said, tears streaming down her cheek.

"Me either," Esperanza replied, fighting back her own tears. "But we're not going to cry."

Esperanza squeezed Dolores's hand one last time and left the room. She had made it as far as the hospital door before a police officer stepped in front of her.[2] He told her to accompany him back to the station to answer some questions. When they got to the station, the officer took Esperanza to an office and checked her bag. After confiscating 100 soles in cash, he raped her right there in the office. As he was getting dressed afterward, Esperanza bolted for the door and ran out of the station.[3] She had endured a most heinous trauma to her body, mind, and spirit, one that would haunt her for the rest of her life. And it happened because she chose to give a stranger comfort during her moment of darkest despair. It was also, Esperanza believed, a worthy sacrifice. As she later discovered, Dolores made a full recovery and would go on to live a full life long after the war had ended.

■ After the Moyobamba attack, Néstor Cerpa and Miguel Rincón fled San Martín to avoid detection by authorities. Lucero Cumpa remained behind as the sole commander of the Northeastern Front. She had to arrange all communications to Lima through a single radio that Teresa, a comrade in Tarapoto, controlled. In April 1993, Teresa went off the grid for three days straight without checking in, leaving Cumpa completely cut off from the Directorate in Lima. Cumpa sent runners down to the city to find houses where they could attend to the wounded. When they didn't return, she sent a second team, which reported back that the city was swarming with soldiers. Then, out of nowhere, Teresa showed up. Cumpa couldn't help but wonder if Teresa had turned army informant, but she didn't feel she had much choice but to trust her, desperate as she was to reach the Directorate. Teresa explained that she had set up a new communications team in Tarapoto and that the Directorate would convene there soon. Cumpa made the trip on foot, accompanied by Tigre, her trusty teenage foot soldier. The following morning, Teresa drove her to the meeting center. As she pressed her body to the truck bench, Cumpa felt the vehicle come to a sudden stop. She could hear military personnel surrounding the truck. Teresa had sold her out.[4]

The soldiers transferred Cumpa to police custody, and after confirming her identity, they sent her by helicopter to DINCOTE headquarters in

Lima. Once there, police yanked her, blindfolded and with her hands bound behind her back, down a flight of stairs into a basement. As she later testified, her interrogators stripped her naked and tortured her before leaving her on the floor. The following morning, her captors removed the blindfold and told her to get dressed. A few minutes later, Vladimiro Montesinos, Fujimori's spy chief and advisor, walked into the room.[5]

"So it's you," Montesinos said. "Tell me, how did you get in and out of the country?"

"There are lots of rivers and ports in this country," Cumpa said.

Montesinos snorted. After making an offhand comment to the guards, he stood and left the room.

Later, the police took Cumpa to a bathroom, their chamber of choice. It was here that the real torture began. According to Cumpa's sworn testimony, the police burned her skin with cigarette butts and punished her for seven days straight. "I really thought they were going to disappear me," she said, referring to the dirty war practice of killing suspected terrorists without a trace.[6]

On the fifth day, the police finally let Cumpa's attorney visit her.

"Your daughter is safe," he said, anticipating her first question.

She breathed a sigh of relief. The rest of the conversation was a blur. She was sure her lawyer was relaying important information regarding her case, but she didn't hear it. Karina remained hidden. That was all that mattered.[7]

On the seventh day, the police released Cumpa back to the army, where she was presented to the press. Her arrest and the failed Moyobamba attack marked the end of the MRTA's dominance in San Martín. From that point on, the remaining guerrillas in the Northeastern Front would be on the run, cut off from the rebel command structure and left to their own devices while army and police forces, now in full control of Moyobamba, moved in for the kill. Back in Lima, the rebel hard-liners, desperate to fund their floundering operation, began stepping up the kidnappings for ransom, once again replacing political theater with shortsighted acts of violence that only further turned popular opinion against them.

■ Complicating the situation further, Fujimori implemented a sweeping amnesty law, the Law of Repentance, offering guerrillas reduced sentences in exchange for information about their active comrades. Many top-level Tupac Amaristas, such as Sístero García, former leader of the Northeastern Front, took advantage of this new law. Now the guerrillas in the field had to contend with a new wave of desertion and betrayal from within their own ranks. Guerrillas found themselves cut off from their superiors, wandering around looking for cover and mistrusting their fellow comrades-in-arms.

Daniel Bravo experienced this crisis firsthand. In June 1993, Manuel, his column leader, gave him 200 soles to buy some food and told him to meet him in town the next day. When Daniel told a comrade about this, he objected.

"I think that he's struck a deal."

"I don't think so," Daniel said. Manuel had stuck with them through thick and thin. He was reliable.

"I don't know," said the comrade, "I have a bad feeling about this. When he saw me he looked nervous."

Daniel heeded his comrade's advice and chose not to go to the rendezvous point. Days later, he heard Manuel's voice over the radio declaring that he had indeed taken advantage of the amnesty law and imploring his comrades to surrender.

The mood around the camp began to sour. Manuel knew where the rebels camped, and he could lead the army straight to them.

"Let's get out of here!" said one of Daniel's comrades one night.

"Tomorrow, first thing," Daniel said, exhausted. "Why would we leave in the middle of the night? Let's try to get a couple of hours in and we'll leave first thing in the morning."

The next morning, Daniel went out to stash some weapons. When he returned, two more comrades were debating leaving.

"Come on, whoever stays here is going to repent," one said, referring to the amnesty law.

"How do you know?" Daniel asked.

"Why do you think they're not going anywhere? I'm going to shoot them now, because they're just going to rat on us and offer us up to be hunted down."

Daniel never thought it would come to this. "To think that we would wind up killing each other," he said years later, "is something that, *pucha* [shoot], it's something extreme."

He finally relented and joined the small band of young men fleeing the camp. They hid in a hut to wait out a tropical rain. He stepped outside and saw a dog running toward him. Behind the dog was a group of soldiers. He ran back into the hut to alert his comrades as bullets riddled the bamboo structure. As he ran for cover, he could hear the voice of Cricket, his camp leader, emerge from among the soldiers as they reloaded.

"Turn yourself in, Daniel!" Cricket cried. "Your other comrades have already turned themselves in. We can all walk out of here alive together!"

Daniel managed to slip away under the pouring rain before regrouping with his comrades. There were forty-seven, all that was left of the entire Northeastern Front. Miguel, the commander, stood forward and said, "Today is the day of deciding. Any comrade who doesn't feel up to the task to stay with us, raise your hand now."

Of the forty-seven guerrillas, twenty-seven raised their hands. True to his word, Miguel let them leave without consequence. "That was the hardest moment of my life," Daniel lamented. "After so many nights spent together, so many lives lost," his band of brothers was going to abandon the cause and head straight to the next military base to turn him in. From that point forward, the MRTA continued to hemorrhage combatants. A few nights later, five more snuck out, followed by two more the following night. And then another. And two more. Finally, they had to let a woman go who suffered from anemia. The mighty Northeastern Front, which had formerly taken towns with ease and, as late as January 1993, boasted a fighting force 300 strong, was down to just eleven fighters; they could barely field a soccer team.

The worn-down Tupac Amaristas roamed aimlessly in the jungle, living on plantains and leaves. They were tired, hungry, and increasingly paranoid. "Everyone was looking at each other out of the corner of his eye," Daniel said. Finally, after seventeen days of wandering in the jungle, they came upon a remote hamlet. The villagers fed them and gave them shelter. As they rested, one of the guerrillas volunteered to pick up some money in the district capital, but the military picked him up along the road and killed him. The ten remaining Tupac Amaristas began to wonder how their comrade had been discovered so quickly. This could only mean there was an informer among them. One day, Renzo, the second-in-command under Miguel, pulled Daniel aside.

"Look," said Renzo, "I'm going to go get the money from our comrades [in town]. You stay here with Challo and Ronald on guard. If I don't come back, if they kill me, that means that Miguel is working with the army. If I don't come back, you need to shoot Miguel and run away and hide."

Renzo had not been gone long before Daniel heard gunshots in the distance. Moments later, Renzo returned out of breath. Ronald and Challo came running from their lookout posts, followed by another guerrilla named Márquez. They had been in a firefight with the army not far down the road, but they had escaped. This was all the confirmation they needed that their commander was working with the army.

"I'm going to kill Miguel, I'm going to kill him myself," Márquez said, turning on his heel and heading to the camp. Márquez walked right up to Miguel, grabbed him by the collar, and held his gun to his head.

"I'm going to kill you, you rat bastard! You're working with the enemy!"

"No!" Miguel cried.

"Well then, how does the enemy know our every move and where we're headed?"

"Kill him! Kill him!" urged one of the others.

"Maybe he's not the one," Daniel said.

"No, *huevón*, fucker," said Márquez, "he's the one!"

"No I'm not!" cried Miguel.

"Fine," said Renzo, turning to Márquez. "Leave him be and take his radio. You're in charge of the radio now. He doesn't come near it."

Daniel's intervention that day saved Miguel's life. They would later learn that the informer hadn't been Miguel but, rather, the dispatcher on the other end of the radio. Miguel, however, never forgave his subordinates their mutiny.

Daniel and his nine comrades spent the remainder of the year traversing the jungle in search of a way back to their comrades. One day, they came across a river bordering indigenous lands. Tigre, who was among the remaining rebels, had seen firsthand the consequences of not seeking permission from the natives during his early incursions into Asháninka territory. Still, they had to keep pressing forward if they wanted to find food and shelter. Daniel volunteered to swim across and check it out. No sooner had he taken off his clothes did the first shots ring out. Still naked, he hit the ground.

"I'm hit! Save yourselves, comrades!" Renzo called out.

Renzo covered his comrades while they retreated. As he ran into the brush, Daniel could hear the soldiers crying for Renzo to die already.

Only six rebels made it out of the ambush alive. Now the group was down to Daniel, Tigre, Miguel, two other men, and a woman.[8] They made their way over to a coca farm in the valley. A peasant woman told them to stay as long as they pleased. They stayed for two months, cultivating coca leaf by day and hunting monkeys in the evenings. It was a long-overdue reprieve from the war, and Daniel wondered if he might not settle there and live as a coca grower, leaving the rebellion behind.

Then, one day in late 1993, a wood salesman came to the farm. Daniel recognized right away that this was no ordinary wood salesman. It was Rolly Rojas, also known as the Arab, chief of MRTA operations in Amazonas. The Arab had learned over the radio of the killing of Renzo and his three comrades and figured, correctly, that there must be survivors in the area. Posing as a wood salesman and bringing two of his men as guards, he had gone to the site of the battle and asked around about the fate of the surviving Tupac

Amaristas. The townspeople sent him on the trail that led him to Daniel, Tigre, and the others.

"Well," said the Arab, "we'll take whoever's left of us and head back through Amazonas."[9]

Just after midnight on Christmas Day 1993, Daniel and his comrades grabbed their weapons and followed the Arab out of the village. "Had the Arab not come," he said looking back, "maybe we would have stayed there living out our lives as peasants."[10] Instead, he continued on his journey, falling deeper into the jungle.

18
The One-Legged Chair

Esperanza Tapia spent most of 1994 living in Arequipa with little direction or personal finances. She had changed her physical appearance so many times that she hadn't seen her natural hair in years. Her most recent look was the bleach-blonde Princess Diana bob so popular in the mid-1990s. No longer able to afford rent or food, she called the one comrade she could still trust in Cajamarca and asked if he could float her some money while she awaited orders. The contact arranged to meet her at a prearranged spot and time. When she reached the rendezvous point, she found her comrade right where he said he would be. The two began walking in tandem and hadn't gotten far before a team of squad cars cut them off. Outnumbered and outgunned, Esperanza had no choice but to surrender.[1]

The police transferred her to DINCOTE headquarters in Lima for processing. As she stood there getting booked and contemplating the many years of prison that awaited her, one of the officers remarked, "Who would have thought that with those nails you could be a terrorist!"[2]

Like Dolores, Daniel Bravo had spent most of 1994 in Arequipa, awaiting his marching orders.[3] Finally, in 1995, he received instructions to head to the rebel camp in Chanchamayo. There, Néstor Cerpa and Tito Cruz, his former column leader from the aborted Moyobamba attack, gathered forty-five combatants to train for a top-secret mission. They performed drills for three possible operations—one on a public administration building, another on an airport, and a third on an embassy—not knowing which one the commanders would select. The recruits built to-scale models of each location in the middle of the rainforest and began running drills on each one.[4]

Once they had completed their training, Cerpa hand-selected twenty fighters to return to Lima for further instructions. The trek began in the back of a fruit truck headed for the capital. Once there, they got inside a *combi* van, where they were driven blindfolded to a hideout in Molina district. There, a mysterious woman held them by the hand and escorted them to the fourth story. Once the ribbon had been lifted from their eyes, they found themselves standing face-to-face with Miguel Rincón, the potbellied commander with the thick-lensed eyeglasses. Rincón greeted the arrivals, handed them clean clothes, and told them to shower, shave, and make themselves at home. That fourth story would serve as their new bunker for the coming weeks. The eighteen young rebels, who included Daniel and Tigre, passed the time playing cards and video games and watching VHS movies. Cloistered inside the tight space, they grew close with one another during those weeks. Daniel and Tigre, who had already been through hell and back in San Martín, shared a room.[5]

Daniel still didn't quite know what he had signed up for. One day, as he was inside sitting around bored, a slender man with sunglasses over his hood tapped him on the shoulder.

"Come with me, comrade."

When they rounded a corner, the slender man removed his hood. "Remember me?"

"Yes, of course!" Daniel said. Néstor Cerpa was much thinner than he remembered, but he had kept his signature gut.

"Look," Cerpa said, "we're planning on hitting the dictatorship when it's down. Right now it's sitting on a one-legged chair, and we need to knock out that leg."

Cerpa led Daniel to a room where a collection of military uniforms had been laid out. The rebels, he divulged, were going to pose as army soldiers and occupy the national congress building while congress was in session. "Our political objective was to turn the congressmen into our prisoners of war," Cerpa later explained. "They were to be set free once the government agreed to free our comrades."[6]

Daniel looked down at the crisp uniforms. "They look brand new."

"You're right," Cerpa said. "These do look brand-spanking new. We'll need to rinse them with water and a little bleach to make them look more faded and worn."[7]

Cerpa left the Molina safe house the next day, leaving fellow hard-liner Miguel Rincón in charge of planning the remainder of the attack.

■ Javier Caminero was among the guerrillas in the Molina safe house. Unlike his comrades, who came from the provinces, Javier had spent most of his life in Lima and knew the city well. As a student at San Marcos, he had headed up the MRTA's political apparatus, ensuring that the movement had established a foothold in the legal political sphere. In 1995, Javier, whose wife was pregnant, had gone to Bolivia to take part in operations across the border. He was pulled out of the field in mid-1995 and brought to Lima for an urgent operation. That operation was the storming of the Peruvian congress. Because he was so comfortable living and operating in the city, and because he had a day job that served as a convenient cover, Javier remained aboveground throughout the planning stage. While the other insurgents in the house wore bags over their heads all day, Javier was one of the few, along with Rincón, who went around unmasked and came and went as they pleased.

Javier was of the belief, like Alberto Gálvez and others before him, that the time had come for the MRTA to demilitarize and embrace the democratic process. In this post–Cold War moment of the mid-1990s, after more than thirty years of armed struggle, state-sponsored terrorism, forced disappearances, paramilitary death squads, and genocide against indigenous populations, the popular appetite for nonviolent protest and participatory politics was high throughout Latin America. Across the region, the armed left was laying down arms and opening peace talks. FMLN guerrillas had already negotiated a peace with the Salvadoran government in 1992, and Guatemala's URNG would do the same four years later. Even Mexico's Zapatistas, who had risen as recently as January 1994, appeared to be moving away from armed action. Javier and others correctly predicted that the Tupac Amaristas ignored these political realities at their own peril. All it took was one trip up to the fourth floor to realize that Cerpa and Rincón had no intention of laying down arms. There were weapons everywhere, enough guns, AKs, and grenades to take out a small brigade. "Those *huevones* looked more lethal than Rambo!" Javier recalled.

After weeks of training, Rincón finally gathered the troops to fill them in on the plan.

"We're going to strike a heavy blow that will allow us to reverse course. We're going to strike deep in the heart of the enemy so that we can recover our protagonism, recover our political initiative, recover resources. What we are about to do will enable this, and you all are going to be the ones to write this new page in history!" They were going, Rincón said at last, to seize the Peruvian congress while it was in session.

If the speech was meant to rally the troops, it had the opposite effect on Javier. Afterward, he pulled Rincón aside and raised his objections.

"Comrade, we came here on the understanding that we were going to develop our short- and long-term political strategy," Javier said. "If you ask me to take part in this operation, know that it will be against my will."

"Well, comrade," Rincón said, "I invite you to think on it, because this is a once-in-a-lifetime opportunity to make history."

Javier went back to his roommates and asked them what they thought. To his disappointment, they too had adopted the hard line.

"You're just having cold feet, comrade," they said. "You lack conviction."

"It's not a question of conviction," Javier said. For him, this was a matter of political prudence.

One day, Javier left the safe house to vote in the municipal elections and never came back. When he learned of Javier's departure, Miguel Rincón set up a meeting with him on the busy Rosa Toro Street in San Isidro. The two began walking and talking.

"As I told you before, comrade," Javier said, "the only way I'll stay for that kind of an operation is against my will. If you order me to go back, I will, but know that it will be against my will."

"No, comrade, that's not necessary," Rincón said. So that Javier knew there were no hard feelings, he handed him $200 in cash to assist with the delivery of his unborn child. "If there's anything else you need, just let us know."

Javier took the money and thanked his commander for his understanding. He returned home to his wife, not knowing if he would see Rincón alive again.[8]

■ The Molina house belonged to a twenty-six-year-old American named Lori Berenson. Berenson was a New Yorker with a flair for the arts. As a preteen, she had taken the lead role in her junior high school's rendition of *Annie*. Later, she enrolled in the LaGuardia High School of Music & Art and Performing Arts, a Manhattan school in whose halls Jennifer Aniston and Chaz Bono once walked. Berenson, who loved to sing, joined the school choir and performed all over the city. Surrounded by such talent, the pragmatic Berenson realized she would never make it as a professional singer or actress. She continued to write music and play her guitar, but she mostly focused on her studies. When college season came around, she turned down scholarships to Oberlin and Carleton to seek out a major in music engineering at MIT in 1987.[9]

At MIT Berenson became enamored with Latin America. During her freshman year, she took a course on Latin American socioeconomic history with Martin Diskin, an anthropology professor specializing in Caribbean politics. Diskin had been an outspoken critic of U.S. Cold War policy and the right-wing dictatorships of Central America, even getting arrested during one protest against the Nicaraguan Contra war.[10] The professor took the curly-haired freshman under his wing, inviting her to attend his graduate seminars and offering her employment as his research assistant. "She adored him," recalled Berenson's father, Marc.[11] The more she learned of the manifold injustices by the Latin American right, the more outraged Berenson became. During her spring semester, Berenson, not yet nineteen, joined a Quaker group expedition to El Salvador. The trip proved eye-opening, an up-close-and-personal look at U.S.-funded dirty war: the helicopters, the tanks, the bombs, the army raids. "I feel so guilty," she told her father during one long-distance phone call. "These people are so poor. They're so good. All they want is to be left alone."[12]

That freshman-year trip changed Berenson's life. When she returned to Cambridge, she became active in CISPES, the Salvadoran solidarity group, petitioning U.S. Congress members to stop the Central American dirty war. Then, during her second year at MIT, Berenson announced that she was dropping out of school and moving to Nicaragua to work for the left-wing Sandinista government.

Lori's decision concerned her father, a college professor who understood the importance of a good education.

"Lori, don't," Marc pleaded. "Get your degree. From the degree you'll have power and be able to do things."

"Dad, I can't," Berenson said. "I've got to help the people now. I'm young. I will go back to school. I will get an education, but now is the time I've got to help."[13]

In Nicaragua, Berenson worked with both the Sandinista and the FMLN, a Salvadoran guerrilla group with aspirations of becoming a legitimate political party.[14] It was through her work with the Salvadoran leftists that she first came to Peru. The year was 1991. Fujimori had recently taken office, and some in the MRTA Directorate, fresh off their historic jailbreak, were still seeking a way into legal politics. At the same time, Shining Path, whose leader Abimael Guzmán was still a year away from capture, was at the height of its power, tightening its noose around the capital. As was becoming increasingly clear, Fujimori had no interest in negotiating with armed groups. The Grupo Colina, a paramilitary death squad run by current and former members of state security forces, had been terrorizing unarmed civilians suspected of guerrilla support.

For Berenson, the tension was palpable. "I felt there was fear," she recalled, "not fear of violence, but fear of . . . You just feel that everyone is just sort of looking at each other [suspiciously]. I had that feeling."[15]

It was during this trip that Berenson first met members of the MRTA. She ended up settling in Peru and, by 1995, was subletting her four-story Molina house to Miguel Rincón's combatants. She would deny knowing much about the hideaway, claiming to have minded her business and paid no attention to the guerrillas upstairs.

Another of Berenson's roommates was Néstor Cerpa's wife, Nancy Gilvonio. Both women would deny any involvement in or collaboration with the MRTA, although Gilvonio would concede to being aware of her husband's involvement in the organization. Whatever or not their involvement, Berenson and Gilvonio soon found themselves in the center of a legal and media firestorm.

It began the morning of 30 November 1995. Having secured press passes, Berenson and Gilvonio went down to the national congress building. The pair claimed to have legitimate reasons for being there, Berenson the reporter, and Gilvonio the accompanying press photographer. Their credentials, by all accounts legitimate, granted them entrance into the halls of congress when it wasn't in session. While there, Berenson made a detailed sketch of the seating chart, noting which senators sat where. This was all, she maintained, for a report she was writing for a small left-wing paper back home. Afterward, the two hopped on a bus and headed down Lima's congested Wilson Avenue. As the bus reached its stop on the corner of Tacna Avenue, several men in street clothes boarded and hauled the two women violently from the bus in front of the nervous passengers, put them in an unmarked car, and sped away. "I was reluctant to realize that I was getting arrested," Berenson recalled, thinking it a kidnapping.[16] Only when the car pulled up at the tall DINCOTE station on nearby España Avenue did she realize what was happening. The plainclothes agents confiscated all of her belongings, including her eyeglasses, which had been knocked off her head during her arrest, and showed her the sketches of the congressional seating plan that she had drawn. They asked if this was her handwriting, but she denied it. "Lori can't see without her glasses," her father reasoned. "When they showed her: 'This. This is yours,' she said, 'no.' She couldn't see it. . . . And she's had this problem [with her eyesight] verified, documented, here in the U.S., since she was like seven years old, six years old. So she really didn't know what the hell they were showing her."[17]

Whatever the reason for the denial, the counterterrorism agents weren't buying it. Four agents took Berenson in the back of a police truck to her

Molina home and demanded that she open the door. "I refused to do it," she later admitted. Frustrated, the police shoved her facedown onto the floor of the truck. "That was when the shootout started."[18]

■ It was 9:00 P.M. when Miguel Rincón heard a knock at the door. "Almost as soon as they knocked on the door they started firing on us," he told the Truth Commission years later.[19] He ran over to Daniel and Tigre, who were watching TV.

"Well, boys, they've found us and now we've got to get out of here."[20]

The young men scrambled to grab their weapons as bullets riddled the compound. Some of the rebels took up posts and fired back while others activated the escape plan. They were to make their way to the backyard, where they would scale a ladder onto the neighboring rooftops and out of harm's way. Daniel and Tigre hurried down the grand stairway to the first floor and ran outside into the backyard. The first to make it to the doorway was a woman named Lucinda Rojas. A barrage of bullets laid her out flat. Running for their lives, Daniel and Tigre didn't have time to check if she was alive or dead. They made it to the ladder and climbed it while others scaled the fence and made a run for the public park across the street.[21]

José Mejía was one of those who attempted to climb the fence, not realizing that it was electrified. As soon as he reached the top, shockwaves ripped through his body, knocking him back into the neighboring yard. Having lost his rifle in the fall, Mejía sprinted toward the street. There, he came face-to-face with a plainclothes policeman.

"Turn yourself in and follow me across the street into the squad car," the agent ordered.

Before Mejía could react, a group of army soldiers arrived on the scene, firing on them both. Mejía took hits to the leg and arm, falling over.

The agent also took a hit to the leg. "I'm a lieutenant, don't shoot!" he cried. The soldiers stopped shooting and carried the officer away.

A short while later, another group of soldiers came across Mejía as he lay in a pool of his own blood. One of the soldiers proceeded to ask him a series of unhelpful questions.

"Why are you lying there?"

"I've been hit," Mejía stated the obvious.

"Who shot you?"

"I don't know."

The soldiers looked at the gashes on Mejía's hand and leg. He had lost a lot of blood.

"He's fucked," remarked one of the soldiers.

"Better kill him," said another, removing his pistol and holding it to Mejía's temple. As soon as the soldier pulled the trigger, Mejía whipped his head back to avoid the impact. The bullet only grazed his temple, but the soldiers didn't seem to notice, leaving him for dead. He would remain there until Red Cross members found him, barely conscious, the next morning.[22]

Another rebel made it to the park, only to find himself completely surrounded. Shirtless and clutching his rifle, he crouched behind a Toyota while two policemen yelled at him from their cover behind the fountain.

"Identify yourself! Identify yourself! Shout your name!"

"Rodríguez, Rodríguez, I'm a policeman!" replied the Tupac Amarista.

"I don't believe you, motherfucker! Stand up slowly with your hands up! Hurry up, dammit!"

"I'm Rodríguez. I'm a policeman!"[23]

There was a long silence. And then the police opened fire, dropping him before he could get a shot off.[24]

While their comrades rumbled in the park, Daniel, Tigre, Miguel Rincón, and a handful of others ran across the rooftop of a neighboring home. Down below, resident Carla Figari was hiding in the bathroom with her housekeeper and children. She listened closely to the urgent voices and noises from Rincón's rebels. They were clearly trying to break into her home, but she had managed to lock all the doors as soon as the shootout got under way.[25]

Finally, the Tupac Amaristas gave up and went on to try their luck in the next house. Inside, Ada Sesarego had gathered her mother and two boys in the hallway, away from the windows. She tried to call Alaska, the family dog, to join her, but he had worked himself into a frenzy amid the gunfire and heavy footsteps on the roof.[26] Then there was a loud noise from inside the house. It sounded like broken glass.

"They're inside!" Sesarego cried, ushering her mother and boys underneath the office desk. Alaska barked incessantly as the rebels ran down the hall. And then the barking stopped. "My dog is brave," one of Sesarego's boys told reporters, "but there was nothing he could do against people with guns." Daniel, Tigre, Rincón, and the remaining Tupac Amaristas shuffled down the stairs and erected mattresses in front of the broken window frames for protection from the onslaught of bullets.

At first, Rincón didn't realize there was anyone inside the home, as he was too preoccupied with the assailing security forces. "When we got to the house we didn't hear any voices, and when we were in the middle of the shootout there was no family to be found."[27] Then, as if out of nowhere, Sesarego came out of hiding. The rebel commander asked her if there was any part of the house that wasn't penetrable from the outside.

"In the bathroom," Sesarego said.

Rincón's rebels ushered the family into the bathroom and told the boys to hide in the bathtub. Sesarego pleaded with Rincón to let them go, but he demurred. As he told the Truth Commission, "If we would have let them go, [the family] would have been killed as soon as they stepped outside."

"Nothing's going to happen to you," he assured Sesarego.

He, Daniel, Tigre, and the others hunkered down for the fight of their lives. Outside, police, army, and navy tanks and trucks surrounded the house while helicopters swirled overhead. By 11:00 P.M., the tanks had begun firing on the house, lobbing explosives and ramming the outer wall.[28]

Rincón, whose name means "corner" in Spanish, now found himself backed into one. He asked Sesarego to pick up the phone and make contact with the police. Police responded that they were sending someone over to negotiate, but the line was promptly cut off.[29]

The bombardment continued well into the following morning. Throughout the night, Sesarego attempted to renew contact with the police via the telephone, as some of Rincón's men were in sore need of medical attention, but to no avail. It was almost daylight when Rincón told the sleep-deprived mother to go outside and ask police for a walkie-talkie so they could negotiate the terms of their surrender.

Sesarego screamed for the police and military to cease firing as she approached the door. The rebels had lost, she said; all they wanted was a guarantee of their safety.[30] Sesarego returned shortly with the walkie-talkie.

"This is a surrender for a lost battle," Rincón radioed Domínguez Solís, head of the police operation. "However, the armed revolution will continue without us."[31]

Rincón went on to specify the terms of surrender. He requested the presence of representatives of the Red Cross, the Catholic Church, the press, and the district attorney. His men would turn themselves in only after signing an official document of surrender in the presence of these outside witnesses, he said. Then, one by one, each rebel would leave the house unarmed, arms raised in a defiant fist or forming the letter V with their index and middle fingers.[32] "We wanted guarantees of an honorable surrender," he recalled.[33]

Domínguez Solís found the terms agreeable and began making the necessary arrangements. The Red Cross refused to comply, arguing that its bylaws did not allow it to negotiate in what amounted to a hostage situation. The other requested witnesses did their part, and the rebels signed the document in their presence. Rincón was the last to turn himself in, leaving the house with fist raised, with his button-down striped shirt protruding well past his belt, in his black jeans and white socks, at around 8:45 A.M.[34]

It was a new low point for the MRTA. In addition to capturing most of what remained of the struggling insurgency, authorities had raided its principal weapons arsenal. "THE MRTA IS FINISHED," headlined one newspaper.[35] The task remained only to locate Néstor Cerpa, the elusive commander who had yet to fall into police custody. No one really knew where *El Gordo* was. Some believed he had slipped across the border into Bolivia and was now participating in armed actions there. Others believed he had been captured in the Andean country, but it was difficult to say for sure.[36] Whatever the case, there was a mounting feeling that it was only a matter of time before the entire guerrilla operation crumbled. "Their days are numbered!" *La República* prognosticated, predicting that the rebel chieftain would fall within "a matter of days."[37] It was all wishful thinking. Cerpa not only evaded capture, but he spent the next year hatching a plan that he hoped would return the MRTA to its former glory.

19

Gone with the Wind

It was the biggest event in town that evening. The 500-person guest list for the party at Japanese ambassador Morihisha Aoki's residence was a veritable *Who's Who* of Lima high society. There was Sally Bowen, the BBC journalist. There was Francisco Tudela, the Peruvian chancellor. Even Alejandro Toledo, the future president of the republic, was in attendance. The current president was also scheduled to make an appearance at some point in the evening, joining his mother, brother, and sister, who were already mingling in the crowded mansion on the night of 16 December 1996 to celebrate the birthday of the Japanese emperor.[1]

Aoki's compound was an architectural anomaly on Thomas Edison Street. The pearly white building, with its towering Roman columns, wide front porch, and tiered steps, seemed more befitting of a plantation home in the antebellum South than it did a twentieth-century Latin American house. The interior was equally lavish, with a sprawling grand stairway that Scarlett O'Hara could have easily scurried down in her wide hoopskirt. The building's likeness to the fabled Tara of the Margaret Mitchell classic, *Gone with the Wind*, was no accident. Its original owner, Antenor Rizo Patrón, had ordered the manor's construction following the release of the 1939 technicolor hit. Rizo Patrón's young wife, Beba Basurco, dreamed of living in a mansion as splendid as the one inhabited by the movie's protagonist. The exceedingly wealthy Rizo Patrón contracted the architect Dammert Muelle to design for the much younger Beba her very own Tara in Lima's upscale San Isidro district.[2]

Luis Giampietri and his wife, Marcela, had been among the guests in attendance that evening. A former admiral in the Peruvian navy under Alan García, Giampietri had previously been implicated in the 1986 massacre of Shining Path prisoners. Giampietri had always denied any wrongdoing or knowledge of the massacre, but the episode seemed to follow him wherever he went. Tonight, however, Giampietri was attending Aoki's party as a civilian. He only wanted to pay his respects to the ambassador, mingle a little, and slip out before 8:30.

Luis and Marcela left their home in Callao's historic naval neighborhood at 7:00 P.M., the time that the reception had kicked off. If traffic was light, they might arrive at 7:30, fashionably late by Peruvian standards. Traffic in Lima is never light, though, and this Monday evening was no exception.[3] It was 8:00 P.M. by the time the driver pulled up to the gate, where a single guard checked their invitation card and let them through to the grounds. As he and Marcela made their way up the steps, Luis noted how light security had been compared with the Guantánamo-like security at the American, Canadian, and British embassies.

"That was easy," he muttered to Marcela as they walked through a metal detector with most of their possessions still in their pockets.[4]

The smiling Aoki was standing in the parlor, greeting every guest that walked in. Luis and Marcela got in the back of the line and waited their turn. After exchanging pleasantries with their Japanese host, they meandered over to the garden.[5]

The yard was resplendent: a beautiful arrangement of red and white flowers, an elegant spread of the finest Japanese fixings, and tuxedoed waiters serving cocktails. Most of the guests stood talking while the elderly women, Fujimori's mother, Matsua, included, sat in chairs.[6]

Just as Luis had hoped, Aoki came out to entertain his guests in the garden at half past eight. This was the admiral's chance to make his exit. He and Marcela exchanged glances and initiated that sidestepping sashay of smiles, small talk, and salutations toward the front door.[7]

Marco Miyashiro, the DINCOTE agent who twice captured MRTA leader Alberto Gálvez Olaechea, was also in the garden that night. The former scout mate of Víctor Polay now headed up the Special Investigations Tributary Unit, or SUNAT. He had come with his wife to celebrate the birthday of the Japanese emperor in the ambassador's home. A Japanese Peruvian, Miyashiro must have felt honored to be among the ambassador's guests.

There in the garden he came across his old colleague, Luis Valencia. Together with Benedicto Jiménez, now a pseudocelebrity in Peru, Miyashiro and Valencia had led the special intelligence unit that had captured Abimael Guzmán, leader of the Shining Path guerrillas, five years earlier. Now they could lift a glass together in a country whose worst days seemed behind it and in which armed insurgency seemed on the decline.

The officers hadn't been talking long before they felt a violent explosion from somewhere in the garden. Miyashiro instinctively told Valencia to hit the deck and did the same while the other panicked guests began pushing and shoving their way into the mansion, nearly trampling some.[8]

Inside, one of the guests caught a glimpse of men in black uniforms carrying assault rifles.

"Thank God," she cried. "Embassy security is here."

Peruvian diplomat Carlos Yrigoyen, another of the guests, knew better. "I don't think so, ma'am. Those are our attackers."

"No," replied the woman, "it's a ninja!"

"Alright, dammit," interrupted one of the uniformed men. "Everyone on the floor. From this moment on you are all prisoners of the MRTA!"[9]

The man was Tito Cruz Sánchez, the young rebel who had led the assault on Moyobamba with Daniel Bravo three years earlier and who had helped Lucero Cumpa escape Canto Grande prison three years before that.

Groups of armed guerrillas, their faces masked in red-and-white bandanas bearing the likeness of Tupac Amaru, fanned out through the residence, lining the doors with bombs as booby traps.

"Heads down, everyone on the floor, don't look at us!" they ordered. One of the rebels fired his semiautomatic into the air for good measure.[10]

■ The storming of the Japanese ambassador's residence had been an operation a long time in the making. There were fourteen assailants in all, twelve men and two women. To get inside the residence, they had infiltrated the waitstaff, taking advantage of the fact that few high-society types ever looked their brown-faced servers in the eye. Others had dressed as paramedics, parking their stolen ambulance down the street. Not even Néstor Cerpa, the brains behind the operation, dreamed it would go so smoothly. On the night of the attack, he had noticed serious security oversights. "We went through the trouble of preparing an ambulance for the assault and we didn't even need it," Cerpa said. "There weren't even any police on the back street."[11]

Within minutes, Thomas Edison Street was glittering with police lights. Some of the officers fired on the compound from the street as the guests lay facedown on the floor.[12] The efforts of the police were futile. The mansion was a veritable fortress, enclosed on all sides by large concrete walls designed to withstand the impact of bullets and bombs, with caged windows.[13]

"We have you surrounded, stand down!" shouted an officer from the street.

"*Patria o muerte, venceremos!*" replied the masked rebels as they returned fire. "Fatherland or death, we will prevail!"[14]

Luis Giampietri lay face down in the main parlor with Marcela. "It's usually in the first ten minutes that one has the best chances of resolving these problems," Giampietri knew.[15] He tried to assess who these assailants were and what they wanted. "Once I realized that it was the MRTA I thought, 'Alright, things [aren't that bad]. Let's see what they want.' Because if it had been Shining Path, they probably would have shot us all right then and there." At least the MRTA could be reasoned with, he believed.

Then the police started lobbing canisters of teargas. Some of the guests immediately headed for the windows to let the smoke out, but Tito would have none of it.

"Heads down, sons of bitches!" he barked, firing over the guests' heads. "Don't look at us, motherfuckers! All you goats get on the floor!"[16] As Tito stood there, a bullet caught him in the leg, forcing him to retreat.

At this point Ambassador Aoki took matters into his own hands. Hostages or not, the nearly 500 men and women inside the mansion were his guests, and he had a responsibility to look after them. He pleaded with the Tupac Amaristas to respect the lives of his guests. He asked that the rebels take him as their hostage and free his visitors.[17] When the rebels demurred, he tracked down a bullhorn and, in broken Spanish, addressed the police in the street.[18]

"Hole [*sic*] your fire!" Aoki said, butchering the Spanish command.[19]

Police returned the ambassador's pleas with a barrage of teargas. Some of the canisters broke the windows. Smoke seeped into the room and crawled up the walls and across the ceiling. Unfazed, the Tupac Amaristas put on the gas masks that they had brought and continued to fire on the police while their hostages coughed and cried uncontrollably.[20] "Marcela wasn't one to cry," Luis Giampietri knew, but he wondered how she would handle the teargas.[21] He removed the handkerchief from his pocket, soaked it in a nearby glass of water, and handed it to Marcela. The two took turns covering their faces to alleviate the feeling of asphyxiation.[22]

"Stop throwing teargas, there are women present!" someone cried.[23]

Ambassador Aoki went into a room to phone the president. When the palace receptionist picked up, he explained the situation and demanded to speak with Fujimori.

"The President is very busy, he can't take your call," replied the receptionist.[24]

Aoki hung up and tried again. And again. And then a third time, hoping someone would eventually patch him through. He was still attempting to get through when Néstor Cerpa appeared in the doorway, a red-and-white bandana over his mouth and nose.

"Go ahead, ambassador, keep calling," Cerpa said amusedly.

Aoki made no fewer than ten more attempts, each time getting nowhere.

"Isn't Fujimori your friend?" Cerpa mocked. "Didn't he always take you around to inaugurations and gift drives? Why won't he talk to you now?"[25]

Once the smoke had cleared in the parlor, the guerrillas separated the guests by gender. Were the president's mother and sister in attendance, they asked? Nobody answered. They repeated the question. Still no reply. Of course, most of the guests knew Fujimori's family were inside the residence, but they refused to give them up.[26]

Back in the main lobby, a slender forty-four-year-old with thinning blonde hair rose to his feet. He identified himself as Michel Minning, a ten-year veteran of the Red Cross. Minning hailed from Switzerland but had worked in Iraq, Lebanon, Bosnia, and Nicaragua. In August 1995, he had been appointed head of the Peruvian Red Cross in what he must have considered his most low-key assignment yet. Now he found himself in the center of perhaps the most dangerous crisis of his career, at a time when Latin American insurgencies were on the decline.[27] Minning offered to mediate the situation. Cerpa relented, handing him the megaphone.

"Officers," bellowed Minning. "For the sake of the safety of the guests inside the residence, please don't shoot."[28]

It was the second time a foreigner had tried to communicate to police through this device. Fortunately, Minning's Spanish was much better than that of his Japanese host, and the police complied. He turned to Cerpa and took a list of demands, imploring the rebel chieftain to respect the lives and well-being of the guests.[29]

Minning's intervention paid off immediately. Just before 10:00 P.M., a group of fifteen women in kimonos and evening gowns doddered past the mansion's white columns. Moments later came a second group, this time about thirty strong. The women continued in this way, released in small groups, until all—including President Fujimori's mother and sister—had filed out of the home.[30]

Half an hour later, a rebel, face covered, appeared before the anxious

Néstor Cerpa addresses media in doorway of Japanese ambassador's residence, 1996 (photo by José Vilca, *Caretas*, with kind permission)

press corps to articulate his group's demands. They wanted a prisoner exchange, simple and plain: all 450 Tupac Amaristas currently incarcerated in the penitentiary system for the remaining guests in Aoki's home. "We have 250 hostages in our possession," said the masked man. "Their lives depend on President Fujimori. If he doesn't give in to our demands, we will begin to eliminate each one of them." When asked his identity, the rebel said only that he was a commander of the MRTA special forces. In all likelihood, this was Cerpa himself, although some in the press corps reported a Central American accent.

"We are here to accomplish a mission and surrender is not an option," he added. Then, as if addressing the president directly, he warned, "Set them free or everyone here dies. *Patria o muerte, venceremos!*"[31]

It was after midnight when the rebels released the catering staff. Their fight, after all, was not with the working class. The guerrillas then did a roll call, sending the most high-ranking officials upstairs and leaving the remaining guests in the parlor.[32] With Tito out of commission due to his gunshot wound, the job of second-in-command fell to Rolly Rojas, the "Arab," the short young lieutenant with a hooked nose and wry sense of humor who had delivered Daniel Bravo from the depths of the jungle three years earlier. The Arab had only gone to high school but fancied himself an intellectual.

Standing in the grand staircase, the Arab checked the ID cards of every policeman and soldier before sending them to their second-floor quarters. As he stood in line, ID in hand, a terrible thought raced through counter-terrorism police detective Marco Miyashiro's mind: "What if they recognize me?"[33] He was still deep in thought when he overheard an exchange between the Arab and the guest in front of him in line.

"You are a priest," the Arab said respectfully. "You may go back down because you will be released later."

The priest, a Catholic named Juan Julio Wicht, replied, "I am a priest, but I would like to stay because I can be of more use in here than out there."[34]

The Arab conceded reluctantly. "Let it be known, Father, that you are staying of your own volition."

Miyashiro stood there stupefied. "Amid all the confusion, terror, and uncertainty," he wrote of the exchange, "a response of that nature was completely out of place." Wicht's example had a disarming, almost soothing impact on the colonel. "Well, if a priest like him can stay, so can a policeman like me," he thought, stepping forward and handing over his police ID. The Arab inspected the document and said, "Well, the SUNAT is doing good work."

"But I'm also a policeman," Miyashiro said.

The Arab turned to one of his comrades: "Make a note that he's a retired law enforcement officer." Miyashiro took back his ID and walked up the stairs to a second-floor bedroom.[35]

Luis Giampietri, the navy admiral, had been visiting a similar dilemma in his head. Like Miyashiro, he identified himself according to his military rank.[36] With an air of hostility, the Arab asked Giampietri if he was active duty or retired. When he replied the latter, the Arab ordered him to a room on the second floor where the rebels had put their most high-profile hostages: congressmen, cabinet members, and high-ranking military and police officials. Giampietri was placed in room Alpha with thirty-one other high-priority hostages. Across the hall, in room Bravo, remained other high-ranking military and police personnel, including its newest inhabitant, Marco Miyashiro.[37]

■ The following afternoon, Néstor Cerpa began the first of what would become customary grad-school-like seminars with the hostages. During these occasions, the guerrilla boss would round up a group of hostages and attempt to explain the MRTA's perspective on different societal issues. In this first chat, he discussed social theory. The problem with the current economic order, he said, was that it was designed to "make the rich richer and the poor poorer." What Cerpa envisioned was a socialist model, but one rooted in Peru's own history and that paid attention to its most neglected masses.[38] The chats could take on a lighthearted tone. During a particularly heated exchange about the free market, a hostage named Romero tried not so subtly to change the subject. Everyone, Cerpa included, burst out laughing. Hearing this, the rebels on the second floor came running down the grand staircase to order the hostages to fall in line. "When they realized the person responsible for the antics was their own boss," one hostage wrote in an improvised diary, "they returned to their posts as quiet as little mice."[39]

Cerpa's seminars were often interrupted by Red Cross representative Minning's frequent visits to the mansion. Cerpa allowed the Swiss diplomat to come and go at will, and he quickly emerged as the most critical agent in the negotiations with the Peruvian government. Before long, the Red Cross was bringing a stream of five-gallon jugs of water to the residence, along with shipments of apples, bananas, bread, ham, cheese, and other essential supplies. Minning's team also arranged for the hostages to send and receive letters to and from their loved ones, following a thorough inspection by the Arab.[40] Then, on 20 December, Minning helped coordinate the release of the first group of hostages since the night of the takeover.

Cerpa was in good spirits that night, chatting with the group of lucky hostages next to the curved staircase. The group included prominent politicians like Senator Javier Diez Canseco and future president Alejandro Toledo.[41] Francisco Sagasti, a *Caretas* reporter who had penned his plight on the back of a calendar, also had his number called that night. Before departing, the bearded reporter grabbed a slab of cardboard from a box of Japanese Fuji water and asked if the rebel commander and first lieutenant would autograph it as a keepsake. The two were happy to comply. "To Mr. Segástegui [sic]," wrote Cerpa, misspelling the hostage's name, "with much respect." The Arab did the same: "To Mr. Sagasti, with all due respect." The commanders were equally respectful of the other soon-to-be-released hostages, exchanging, in at least one case, hugs.[42] Then the doors opened, and the hostages began their long march to freedom.[43]

The whole world was watching. In the coming days, journalists and photographers from around the globe flooded the upper-class district, setting up video cameras, high-zoom photographic cameras, and walkie-talkies on the surrounding rooftops to catch a glimpse of the action.[44] Thousands of civilians poured into plazas and churches throughout Lima to march, sing, and pray for a peaceful end to the crisis. Others laid floral arrangements and held candlelight vigils across the street from the embassy.[45] U.S. president Bill Clinton reached out to Fujimori to offer his support and solidarity in this time of crisis.[46] For the moment, Cerpa was winning the public relations war. The foreign press hung on to his every word, waiting for him to rear his head and make a statement.

On 21 December, a voice came over the radio waves: "This is Néstor Cerpa of the MRTA National Directorate, with a message for the families of all the people who are being held here at the residence by our organization. We would like to assure you that we will continue releasing anyone who doesn't have anything to do with the government." While insisting that the remaining hostages had "no reason to fear that we will cause them any physical or psychological harm," he maintained that their fate was solely in the hands of Fujimori. Only once the president released political prisoners, Cerpa said before signing off, "can we begin to speak of a true peace, peace with social justice."[47]

Later that night, the president responded with a television broadcast of his own. The address, evidently prerecorded, went out at the eleven o'clock news hour, a time when the most Peruvians would be tuning in to their television sets. The MRTA, Fujimori said, "the same group that has been sowing destruction and death in Peru for the past decade, and whose most characteristic representatives include Víctor Polay Campos, Peter Cárdenas Shultze, and Lucero Cumpa, among others, now wants to enter a dialogue toward a peace treaty. That is, it seeks a dialogue with an AK rifle pointed at their hostages' heads." The Peruvian government simply could not succumb to the demands of "terrorist commandos." While maintaining that his government did not seek "remedies of force," Fujimori insisted that he would only accept a total disarmament and unconditional hostage release. "This is the government's proposal before the nation and international community, and I can only hope for a resolution that respects the lives of the innocent. Good night."[48]

There it was. Both sides had drawn their battle lines, unwilling to cede an inch. Cerpa, always the hard-liner, would accept nothing short of the release of MRTA prisoners, and Fujimori wouldn't begin to talk until the fourteen rebels at the Japanese ambassador's residence laid down their arms. The only silver lining was that, for the time being at least, neither side appeared willing to resort to violence. Víctor Joy Way, president of the Peruvian congress, confirmed as much that day, reassuring reporters that the government had ruled out a military operation to rescue the hostages.[49]

20

Captivity

At 9:40 in the evening on Sunday, 23 December 1996, the large doors to the Aoki mansion opened, and Red Cross negotiator Michel Minning appeared in the doorway with four hostages. Minning lifted a megaphone to his lips and announced that 225 of the hostages would be coming home that evening, a good-faith gesture by the Tupac Amaristas to illustrate their willingness to negotiate with Fujimori's government.[1] Camera clicks and flashing lights filled the night sky as the hostages silently walked past the international press corps. Then, as if to wake them from their stupor, a young woman's voice emerged from the crowd of spectators in front of the Italian clinic on the corner.

"Papá, papá!"

The woman erupted into tears. Her father would be among the fathers, sons, and brothers coming home for Christmas.[2]

Inside the residence, there were still 140 government officials, security forces personnel, and Japanese diplomats whose hopes of a Christmas Eve with family had now vanished. With Christmas around the corner, leaders from across the world began to chime in. In Washington, Bill Clinton praised Fujimori for respecting the lives of the recently freed American hostages and called on the Tupac Amaristas to send all remaining hostages home.[3] In Uruguay, the courts released two suspected MRTA guerrillas being held in connection to the kidnapping of a Bolivian businessman.[4] Cuba's own bearded rebel, Fidel Castro, indicated his willingness to grant Cerpa's band political asylum as part of a negotiated settlement.[5]

The hostages found some minor consolation on Christmas Eve when several fruit baskets made their way into the residence, a gift from the Market Vendors Association. Perhaps warmed by the holiday spirit, Néstor Cerpa allowed the Red Cross to distribute the fruits to rebels and hostages alike. It was the first fresh fruit many of them had tasted since the crisis began a week earlier. Later that night, the Red Cross brought another surprise in the form of a full Christmas dinner. The dinner, always consumed on Christmas Eve in Peru, had been a gift from the divorced president's teenaged daughter and de facto First Lady, Keiko Fujimori. The hostages watched in wonderment as the Red Cross workers lit candles inside plastic cups and set chocolates on top of a stretcher to bring upstairs. At the stroke of midnight, the hostages, their bellies filled with holiday food and cheer, shouted *"Feliz Navidad,"* exchanging good tidings and warm hugs. Afterward, Juan Julio Wicht, the priest who had elected to stay in captivity with the other hostages, oversaw a Christmas mass.[6]

Yet it was another ecclesiastic who emerged as the unlikely protagonist during the crisis. Juan Luis Cipriani, an Opus Dei bishop from Ayacucho, the war-torn Andean department that incubated the Shining Path insurgency, was no friend of the left. He had famously downplayed state terror while condemning the nation's guerrillas as "traitors, murderers and cowards."[7] On Christmas Day, the bald bishop accompanied Minning into the ambassador's home without any prior announcement or warning. Cipriani donned his typical black cloth and waist sash, a crucifix hanging from a long chain just above the navel. The bespectacled bishop's visit was ostensibly to perform a mass for the hostages, but such an explanation is unlikely, given that Juan Julio Wicht had already been among the original hostages. Add to this the fact that the monsignor's visit spanned seven hours, and such an explanation unravels still further.[8] The following day, Cipriani returned to the residence, remaining another three hours before leaving. From that point forward, his visits to the mansion became a regular occurrence. Evidently, this was perfectly fine with Néstor Cerpa, who later remarked that Cipriani was welcome to come and go as he pleased.[9] Although Cipriani insisted that he was only there in a "pastoral" role, it soon became clear that he was serving as an unofficial negotiator on behalf of the government.[10] The bishop's interventions appeared to bear fruit. Within a week of Cipriani's Christmas Day surprise, Cerpa released another twenty hostages, followed by seven more on New Year's Day, bringing the remaining number to seventy-four.[11] Peace, it seemed, was on the horizon.

Fujimori assigned Education Minister Domingo Palermo as the government representative in the ensuing talks. On Friday, 10 January 1997, Palermo reached Cerpa via walkie-talkie.

"OK, don Néstor, so is it alright with you if we meet briefly this weekend?" Palermo confirmed after a brief conversation with the guerrilla boss.

"Forgive me for saying so," Cerpa radioed, "but there's no problem on our end. It's not like we're going anywhere."

"I congratulate you on your good sense of humor," Palermo said with a chuckle. "See you soon."[12]

Come Saturday, however, Cerpa changed his mind. Apparently, he had expected Palermo to come with an offer to release political prisoners. When he learned that no such proposal was forthcoming, he called the meeting off.[13]

The spirit of negotiation was breaking down fast. The same day as the aborted talks, police began encroaching on the outer perimeter of the residence. As Cerpa told the Agence France-Presse, some of these policemen had even begun lobbing rocks into the garden. The Tupac Amaristas responded by opening fire, causing a frenzy among the assembled press corps but resulting in no injuries.[14] Two weeks later, another incident with police almost ended in tragedy when a Tupac Amarista put up two fingers, making a V sign to a cruising patrolman. The patrolman responded with a gesture of his own, most likely the middle finger. Raising the stakes, the rebel took four potshots at the armored vehicle. Within minutes, more than sixty policemen had descended on Thomas Edison Street in Hummers and tanks, while the Tupac Amaristas took up defensive posts throughout the residence. Fortunately, a coolheaded commanding officer instructed his troops to stand down, de-escalating the situation.[15]

Despite the scare, Cerpa still appeared willing to talk. When the government proposed the appointment of a special delegation to help negotiate a rapprochement, the rebel ringleader acquiesced.[16] And when two of the remaining hostages—one of them Marco Miyashiro's old partner, Luis Valencia—fell ill over the course of the next month, Cerpa released them both.[17] That, Cerpa insisted, was the extent of his magnanimity.

"If anyone else gets sick," he told the remaining seventy-two hostages, "they'll die in here."[18]

■ As days slipped into weeks, weeks into months, the crisis enveloped a colorful cast of characters. Pope John Paul II chimed in from the Vatican to offer his solidarity with the hostages and commend the efforts of his Peruvian bishop.[19] Among the figures who either volunteered or whose names were floated to help mediate a solution were Víctor Polay's mother, Otilia; Argentina's Madres de Plaza de Mayo; Cuba's Fidel Castro; and South Africa's Nelson Mandela.[20] Some of the recently freed hostages reported that their Peruvian captors had expressed their desire to spend their years of exile with Subcomandante Marcos, the balaclava-wearing, pipe-smoking Mexican rebel who just three years earlier had launched an insurgency of his own in the jungles of Chiapas.[21] Even Vicky Peláez, the former *90 Seconds* reporter whom Cerpa had kidnapped when the MRTA was in its infancy, returned from New York to join the assembled press corps.[22]

The media attention played right into the MRTA's hands but did little to assuage the concerns of the hostages. Marco Miyashiro, the DINCOTE detective, believed his death could come at any moment. One night, some of the Tupac Amaristas rushed into the room where he was sleeping and awoke everyone at gunpoint.

"Face down and hands behind your head, dammit!" they barked.

As he lay there, Miyashiro could feel the barrel of a gun press against the back of his head.[23] Fortunately, the situation did not escalate, but Cerpa made it clear that police and military would be the first to die in the event of a rescue attempt.

"If the government comes in guns blazing," Cerpa told Miyashiro's group one day, "we're going to kill you guys first. If the government tries to rescue you, we're all going to die. None of you will make it out of here alive if the government doesn't give in to our demands."[24]

Miyashiro sought some comfort in establishing a daily routine. A second-generation Japanese Peruvian, he passed most of the time getting tutored in his ancestral tongue by the embassy staff. The routine was straightforward enough: "Breakfast. Japanese lessons. Lunch. Nap. Continue my Japanese lessons. Dinner. Visit with the other hostages." Then he would go to bed, only to repeat the entire ordeal the following day.[25]

Each hostage came up with his own little games to lift his spirits and keep hope alive. Some allowed Rodolfo Masuda and Felipe Ramírez, two vice ministers in the president's cabinet, to cut their hair with a pair of rounded kindergarten scissors. For Miyashiro, not cutting his hair was what gave him hope. He told himself that he wouldn't groom himself until he was on the other side.[26] When his hair grew past his ears, however, the normally clean-cut agent did try to give himself a good combing before mass one day.

"Hey Marco, where's the party?" asked priest Juan Julio Wicht.

"Look, Juan Julio," Marco said. "I figured that since we're going to pray for an end to the crisis and for our safe return home, I might as well dress for the occasion! I don't want to be like those peasants in the Andes, where everyone goes to church to pray for rain but no one brings an umbrella!"

Wicht let out an infectious laugh. "Yes, it's good to come to mass prepared."[27]

Wicht's masses offered a semblance of normalcy for the hostages, a routine performed on the outside that could be simulated inside the compound. The father even persuaded the rebels to donate a bottle of wine from the ambassador's house to use for the communion. As the wine was a valued commodity, he put Miyashiro and the other eleven men in his bedroom in charge of its safekeeping. The colonel and his mates performed their task dutifully. However, when air force colonel Pepe Garrido received word that his wife had given birth to a bouncing baby boy, the hostages couldn't resist a celebratory toast.

"Whose wine are we charged with safekeeping?" asked one of the men.

"The father's!" Miyashiro and the others replied.

"And who is the father?"

"The colonel, of course!"[28] they replied, downing the wine.

Humor, even dark humor, was one of the main ways the hostages kept up spirits. In response to the sporadic night raids where he and his mates would be forced to the ground, Miyashiro and the other policemen joked that, long after they were free and the hostage crisis was a distant memory, they would open their own restaurant called Hands on the Back of Your Head! The waitstaff, clad in MRTA bandanas and black uniforms, would greet every customer the same way: "Facedown on the floor, dammit!"[29]

■ Across the hall, Luis Giampietri had developed his own coping mechanisms. Some hostages chitchatted with their captors. Others offered them language classes or invited them to play board games. According to Giampietri, one high-ranking police chief went so far as to teach the rebel Tito the *marinera*, the folkloric dance from the coastal *criollo* tradition. For the proud admiral, this was a bridge too far. "He was giving *marinera* lessons to terrorists! Can you imagine? A general all decked out in his green suit and white shoes, twirling around, handkerchief in hand . . . with Tito! Motherf— I mean, get the fuck outta here!"[30]

Giampietri preferred to keep to himself. An early riser, he would get up before daybreak and walk up and down the curving staircase for some morning exercise. Afterward, he would go into the bathroom and wash up with splashes of water and wet wipes that the Red Cross had brought in. He tried to take advantage of these quotidian tasks to gather his own intel on the enemy. Where did each Tupac Amarista stay? What kind of routines did they settle into? Where were their watch posts? He thought this information might come in handy if the hostages ever established contact with the outside.[31]

He volunteered for any chore that would get him out of his room. Not only would this give him a bit of exercise and occupy his mind, but more important, it would enable him to continue his internal assessment of the compound and identify weaknesses in rebel security. It wasn't uncommon in early 1997 to see the balding, six-foot three-inch admiral changing candles or emptying buckets of excrement from the upstairs bathroom.[32]

In the afternoons, Giampietri would head over to room C, where a group of hostages were allowed a small battery-operated radio. Radio personality Zenaida Solís used her show as a platform through which loved ones could relay messages of hope and encouragement to the hostages. "Those were very sad times for us," Giampietri recalled, noting how the most-decorated generals had been reduced to tears hearing their wives' voices. He decided not to give his captors the satisfaction of seeing him so vulnerable, writing his wife and imploring her not to appear on Solís's program. Marcela heeded his advice, but no one could stop his mother from calling in to the show. Giampietri's mother was of advanced age and had cancer; he didn't know if he would ever see her alive again. Hearing her frail voice over the airwaves was almost unbearable, but he tried to maintain his composure. In a further test of his resolve, he overheard Néstor Cerpa, leaning back with his legs crossed over a desk, talking to his comrades.

"Tell Popeye to come here so he can talk to his mother," Cerpa offered.

Popeye was the nickname Cerpa gave Giampietri, a nod to his background as a sailor. Cerpa's offer sounded sincere, probably coming from a place of genuine empathy for his captive. The time lapse between overhearing Cerpa's offer and receiving the message from his subordinate gave Giampietri just enough time to consider it. In the end, he decided against talking to his mother. "I couldn't let . . . him see me being moved by what my mother was saying," he later explained.[33]

"Tell Cerpa," Giampietri said when he got the message, "to go fuck himself."

Generally speaking, Giampietri tried to keep his exchanges with the MRTA leader to a minimum. "I had nothing to say to him," he explained.[34] Sometimes, however, these interactions were unavoidable. One day in January, Cerpa learned through press reports that Giampietri had headed up navy special forces as part of the state counterinsurgency campaign in the 1980s. The information landed Giampietri on the receiving end of a heated interrogation. Usually, Cerpa presided over ad-hoc tribunals on the first floor, sitting in a chair like a judge while Tito and the Arab stood watch.[35] On this hot January day, however, Cerpa didn't wait to summon the admiral to him. He had just learned of the reports on the radio and stormed into Giampietri's quarters to confront him directly.

"Are you admiral Giampietri?" Cerpa demanded.

"Yes."

"Were you navy Chief of Operations?"

"Yes."

"That means you are an enemy of the revolution. You participated directly in the execution of our comrades."

"No," Giampietri said. "The navy Chief of Operations is in charge of naval forces; you know, ships, planes, submarines."

Cerpa wasn't buying it. He continued to interrogate Giampietri over the details of his job, accusing him of commanding an operation in Ucayali that resulted in the death of one of Cerpa's comrades from his Cromotex days.

"What year did that happen?" Giampietri asked.

"In 1989."

This was good news. Giampietri explained that he had been in the naval academy in the United States in 1989. He would have had no knowledge of, or oversight over, the Ucayali operation.

Cerpa still wasn't convinced. He stormed out of the room and into the neighboring room to ask if any of the policemen could attest to Giampietri's service in Special Operations. One of the policemen, an even-keeled man named Landy who was friends with Giampietri, declared without equivocation that he had been with Giampietri in the aforementioned unit and that they had been in charge of aviation. That seemed to appease Cerpa, and he ended his investigation convinced, according to Giampietri, that "Popeye" was nothing more than "a harmless old retired sailor."[36] From that point on, Cerpa's suspicions regarding Giampietri abated, and the rebels eased their surveillance of his movements throughout the house.

■ For the two lone women Tupac Amaristas, the hostage crisis put MRTA misogyny on full display. Herma Luz Meléndez hailed from the Asháninka lands of Oxapampa, but her light complexion earned her the nickname *La Gringa*, the White Girl, among her comrades. Just a year earlier, when she was sixteen years old, La Gringa joined a band of Tupac Amaristas that had been passing through her community. The circumstances of her conscription into the guerrilla army are unclear, although her mother claimed she had been kidnapped.[37] The other woman among the rebels was Luzdina Villoslada, a petite and reserved seventeen-year-old with dark brown skin who went by the *nom de guerre* Melissa.[38] Although these young women performed sentry duty throughout the residence, Cerpa displayed unease in allowing them to intermingle with the hostages, assigning them mostly to guard the front door.[39] In addition to keeping them isolated from the men, this assignment effectively turned them into cannon fodder, as they would be the first line of defense in the event of a military raid. The rebel men verbally and physically abused the women, and some became aggressively territorial over them. Prime Minister Tudela, the rebels' most prized prisoner, claimed to have personally witnessed Cerpa kick Melissa and La Gringa whenever they fell asleep on sentry duty or failed to bring him his food promptly.[40] While Tudela certainly had reason to paint an unflattering portrait of his captor and would-be assassin, his description fits within the larger pattern of daily micro- and macro-aggressions experienced by other rebel women.

By all accounts, the two women were ambivalent about their predicament. Given the number of testimonies, it is likely that La Gringa considered herself to be there against her will or, at the very least, that she regretted her decision to join the rebellion. When La Gringa's mother appeared before the press begging her daughter to come home, Cerpa ordered her not to respond. La Gringa obeyed the order but confessed to several hostages that she had been "practically kidnapped" into service with the rebel army, a confession that would seem to support that of her mother in Oxapampa.[41] At night, when no one was looking, she wept, according to multiple hostages who could hear her cries. If true, her forced conscription into the rebel army further illustrates the sense of racial entitlement that mestizo rebels held over their indigenous countrymen and women. Earlier in the war, when conscription in the rebel army was high, mestizo commanders didn't allow Asháninka villagers to join the rebel ranks, assigning them instead to menial tasks. Now, rural commanders felt empowered to kidnap those same indigenous villagers in order to fill their depleted military ranks. Evidently, La Gringa wasn't alone. According to one hostage, Melissa at one point considered escaping in laundry carts that the Red Cross occasionally rolled out of the residence for cleaning.[42]

The hostages, particularly those with military and police backgrounds, exhibited their own prejudice toward their women captors. Their claims about the weeping women may themselves be ex post facto inventions, a way of juxtaposing the supposedly delicate Tupac Amarista women with the fearless soldiers and policemen. After all, it was admiral Giampietri who proudly pointed out his refusal to cry upon hearing his mother's voice on the radio. The presumption of the emotional weakness of their women captors led some hostages to conclude that they could be manipulated psychologically. "I looked for a way in with La Gringa with the hopes of learning her commander Cerpa's intentions," General Carlos Rosas testified, "and at the same time to dissuade her from the action she was taking."[43] Marco Miyashiro tried a more direct approach.

"Hey, Gringa, now that we're friends and all, do you think you could shoot me if your commander ordered it?" Miyashiro asked as she hovered over him while he played cards one day.

"Please, Colonel," La Gringa replied, "don't try to escape because we're under strict orders to shoot anyone who attempts to flee. And that's a direct order from the commander from a meeting we had a few nights back."[44]

No matter their attitudes about the rebel women's ambivalence or inherent psychological weakness, none of the men in captivity dared attempt an escape on their watch. They knew all too well that neither woman would hesitate to put a bullet in their head.

■ All hope was not lost for the hostages. In late January, Alberto Fujimori promised their families that "the problem will be resolved peacefully."[45] As if to reiterate this point, the president conceded to the first round of face-to-face talks with a newly created negotiation commission. The commission consisted of several members who had already served as de facto negotiators in the crisis: Red Cross representative Minning, Bishop Cipriani, and Minister Palermo. It also included some additional members deemed acceptable by the MRTA: Canadian ambassador Anthony Vincent and Terusuke Terada of Japan. For the first meeting, Cerpa chose his second-in-command, the Arab, to represent the subversives. The meeting took place in the foreign press's London Club, directly across the street from the Japanese ambassador's home. At 3:22 in the afternoon of 11 February, a white sedan carrying Minning and Vincent pulled into Aoki's gated residence. Within minutes, the Arab, still sporting the white-and-red bandana across his face, hopped into the backseat and crouched down to avoid detection from the outside. At 3:25, the car pulled out of the gated walls and into a building directly across the street, where a conference room had already been set up. The guests met for four hours in the small conference room, with the Arab sitting at the head of the table. Ambassador Vincent, who had been appointed as the neutral head of the commission, sat to his left, while the other four members sat directly across the table from the Canadian ambassador. If the Arab suspected that Peruvian intelligence was listening in on the conversation, he was right. The National Intelligence Service (SIN), headed by the president's right-hand man, Vladimiro Montesinos, had installed video cameras and microphones throughout the location, and SIN agents watched from the adjacent room. This preliminary meeting went on much longer than anticipated, however, and when the videotapes ran out, an agent awkwardly came into the room to replace them.[46] Four hours later, the sedan pulled back out and returned the Arab to the residence.[47] The talks continued three days later over sodas and mineral water, with the Arab communicating directly via walkie-talkie with Cerpa, who followed the talks from a closed-circuit television inside the Aoki mansion.[48] Apparently, not being there in person frustrated Cerpa, and by the next week's meeting, he had joined his comrade at the negotiating table.[49]

The talks appeared to be moving in the right direction. An eager Fujimori embarked on a state visit to Cuba in early March. Sipping on mojitos with the olive-green-clad Caribbean leader, the president discussed the ongoing talks and the role that Cuba might have in them. Fidel Castro, once a leftist rebel who had fought alongside Che Guevara, the man so venerated in MRTA iconography, was more than willing to do his part. The aging revolutionary offered to grant Cerpa and his guerrillas political asylum as part of the rapprochement between the Peruvian government and the MRTA.[50] Afterward, Fujimori announced his government's latest offer. In exchange for releasing the remaining seventy-two hostages unharmed, the government would drop all charges against Cerpa and his fellow hostage-takers and submit a formal request for Cuba to accept them as political exiles. Additionally, the Tupac Amaristas' exile would come with guarantees against future extradition to Peru. This, Fujimori indicated, was his government's best and final offer.[51]

This may have been Cerpa's best chance at a peaceful resolution to the crisis. Accepting the offer, however, would have required him to compromise his own hard line. He had orchestrated the hostage situation in order to secure the unconditional release of his imprisoned comrades, ostensibly so that they could keep on fighting. The very notion of compromise, of laying down arms and walking away, had never been in the hard-liner's vocabulary. "We have no intention of seeking exile or political asylum," he told the media via walkie-talkie. "We only seek the liberation of our imprisoned comrades." Without the prisoner exchange, there would be no deal.[52]

Cerpa followed up this message with an even bigger bombshell on 6 March. Speaking from his two-way radio, he declared, "For the past three days we've been hearing some sounds that seem to be coming from underneath the residence. And now, early this morning, they became more intense. All this, we believe, indicates that a military attack is imminent, or at least that there is one in the works. . . . Therefore, we are taking, logically, the necessary precautionary and security measures. Because, as we've said, we are determined to confront any situation." Given this new development and breach of the government's good faith, Cerpa announced that he would be suspending the dialogue with the negotiating commission, effective immediately.[53]

It was difficult to make sense of Cerpa's claim. If true, the revelation flew in the face of the overtures that Fujimori had been making toward a peaceful end to the crisis. Could it be that everything—the speeches, the trips abroad, the peace commission—had been one big diversion while Fujimori planned a violent end to the crisis? Cerpa seemed to believe so. After all, he knew a thing or two about tunnels, having orchestrated his comrades' escape from Canto Grande seven years earlier. But maybe there was nothing to the allegation. It was possible that Cerpa, having realized that Fujimori would not concede to a prisoner exchange, was looking for an excuse to derail the peace talks. It was just as likely that Cerpa was growing paranoid in his isolation. The truth was anyone's guess. Whatever the case, the revelation ended any hopes of a quick end to the stalemate.

From that point forward, the Tupac Amaristas adopted a bunker mentality. Cerpa moved all the hostages to the second floor, presumably so they would be more difficult to rescue in the event that the tunnel theory proved true.[54] In one of his final communications with the negotiation commission, Cerpa asked to have a message delivered to his wife, Nancy Gilvonio, who had been captured alongside the American Lori Berenson in late 1995. Gilvonio was currently serving time in Yanamayo prison in the cold Andes mountains. Cerpa asked that his companion of twenty-five years understand why he had decided to occupy the Japanese ambassador's residence in the first place, implying that he had been motivated, at least in part, by love. He went on to explain that he would always have "much respect and admiration" for her and that, come what may, she would "always be in his heart."[55]

If rumors of an impending attack on the residency were true, the strategy did not appear to have much support among the Peruvian public. By mid-April, Fujimori, who just two years earlier enjoyed an unprecedented 83 percent approval rating, now found himself in the midst of a public relations crisis. For the first time in his seven-year presidency, the majority of Peruvians disapproved of his job performance.[56] Political analysts cited the president's forty-point plunge as a sign of his political demise, and readers of the daily *La República* awoke on the morning of 22 April 1997 to the headline "'Fujimori Phenomenon' Reaches an End."[57]

21

Chavín de Huántar

One of Cerpa's first orders of business on the morning of 22 April 1997 was to wage the daily battle over symbols. Back in January, government forces had erected large speakers up and down Edison and Barcelona Streets, from which they belted out a daily mix of classical music, *criolla* music (from the Peruvian folkloric tradition), and spirited military ditties for twelve hours at a time.[1] This appeared to be a counterinsurgency tactic to disrupt the rebels' dialogue, thoughts, and sleep. It also had the unwelcome effect of driving the hostages mad. "We felt as if our brains were being scrambled," recalled Luis Giampietri, the navy admiral.[2] More than once Giampietri grabbed the megaphone and gave the police a piece of his mind.[3]

"If I ever get out of here, I swear to God I'm going to piss on those damn speakers!"[4]

At other times, the police performed displays of their might, complete with jet fly-bys, combat drills, martial marches, and plenty of patriotic war music, in a scene that seemed more befitting of a Super Bowl pregame show.[5] That the music represented the patriotic classics seemed to project another, more symbolic message: that of the nation audibly conquering the insurgents' lived space.

Not to be outdone, the Tupac Amaristas found their own way to lob musical grenades right back at the police. Cerpa started every morning with a kind of pep rally that both reminded the Tupac Amaristas why they were there in the first place and responded to the security forces' musical onslaught. This late April morning was no exception.

And so it was that Néstor Cerpa found himself leading his subordinates in a rendition of the "Anthem to the Heroes of Los Molinos" on the morning of 22 April 1997. It was an incredible, two-minute tribute sung in near-perfect harmony.

Something's shaking in Latin America
A free country, on the horizon it is
The children of the Andes are fighting
Tomorrow it will be Socialist [refrain]

Eternal light is reserved for the guerrillas
All of whom gave their lives for peace
By their example the people will be left with
The seeds that they need to become free [refrain]

You live now and always, Tupac Amaru!
In battle you became our immortal son
Los Molinos, example of courage
In the fight for the revolution [refrain]

Dedicated men and women
Are lovers of all humanity
Now they march on, bloodied but alive
Armed with justice, and equality [refrain]

The revolutionary party
Assembles the popular fight
Together, the people and their vanguard
Form the military might [refrain]

You live now and always, Tupac Amaru!
In battle you became our immortal son
Los Molinos, example of courage
In the fight for the revolution [refrain]

The room fell silent for a second before Cerpa addressed his troops.
"Glory and honor to the heroes of Los Molinos!"
"Glory and honor!" the rebels shouted back in unison.
"Glory and honor to the people's heroes of the MRTA!" Cerpa belted.
"Glory and honor!"

"What is the objective of this mission?"

"Free political prisoners!"

"I can't hear you! What is the objective of this mission?"

"Free political prisoners!"

"What is the objective of this mission?" Cerpa asked a third time.

"Free political prisoners!"

Only then did Cerpa move on to the next topic. "One hundred twenty-six days and counting since the sacking of the Japanese Embassy!"

"Never surrender, dammit!"

"One hundred twenty-six days and counting since the sacking of the Japanese Embassy!"

"Never surrender, dammit!"

"With masses and arms!" Cerpa said. "Fatherland or death!"

"Long Live Peru!" they replied.

"With masses and arms! Fatherland or death!"

"Long Live Peru!"[6]

The song was an attempt to establish, musically, the Molinos guerrillas among the pantheon of great national martyrs like Tupac Amaru, Micaela Bastidas, and Luis De La Puente Uceda. That Cerpa's rebels bellowed out the song in response to the security forces' *criolla* music and military anthems added a new layer of melodrama to this Andean opera. Each side attempted to outdo the other, engaging in a kind of pitched musical battle that could last up to eighteen hours a day, beginning each morning earlier than the previous. As Giampietri wrote, "If one day the loudspeakers started playing music at 6 in the morning, the next day the [rebel's] megaphone started at 5:30, and so on and so on."[7]

The battle over these sounds of war was only one of several symbolic tugs-of-war in which the forces of both the MRTA and the state engaged over the course of the standoff now 126 days in the making. Another symbolic battleground involved, as always, the Peruvian and rebel flags. When the rebel occupation was still in its infancy, the Peruvian triband presided over the residence. *La República* put the photo of the still-waving banner on the front page of its 20 December edition with the caption "Flag of Faith." "This Peruvian flag is a symbol of faith in democracy, dialogue and peace," the paper editorialized.[8] The column suggested that as long as the national emblem flew over this and other buildings, a state victory was still possible. Civil society heeded the call. In the days following the takeover, groups of women dressed in white led a march from Miraflores to the steps of the residence, chanting, "We want them freed!" and carrying scores of Peruvian flags on poles over their shoulders.[9]

The Tupac Amaristas responded in kind, tearing down the national colors from the flat terrace and replacing them with the rebel flag bearing Tupac Amaru's likeness. It was the ultimate emblem of their symbolic and physical conquest of the ambassador's space. In the days and weeks to come, the Tupac Amaristas continued to make use of the guerrilla flag, affixing it to windows throughout the manor. Often the rebel flag would appear with other words in all caps listing the rebels' demands or commemorating dates in MRTA history. For instance, on the anniversary of the Cromotex massacre, a favorite date of Cerpa's, the rebels plastered their flag face-out against a window for the media and other spectators to see. Above, the guerrillas had set placards reading, "GLORY AND HONOR TO THE MARTYRED WORKERS OF CROMOTEX, 4 FEB 1979–1997," along with the names of the fallen workers.[10] On this particular April morning, Cerpa's troops prepared more commemorative signs, this time in honor of the upcoming anniversary of the Molinos massacre.[11] As with the anthem and the flag, the signs would serve as a kind of guerrilla calling card designed to insert key moments in the MRTA's historical memory into the wider Peruvian imagination.

After preparing the signs, Cerpa received Canadian ambassador Anthony Vincent. The ambassador had come in his official capacity as a member of the peace commission, hoping to salvage the negotiations that had recently broken down. Vincent found Cerpa alone on the bottom floor of the residence and in a somber mood. After meeting with the ambassador for about forty minutes, Cerpa sent him on his way. To lighten the mood, he called on the Arab, Tito, and a handful of other comrades to join him in a pickup game of soccer right there in the first-floor dining room.[12]

These soccer matches had become a new ritual over the past few weeks, designed to lift spirits and shape bodies. The Tupac Amaristas typically didn't let the hostages join in, keeping them under the watchful eyes of the women rebels, themselves not invited to play, and a handful of others. Cerpa was playing on a bum right foot, having sustained an injury during a previous match. "It's just a little bump, you'll be fine," a Red Cross medic had told him.[13] The game began around 3:00 P.M. La Gringa and Melissa guarded the door while the guys played. They had been going for a good twenty minutes, enough time to loosen up and break a sweat.

And then it happened. An explosion erupted from right under their feet, ripping a hole in the floor amid a cloud of smoke and fire. Tito, who was standing above the detonation, died instantly along with another rebel. Realizing they were under attack, Cerpa, the Arab, and the other players dashed toward the second floor to fetch their weapons. Another explosion tore through the living room, followed almost simultaneously by a third from the study. From the smoky holes emerged a stream of heavily armed commandos, their faces painted in green and black to match their fatigues and helmets. The commandos fired on the fleeing rebels, taking control of the first floor. Another group of invaders arose from a fourth hole in the front lawn, storming through the front door and killing Melissa and La Gringa. As Cerpa scrambled up the curving grand staircase, he caught a stream of bullets to the body, face, and forehead. The rebel hard-liner fell onto his back. His dreams of fighting his way out, of rescuing his imprisoned comrades a second time, of reuniting with his wife, of a future MRTA and a better Peru, died along with him on the bloody stairs.[14]

■ Fujimori had been planning a military operation all along. The president had certainly talked a good game about peace and nonviolence. It turned out that all of it—the overtures to world leaders seeking a peaceful resolution to the crisis, the solemn promises to the families of the hostages that he would not resort to violence, and the creation of the government-sponsored peace commission—had been a stalling tactic while he secretly advanced a military solution. Fujimori had approved the military option in December, within days of the rebel occupation, and the construction of a series of underground tunnels began in early January.[15] Seven meters below the surface, the laborers would load dirt into a police truck and then dump the loads at the SIN base in Las Palmas, where they would await later shipment to the army headquarters in Chorrillos. The planners had installed cables running along the walls and ceiling to bring electricity to the standing fans and lanterns placed throughout the tunnel. They had also reinforced the walls and ceiling with wood beams. Then, officials ordered the construction of an exact replica of the ambassador's residence in a terrain adjoining the SIN and the army First Division so that the soldiers could engage in combat drills in preparation for the rescue.[16]

Only Cerpa and a few other observers in the media took reports of the tunnel seriously. Most had dismissed Cerpa's allegations as pure paranoia.[17] Some news outlets did corroborate the Tupac Amarista's hypothesis in real time, claiming—correctly—that the SIN had orchestrated its construction. "There Really Is a Tunnel," headlined *La República* back in early March.[18] In truth, there were four tunnels, each one leading to a different point of surface inside the embassy compound. Even those who believed in the tunnels' existence, however, thought that their construction had been aborted the moment the guerrillas had discovered the plot. The construction, it turns out, had never stopped. This was why the security forces had insisted on setting up speakers up and down the street. While the symbolic and psychological impact of the noise was certainly part of the calculation, it was only a secondary concern. The first was to muffle the sound of the construction taking place beneath the surface.

On 16 April 1997 Fujimori met with Vladimiro Montesinos and army general Nicolás De Bari Hermoza Ríos, commander of the unit, to go over the final plans for the recue operation. The president agreed that now was the time to put the commandos in the tunnel to await D-Day. They would strike as early as the following afternoon. The 149 commandos waited in the stuffy tunnel for the better part of a week. And then, a little after 3:00 P.M. on 22 April 1997, they received the order. Operation Chavín de Huántar was a go.[19]

Given how early into the hostage crisis Fujimori approved of Operation Chavín de Huántar and the lengths to which his government went to conceal it, it is likely that a military resolution had always been the president's preferred method of resolving the hostage crisis. This does not mean, however, that a violent confrontation was unavoidable. Had Cerpa taken Fidel Castro up on his March 1997 offer of political asylum, the Peruvian president would have had little choice but to call off the operation. The international community, from the press to Western heads of state and the pope, was watching. The Red Cross and other nonpartisan international actors had gotten involved in the negotiations. For Fujimori, whose approval ratings were already plummeting, to go back on his word and send in the proverbial cavalry would have been to commit an act of political suicide on the world stage. Castro's offer was the most opportune moment for Cerpa to recognize that the moment for hard-line guerrilla struggle in Latin America had passed. It was the moment to cut his losses and join the ranks of post–Cold War figures like José Mujica, the former Tupamaro fighter who went on to become a successful politician and beloved president of Uruguay. Instead, Cerpa held the military hard line, preferring to fight his way out of the stalemate. In doing so, he played right into Fujimori's hands, giving the ruthless president all the political cover he needed to green-light the military operation the following month. As Luis Giampietri later marveled, "Fujimori was way colder than Cerpa Cartolini could have ever imagined."[20]

22

Mary Is Sick!

Ever since his January 1997 interrogation by Néstor Cerpa, navy admiral Luis Giampietri enjoyed more freedom of movement inside the residence. During that heated questioning, Giampietri had convinced Cerpa that he posed no real threat. He was simply an old retired sailor. After that, the guerrillas stopped paying much attention to his movements around the antebellum house. Giampietri hoped to use this laxness in security to his advantage.

If his days as a special forces commander had taught him anything, it was that the government would be planning a rescue operation. And if that operation was to stand any chance of success, the agencies would need good intel about the goings-on inside the house. Giampietri knew that, were the shoe on the other foot and he were in charge of the operation, the first thing he would do was smuggle a listening device into one of the many Red Cross carts being brought into the home each day. Of course, as a nonpartisan humanitarian aid agency, the Red Cross would never approve such a course of action. Still, the intelligence community was good, and they could easily attach a listening device to a humanitarian package without the aid workers noticing.

Giampietri also knew that one of his fellow hostages, army commander Roberto Fernández, had been hiding a beeper in his underwear ever since the night of the rebel raid. When, a few days into the assault, the Tupac Amaristas had frisked all the hostages for cell phones, pagers, and other electronic devices, Fernández had stuffed the beeper so snugly under his crotch that it would have taken an act of sexual harassment to find it. Giampietri was one of only a handful of hostages with knowledge of the beeper. Thinking that the device might come in handy some day, Giampietri asked for the corresponding phone number and memorized it.[1] In the weeks following his interrogation, he sneakily picked up every item that made its way into the house and whispered into it.

"This is admiral Giampietri. If you can hear me, page me at the following number."[2]

The admiral waited and waited, but the pager remained stubbornly silent. Meanwhile, he formed a small inner circle to draw up a kind of blueprint of the inside of the building. As luck would have it, one of the hostages was an architect, so he was able to draw the plans to scale. The blueprints indicated where the hostages remained and, equally important, where the Tupac Amaristas tended to stay. But how could they get the plans to the outside? It would be too risky to smuggle them out in anything leaving the house with the Red Cross, as the Arab was meticulous in his inspections. But Marco Miyashiro, one of the members of Giampietri's circle of trust, had an idea.

While Giampietri was assessing the interior of the house, Miyashiro had been taking inventory of the surrounding buildings. Miyashiro knew a thing or two about counterintelligence operations, having led the investigative team that captured Shining Path leader Abimael Guzmán five years earlier. Based on the movement he detected from inside the neighboring houses, he deduced that their occupants had long since been replaced by SIN and DINCOTE agents. It would be a long shot—literally—but if they could find a way to simply toss the blueprints over to a neighboring home, he believed the agents would give them a good look.[3]

Miyashiro and Giampietri, the colonel and the admiral, tied the makeshift map to a rock they found, snuck into the bleach-laden bathroom, and opened the window. They were a stone's throw away from the neighboring house. They knew they would only have one shot. When the coast was clear, they gave the rock a good chuck. It landed right inside the window of the neighboring house. Moments later, the rock and paper came flying back into the ambassador's bathroom, evidently unaltered. There was no way of telling if the recipient had looked at it or not, but it confirmed Miyashiro's theory that whoever was in the house probably worked for the state.[4]

Giampietri continued to test for bugs. It had been weeks since he began whispering into every item that crossed the mansion's threshold, and still nothing from the beeper. The thought occurred to him that the agents had deemed it too risky to page the hostages. If the guerrillas discovered the device, a bloodbath could ensue. He spoke with his inner circle about his predicament. And then Francisco Tudela, the Peruvian chancellor, came up with a brilliant suggestion. By now, the battle of the bands between the state security forces and the MRTA had become a daily ritual.

"Why don't you ask [the agents] to play 'La Cucaracha' when they begin their next musical competition?"[5]

Typically, the music that came out of the loudspeakers was *criolla* music, martial songs, or even classical compositions by the likes of Schubert and Beethoven. If the security forces added "La Cucaracha" to their playlist, it would be no coincidence.

The next morning, the music that blasted out of the speakers was the same as before. The following day fared no better. Giampietri was starting to lose hope. At 6:00 A.M. on the third day, just when the Tupac Amaristas had begun their battle hymn to Molinos, yet another *cumbia* song came blaring over the outside speakers. The dejected sailor listened to the lovesick singer deride his lover. "You're nothing but a cockroach, a *cucaracha*," bemoaned the singer. Giampietri's heart stopped and he perked up. For once, he hung on every note coming out of the noisy speakers. Yes, he had heard correctly. The singer was describing his lover as a cockroach, *la cucaracha*. It wasn't the song he had in mind, the simple jingle sung from Patagonia to Texas, but the song was definitely called "La Cucaracha." This was the confirmation he was looking for. "We knew then that they were listening."[6]

A few days later, SIN agents finally made contact via Fernández's pager. The hostages had since managed to locate the bag where the guerrillas had disposed of the confiscated pagers and cell phones. Rather than steal one of the devices and risk the Tupac Amaristas finding out, the inner circle simply unloaded all the batteries and hid them among themselves. This would ensure that the beeper had power for a good while. The first communication stated that Giampietri would soon be receiving a guitar. Within a few days four guitars made their way into the residence.[7] Bishop Cipriani had hand-delivered some of the instruments on his own.[8] Did the cleric realize he was facilitating a military end to the conflict? Probably not. In all likelihood, he was just as out of the loop as anyone. Three of the guitars became the communal property of the hostages and guerrillas. The fourth had Giampietri's name on it. Written in ink on the wooden frame of the guitar was an inscribed message, written in Marcela's handwriting: "So you can think of me on lonely nights. I love you! Marcela."[9]

It was a sweet gesture, but there was one thing Giampietri knew: it wasn't from Marcela. "I know my wife, but even if it was her handwriting, that's not how she writes," he later wrote. "She would never write something so sappy."[10] Giampietri figured that the agents had dictated the message. Now he had a direct line of communication with the outside. Little did he know that the listening device had been planted inside the guitar case and not in the guitar itself. Fortunately, the instrument was never far from the case, and the frequency was powerful enough to pick up whatever he was whispering anyway.[11]

The guitar was a breakthrough for the SIN agents. They now had an inside man who could give them detailed descriptions of the compound and a blow-by-blow log of where the Tupac Amaristas were at all times. With this information from the admiral's guitar case, they could anticipate the rebels' moves and learn their weaknesses. From that point on, communications between Giampietri and the SIN, via the guitar and, later, a Holy Bible, together with the coded text messages from Fernández's pager, were constant. Giampietri later learned that he had exchanged no fewer than 5,000 communications with intelligence agents in about four months.[12]

Giampietri gave the SIN agents everything they needed. They instructed him via the pager to continue to observe and report and to keep up business as usual so as not to arouse suspicion. When D-Day came, he would be the first to know. His job would be to ensure that all seventy-two hostages were in a safe location on the second floor. H-Hour would come during one of the guerrillas' daily soccer matches. It would be the best chance for a successful operation, as most of the guerrillas would be together on the first floor while the hostages remained upstairs. As April dawned, two separate rescue operations had to be aborted at the last minute because conditions weren't optimal. The agents communicated that the third attempt might occur on the afternoon of 22 April, but this, too, would depend on everything falling the commandos' way. For now, Giampietri should sit tight and try not to arouse suspicion.

Giampietri didn't sleep the night of 21 April. By this time tomorrow he could be free, or dead. He quietly sketched out a last will and testament and slipped it into his pocket.[13]

He was still awake when the guerrillas initiated their daily anthem to Molinos.

At 9:00 A.M., Giampietri whispered the normal report into his Bible. "The sea is a little agitated. It's good fishing. We're down here with the big pigs and little pigs." The code was easy to decipher. "The Sea" was his code name. When Giampietri uttered it, the agents would have confirmation that it was indeed the admiral on the line. The big pigs referred to Cerpa and the other commanders. The little pigs were the subordinates.

"Only the Arab is moving around freely," Giampietri continued. "The rest are down below. The little pigs are mimetizing: one has on an Alianza Lima soccer jersey, the other is sporting Cristal colors, and another is wearing a jersey of the Peruvian national team."[14]

Everything appeared normal on the inside. The guerrillas went about their business and the hostages settled into their daily routines, while Giampietri reported on anything and everything that could be of use to the commandos who were sweating it out three meters below. At around noon, the pager went off again: "This is not an exercise, it is a real operation. Today, during the soccer match, we will come in and rescue you. Using the agreed upon signal, please inform when the match is under way, how many are playing, and how many are on guard."[15] Giampietri's heart skipped a beat. "We soldiers are prepared for these kinds of situations, but that doesn't mean we aren't afraid to die," he later admitted.[16] He informed Fernández and asked to keep the beeper on his person.

The remainder of the day seemed to drag on and speed up at once. Giampietri waited impatiently as the Red Cross delegation arrived, and then for Cerpa's long meeting with Canadian ambassador Vincent. At last, the guerrillas started their match. Giampietri spoke clearly into the Bible: "15:00. Game on; I'm going to verify exactly who is playing." Five minutes went by, and the admiral returned to the line. "15:05. All the piggies are in the sty. The big pig, the three little piggies, and four suckling pigs." After detailing the whereabouts of every single rebel, he said, "Please advise if I can begin preparing the hostages, so I can send them to their posts and make sure no one is out in the halls. I await your orders to open the door [to the terrace]."[17]

It was at this point that Vladimiro Montesinos, the SIN head, phoned the president to request his permission to proceed with the strike.

"Okay, you may proceed," Fujimori said.[18]

After receiving confirmation, Giampietri ran into one of the rooms where Father Wicht and other hostages were playing cards. He solicited their help in opening the doors to the terrace, but they just smiled, thinking it a joke, and returned to their game.

"They are coming to rescue us in three minutes!" Giampietri said. "Stay calm, but I need your help with the doors!"[19]

Realizing he was serious, the hostages sprang into action, loosening the stoppers on the wooden doors so that they could easily swing open during the escape. Giampietri then ran back into the bedroom and got on the floor, along with the other hostages. He could hear helicopters overhead as he made his final report: "I await your orders to open the door. It's 17:14, sorry 15:14." He could hardly think straight. "I can hear helicopters. I'm opening the door. There's one [guerrilla] upstairs, thirteen downstairs. Mary is sick! Mary is sick!" he cried, repeating the code phrase for "anything can happen."

"Then," Giampietri recalled, "I got into my place and asked God for protection."[20]

■ It was about one o'clock when Colonel Denegri cornered Marco Miyashiro and spoke to him in a hushed voice.

"Marco, don't take a nap because today's the day they come and get us."

"Third time's a charm," said Miyashiro.[21] When he saw Giampietri moving nervously in and out of the rooms that afternoon, he could tell this time was different. Giampietri solicited his help in making sure all the hostages were upstairs and in position. Under no circumstances, said the admiral, should the hostages go down to the first floor. Miyashiro was eager to assist. When the first explosion sounded, he began ushering the hostages into the bedroom. With bombs blasting and bullets raining throughout the compound, Marcos, a lazy-eyed insurgent and the sole rebel guarding the hostages during the soccer game, ran over to Miyashiro, weapon raised.

"What's going on?" Marcos asked.

"I don't know," Miyashiro shrugged.

Miyashiro carefully backpedaled into the bedroom, keeping a watchful eye on Marcos, who dashed over to the window to see what was going on. Moments later, another rebel by the name of Coné ran in and pointed his gun at the hostages.

"Go outside! It's not coming from here!" Miyashiro shouted, referring to the gunfire and explosions. Coné turned on his heel and left the room, standing just outside the doorway to guard the entrance.

In all likelihood, Coné was looking for Francisco Tudela, the Peruvian chancellor. The rebels had been told to execute Tudela in the event of a military raid, and Coné was the man charged with carrying out the action. Knowing that he was a marked man, Tudela had already slipped into a room other than the one to which he had been assigned and had taken cover behind one of the columns next to the bathroom. Once the attack got under way, Tudela raced for the door leading to the terrace and scaled the stairs, where a series of commandos were waiting to escort him and the other hostages to freedom. Once the chancellor made it to the top, he crouched down and shuffled forward toward the stairs leading down to the lawn. Apparently, a Tupac Amarista noticed that their number 1 hostage was getting away and lobbed a grenade at him. The grenade bounced off an archway in the middle of the roof, exploding on the spot; it missed Tudela but sent shrapnel flying in his direction. At that moment, a commando named Juan Valer ran forward to insert himself between the chancellor and the Tupac Amarista as the latter opened fire. Valer used his body to shield Tudela as he led him to the stairway at the roof's edge.

The chancellor continued on his run, using the wall for cover as the Tupac Amarista fired from the bedroom. Seconds later, a bullet grazed his right arm and another whizzed past his face, striking the wall and sending shards of cement into his eyes. He had made it so close to freedom, but he was now in the middle of the crossfire. He continued along his path, running on pure adrenaline. He reached the stairway and peered down. A group of camouflaged soldiers awaited him below. The challenge was in reaching them. Bullets continued to rain down, and before he could make it down the stairs, one tore into his left leg. Unlike the previous graze to his arm, this one had struck him true. Still, he plugged forward, down the stairs and into the hands of the commandos. No sooner did he make it into the garden than he heard the chilling words of one of the commanders: "Commander Valer is down!" The soldier had taken a fatal bullet for his chancellor.[22]

Back in the house, Miyashiro, Giampietri, and the other hostages continued to crouch in the corners of the bedrooms. Coné, the cockeyed rebel, was still standing just outside the doorway, blocking the entrance of the commandos. After about a three-minute firefight, Coné finally disappeared from sight, evidently falling in the shootout, and the first commandos entered the room. A navy infantryman approached Giampietri.

"Admiral, we're here to take you home."[23] His words overcame Giampietri, a swirl of emotion and smoke swelling his chest.

The commandos ordered the hostages to make their way toward the rooftop via the second-floor staircase. Giampietri, Miyashiro, and the other hostages followed the commandos up the stairs to the terrace. As soon as he smelled fresh air, Giampietri could taste imminent freedom. He got on his knees, crawling across the roof to make himself a smaller target. He was so focused on the ground ahead of him that he didn't even notice commando Valer's body lying there. He had to take the staircase into the yard with some difficulty, as commandos kept climbing past him. When he reached the garden, he was met by a cluster of navy infantry, "my people." He had never been more proud to be in the navy.[24]

Marco Miyashiro wasn't far behind. Reaching the rooftop, he hunched down and followed the line of hostages down the stairs and onto the front lawn, where dozens of other hostages had already assembled. Out of the corner of his eye, he could see Chancellor Tudela laid out on a stretcher. The chancellor was wounded, but he was still alive, offering a thumbs-up to the quickly assembling press corps. So, for that matter, was Miyashiro. After

126 days of captivity, he was free—free to return to his wife, free to eat ceviche and smoke cigarettes whenever he pleased, and yes, free to cut his hair.[25]

■ Smoke rose into the sky from the house on Thomas Edison Street. Two of the 140 commandos, Valer and Raúl Jiménez Chávez, were carried out on green stretchers, having given their lives to save those of their fellow countrymen. Miraculously, all seventy-two hostages made it out of the compound alive, although one, Supreme Court Justice Carlos Giusti, would later die of complications due to hemorrhaging from a bullet wound to his leg.

None of the fourteen Tupac Amaristas survived the assault. Later forensics reports, together with at least one eyewitness testimony from a rescued hostage, suggested that some of the rebels had been killed extrajudicially. Realizing that they were outnumbered and outgunned, these guerrillas had dropped their weapons and surrendered during the attack. According to this version of events, the commandos then marched them to a location in the compound and killed them with close-range bullets to the head.[26]

None of that seemed to matter now. A general mood of patriotic effervescence filled the smoky air as news teams, many of which had been posted on the surrounding rooftops and lawns, captured the atmosphere in real time. The entire nation watched transfixed as two commandos walked over to the corner of the roof from which the MRTA flag still waved. One commando supported a ladder while his partner climbed onto the edge and unpinned the rebel flag from its pole. Once he had jogged it loose, he emphatically discarded the flag onto the terrace floor. The two soldiers took great pride in grinding their grimy combat boots over the banner, and then, as if it had always been the plan, one of them picked the flag back up and flicked it off the roof. His colleagues watched as the cloth drifted down, down, down, to the garden floor. The thirteen-year-long game of "capture the flag," which the guerrillas had initiated back in 1984 by stealing the battle flag of San Martín, was over. The state had triumphed in the end.

Never one to miss a public relations triumph, Fujimori arrived on the scene in no time looking as if he had personally participated in the operation. He sported a white button-down shirt with the top button undone and the sleeves rolled up. A bulletproof vest hugged his shirt, and he carried a walkie-talkie. Microphone in hand and cameras rolling, the bespectacled president stood before hostages and commandos alike and gave a not-so-impromptu speech reminding them of his solemn pledge to never give in to terrorists.

"I promised, and I delivered," Fujimori said.

Operation Chavín de Huántar, 1997 (photo by Oscar Medrano, *Caretas*, with kind permission)

Later, Fujimori saw each prisoner onto a bus bound for the hospital and hopped aboard. Crowds of jubilant spectators lined the sidewalks as the president made his victory lap. Fujimori hung out of the open doorway like a young bus-driver's assistant. Smiling from ear to ear, he hung off the open passenger door waving the Peruvian flag. The flag flapped proudly in the president's hands as the bus barreled down the city streets.

And just like that, Alberto Fujimori went from goat to hero. Within two days of the operation, polls showed him sitting on a comfortable 67 percent approval rating, an incredible thirty-point swing in the span of a few days. Roughly nine out of ten Peruvians supported the action of the armed forces, and 86 percent approved of the role that Vladimiro Montesinos's SIN played in the affair.[27] The international community praised the action as a textbook counterinsurgency measure, and a beaming Fujimori offered to share his tactics and technology with heads of state from around the world.[28] The president took full credit for the operation, claiming, improbably enough, that the idea to build an underground tunnel resembling the pre-Columbian archaeological site Chavín de Huántar had come to him in a dream.[29] In all likelihood, the operations' planners were simply copying the same strategy that the Tupac Amaristas had used to escape from Canto Grande prison seven years earlier. Back then, a tunnel had delivered them salvation. Now, a tunnel had sealed their doom.

Conclusion

Alberto Fujimori slowly made his way up the curving grand staircase in the ambassador's home. The bodies of Néstor Cerpa and his comrades, some shirtless and others still sporting soccer jerseys, were still warm, sprawled across the carpeted green steps just as they fallen. The president, in his white-collared shirt and red power tie, his sleeves rolled up to convey a man of action, sidestepped the vanquished rebels, grazing the wooden rail with his hand as he gawked at their blood-soaked corpses.

It was one of the greatest moments of his presidency, surpassed only by the 1992 capture of Shining Path ringleader Abimael Guzmán. Yet whereas Guzmán had been captured alive, his insurgency continuing for years without him, this moment had a mark of finality. Cerpa and his beleaguered band of brothers were all dead, and so was, by all appearances, the MRTA. Operation Chavín de Huántar was the symbolic death knell not just for the Tupac Amaru Revolutionary Movement but also for the Peruvian Cold War. It didn't matter that small bands of Tupac Amaristas continued to fight following their comrades' defeat in the ambassador's home, or that the group itself wouldn't officially recognize its defeat for another twenty years. Nor did it matter that Shining Path continued to fight on, in various forms, up through the writing of this book. While Fujimori would later attempt to use these facts to justify remaining in power beyond his constitutional term limit, for the time being he was content to let the optics of his stairway climb say it all. The rebels had been laid out, annihilated, defeated. The nation, personified by its multicultural everyman, was still standing, headed up, up, up toward the future, toward progress, toward peace.

In the months and years to come, 22 April 1997 would enter collective memory as one of the greatest moments in Peruvian history. On that date, so the story went, brave young patriot men—every one of them a father, a brother, a son—saved the nation from the evils of domestic terrorism. There would be songs, moments of silence, survivor testimonies, and commemorative buttons. Members of the armed forces and intelligence community would write books touting their role in this piece of Peruvian history.[1] To commemorate the tenth anniversary of the operation, acclaimed journalist Umberto Jara would write a popular book, reprinted a decade later, about the "heroism of the Operation Chavín de Huántar Commandos, 149 men who carried out what went down as one of the most brilliant rescue operations in world history." This operation, Jara wrote, "succeeded in saving seventy-one lives, liquidating the MRTA and restoring for Peru the dignity to live in peace."[2] The replica of the ambassador's residence, which had been used by the military in preparation for the rescue operation, would be converted into a museum where visitors could walk the president's steps up the grand stairway, inspect a replica Operation Chavín de Huántar tunnel, or view an exhibit of a "terrorist" mannequin as if it were a relic of some long-vanquished civilization. The names of all the Chavín de Huántar commandos would be on full display inside this museum, with a special room and short film dedicated to the operation's two martyrs. Large posters of fierce-looking infantrymen adorned the museum's outer wall, their faces painted in the red and white of the national flag.[3]

■ The story of Peru's Tupac Amaru Revolutionary Movement is, in many ways, the story of Latin America's Cold War left. It is made up of the voices of women like Lucero Cumpa and Esperanza Tapia, who confronted gender discrimination on a daily basis but still fought for a more equitable revolution; of men like Tigre, who objected to his leaders' mistreatment of indigenous people; of rural boys like Daniel Bravo and Rodrigo Gálvez, who took up arms against a military that violated human rights; and of political operatives like Javier Caminero and Alberto Gálvez, who advocated compromise and democratization. Sometimes these individuals were more successful than others, but they never stopped trying to forge a more inclusive, democratic, social-justice-oriented movement and society. This was the case with Peru's MRTA, and it was the case for much of the Latin American left during this period.

What began as a struggle against imperialism, dictatorship, and social injustice gradually gave way to the impulses of the most authoritarian, truculent wing of the party. This, too, is part of the story of the Latin American Cold War. In Cuba, the cradle of Latin America's Cold War revolutions, Fidel Castro discursively championed gender equality even while his rebels practiced a culture of militant masculinity.[4] In Allende's Chile, as historian Marian Schlotterbeck observes, the MIR's Santiago-based leadership overlooked the democratizing efforts of its grassroots supporters to push through a dogmatic, militant platform.[5] In Peru, too, the rise of Shining Path's "Gonzalo Thought" and its "blood quota" of war came only after Abimael Guzmán purged the party of would-be compromisers.[6] The MRTA's replacement of social justice and democratic socialism with a more draconian revolutionary model thus followed a familiar trajectory of Cold War politics. Party hard-liners believed that, in a late-twentieth-century context in which U.S. imperialism enjoyed such vast reach and the capitalist class held such entrenched power, only the most ideologically and militarily committed vanguard could bring about revolutionary change. These militants were willing to do whatever it took to achieve these aims, even if it meant abandoning the participatory politics and human rights protections in which they believed. In Peru, as elsewhere, the democratizing wing found itself sidelined by its most autocratic, combative sector.

More than anything, the story of the MRTA is a cautionary tale. At various points throughout the MRTA's insurrectionary history, political circumstances presented the rebels with opportunities to put their democratizing rhetoric into practice. This occurred in 1985, when Peruvian voters sent the Aprista leader Alan García into the presidential palace with a mandate to carry out his anti-imperialist, populist agenda. Rather than lay down arms and join the ranks of the growing legal left, the MRTA leadership offered a perfunctory truce and continued to attack nongovernmental targets. In the late 1980s, with most of their core leaders behind bars, regional commanders overlooked the socially progressive statutes of the MRTA national congress and instead began killing party defectors, indigenous villagers, members of the LGBTQ community, and other civilians. Then, in 1990, after staging the most spectacular prison break in Latin American history, Víctor Polay suppressed his own political instinct to democratize, instead placating party hard-liners and consolidating his own authority in the rebel leadership. This refusal to lay down arms and democratize is what led to the arrest of Miguel Rincón and his band of fighters in 1995 and to the tragedy in the Japanese Embassy two years later. For the MRTA, the bigger tragedy was that the leadership's failure to incorporate the demands of its most socially progressive, democratic members precipitated the group's political demise. The story of Peru's Tupac Amaru Revolutionary Movement is thus the story of what happens when a political movement allows itself to be hijacked by the most militant, ideologically inflexible voices within it.

■ Some of the hostages went on to lives of prominence after their rescue at the Japanese Embassy. Francisco Tudela returned to his chancellor's post and gave powerful speeches in honor of his rescuers. Luis Giampietri wrote a popular book about his days of captivity and would become vice president under none other than Alan García.[7] Marco Miyashiro, who made a living capturing Tupac Amaristas before he lived in captivity under them, would be promoted to general and head up National Security before being elected to congress as a member of Fujimori's political party, Fuerza Popular.

None of the MRTA's political enemies fared well after the war. Despite overseeing one of the worst economic recessions the nation had ever seen, losing ground to Shining Path, and conceding a dramatic prison break, Alan García distanced himself from his checkered past and was reelected in 2006. Thirteen years later, however, he became the latest in a growing list of Latin American political figures—among them Alberto Fujimori's daughter, Keiko—ensnared in the bribery and money-laundering scandal involving the Brazilian construction conglomerate Odebrecht. Faced with the near-certainty of spending his remaining days behind bars, García, sixty-nine, locked himself in his bedroom and took his own life.

Alberto Fujimori also underwent a fall from grace as meteoric as his rise. Enjoying unprecedented approval after the Chavín de Huántar operation, Fujimori removed presidential term limits to run for an unprecedented and unconstitutional third term in 2000. He won the majority of the popular vote, despite claims of widespread fraud. Shortly after his victory, however, videos surfaced of Vladimiro Montesinos, his chief advisor and head of the SIN, bribing politicians, military commanders, and media figures with stacks of cash in exchange for their loyalty. The president feigned outrage over these so-called Vladivideos, ordering an international manhunt for his onetime confidant. Montesinos was arrested in Venezuela and returned to Peru to stand trial. His conviction led him to the naval prison, where he would become Víctor Polay's newest cellblock mate. Fujimori's effort to save his own neck by throwing his spy chief under the bus didn't take, however, and tens of thousands of citizens took to the streets to demand his resignation.

Fujimori fled the country to his ancestral Japan, tendering his resignation via fax on 20 November 2000, just four months into his third term. Ambition got the better of him, however, and in 2007 Chilean authorities arrested him trying to reenter the country in an apparent effort to run for a fourth term. Extradited to Peru, Fujimori was tried and convicted on various charges of corruption and human rights violations. In an apparent quid pro quo deal, President Pedro Pablo Kuczynski, himself a onetime foil of the MRTA, pardoned the seventy-nine-year-old ex-president in 2017 before stepping down amid his own corruption scandal involving Odebrecht. The pardon was short lived, however, and the following year the Supreme Court reversed the pardon and ordered the cancer-stricken ex-president back to jail.

Following Fujimori's 2000 resignation, an interim government headed by Valentín Paniagua saw to the democratic transition. Paniagua established the CVR to investigate the many atrocities committed during the civil war. Made up of academics, human rights attorneys, ecclesiastics, and military leaders, the CVR found that more than 69,000 people had perished during the conflict, far more than even the most liberal estimates at the time. The CVR found Shining Path responsible for over half of the casualties, a departure from previous Latin American civil wars in which state forces committed the majority of the atrocities. The CVR did hold government forces responsible for slightly less than half of the deaths and disappearances, finding the MRTA responsible for less than 2 percent.[8]

Alejandro Toledo, the man who took office following the national elections, had also been among the MRTA hostages at the Japanese ambassador's residence in 1996. The Stanford-educated mestizo ran on a campaign of justice and anticorruption, delivering neither. His government did allow for a retrial of convicted guerrilla heads, the so-called *megajuicio*, or megatrial, since they had been arrested and convicted without due process. The state brought out the usual suspects: Víctor Polay, Alberto Gálvez, Peter Cárdenas, Miguel Rincón, and Lucero Cumpa, among others. All were found guilty. Only Alberto Gálvez renounced his membership in the group; he would be released in 2015. As of 2020, Gálvez was living a quiet life in Chorrillos, dedicating himself mostly to writing and translating from English, a language he taught himself during his twenty-seven years in prison. Peter Cárdenas was also released after completing his sentence around the same time as Gálvez. He moved to his ancestral Sweden and also avoided the spotlight. Lucero Cumpa, Miguel Rincón, and Víctor Polay were still in prison as of the writing of this book. In 2019, all of them, Gálvez and Cárdenas included, faced new charges, accused of orchestrating the hate-crime killing of homosexuals in San Martín during the war. As most of them were already in prison at the time the crimes were committed, they maintained that these charges were simply a ploy to keep them from ever seeing the light of day or, as in Gálvez's and Cárdenas's cases, to return them to prison.

Lower-ranking Tupac Amaristas have had a slightly better fate, but only slightly. Daniel, Tigre, and Esperanza all served more than two decades behind bars and are now living quiet lives as ex-cons and convicted terrorists. Daniel returned to his native San Martín, finally living out his once-fleeting dream of becoming a farmer. Tigre married, had two children, and lived briefly in a Lima shantytown before relocating to Arequipa. Esperanza reconciled with her aging father and hoped to one day meet Dolores, the woman whose life she saved.

Some former combatants have spent more years in prison than comrades like Rodrigo Gálvez spent alive. Today, Rodrigo's younger brother keeps his memory alive, maintaining a black-and-white photograph of him inside a golden picture frame with cracked glass. Dressed in the camouflage fatigues and cap of a MRTA guerrilla, young Rodrigo receives a glass of water from a jungle villager, a sparkle in his eye behind the broken glass.

Notes

ABBREVIATIONS IN THE NOTES
In addition to the abbreviations and acronyms used in the text, the following appear in the notes.

ADP   Archivo de la Defensoría del Pueblo (commonly known as the Archivo de la Comisión de la Verdad), Lima, Peru
APJP   Archivo del Poder Judicial del Perú, Lima

Unless otherwise noted, all interviews were conducted by the author. Transcripts/recordings are in the author's possession.

INTRODUCTION

1. Servicio de Inteligencia Nacional [SIN], Grabación secreta del interior de la embajada japonesa [audio], 22 April 1997 (personal archive of Luis Giampietri, Callao, Peru).

2. "La hora cero," *Caretas* 1462 (25 April 1997): 18–19; ADP, Unidad Investigaciones 100337, Chavín de Huántar, Tomo 1.1, SC049501, Manifestación de Francisco Tudela, 3 August 2003.

3. Pablo Brum, *The Robin Hood Guerrillas: The Epic Journey of Uruguay's Tupamaros* (self-published, 2014); Patricia Lara, *Siembra vientos y recogerás tempestades* (Bogotá: Planeta, 2014); Roberto Regalado Álvarez, *FMLN: Un gran tsunami de votos rojos* (San Salvador: Ocean Sur, 2011).

4. Gustavo Gorriti, *The Shining Path: A History of the Millenarian War in Peru*, trans. Robin Kirk (Chapel Hill: University of North Carolina Press, 1999); Carlos Iván Degregori, *El surgimiento de Sendero Luminoso: Ayacucho, 1969–1979* (Lima: Instituto de Estudios Peruanos, 1990); David Scott Palmer, ed., *Shining Path of Peru* (New York: St. Martin's Press, 1994); Deborah Poole and Gerardo Rénique, *Peru: Time of Fear* (Nottingham: Latin America Bureau, 1992); Simon Strong, *Shining Path: The World's Deadliest Revolutionary Force* (Hammersmith: Harper Collins, 1992).

5. Carlos Iván Degregori, José Coronel, Ponciano Del Pino, and Orin Starn, *Las rondas campesinas y la derrota de Sendero Luminoso* (Lima: Instituto de Estudios Peruanos, 1996); Orin Starn, "Villagers at Arms: War and Counterrevolution in the Central-South Andes," in *Shining and Other Paths: War and Society in Peru, 1980–1995*, ed. Steve J. Stern (Durham: Duke University Press, 1998); Nelson Manrique, "The War for the Central Sierra," in Stern, *Shining and Other Paths*; Mario Fumerton, *From Victims to Heroes: Peasant Counter-rebellion and Civil War in Ayacucho, Peru, 1980–2000* (Amsterdam: Rozenberg, 2002); Carlos Tapia, *Autodefensa armada del campesinado* (Lima: Centro de Estudios para el Desarrollo y la Pacificación, 1995).

6. For a journalistic account, see Carlos Paredes, *La hora final: La verdad sobre la captura de Abimael Guzmán* (Lima: Planeta, 2017). For accounts from the security forces community, see Benedicto Jiménez Bacca, *La captura del Presidente Gonzalo* (Lima: Ediciones Rivadeneyra, 2012); Guillermo Bonilla Arévalo, *Golpe Mortal: La verdadera historia de la Pacificación Nacional, Rompiendo Mitos* (self-published, 2015); and Vladimiro Montesinos, *SIN Sendero: Alerta temprana* (Lima: Editorial Rodhas, 2018), vol. 1.

7. Robin Kirk, *The Monkey's Paw: New Chronicles from Peru* (Amherst: University of Massachusetts Press, 1997); Catherine M. Conaghan, *Fujimori's Peru: Deception in the Public Sphere* (Pittsburgh: University of Pittsburgh Press, 2005); Jo-Marie Burt, *Political Violence and the Authoritarian State in Peru: Silencing Civil Society* (New York: Palgrave MacMillan, 2007); Carlos Iván Degregori, *La década de la antipolítica: Auge y huida de Alberto Fujimori y Vladimiro Montesinos* (Lima: Instituto de Estudios Peruanos, 2001); Fernando Rospigliosi, *Montesinos y las fuerzas armadas: Cómo control durante una década las instituciones militares* (Lima: Instituto de Estudios Peruanso, 2000); Julio Cotler and Romeo Grompone, *El fujimorismo: Ascenso y caída de un régimen autoritario* (Lima: Instituto de Estudios Peruanos, 2001); Coletta Youngers, *Violencia política y sociedad civil en el Perú* (Lima: Instituto de Estudios Peruanos, 2003).

8. CVR, *Informe Final*, 9 vols. (Lima: CVR, 2003), 1:31.

9. Caroline Yezer, "Who Wants to Know? Rumors, Suspicions, and Opposition to Truth-Telling in Ayacucho," *Latin American and Caribbean Ethnic Studies* 3, no. 3 (November 2008): 271–89.

10. Cynthia E. Milton, ed., *Art from a Fractured Past: Memory and Truth-Telling in Post–Shining Path Peru* (Durham: Duke University Press, 2014); Edilberto Jiménez, *Chungui: Violencia y trazos de memoria* (Lima: Instituto de Estudios Peruanos, 2010); Oscar Medrano Pérez and Roberto J. Bustamante Flores, *Nunca más! Los anos de crueldad: El terrorismo en el Perú* (Lima: Fondo Editorial del Congreso del Perú, 2015); Jonathan Ritter, *We Bear Witness with Our Song: The Politics of Music and Violence in the Peruvian Andes* (New York: Oxford University Press, forthcoming); Juan Carlos Ubilluz, Alexandra Hibbett, and Víctor Vich, *Contra el sueño de los justos: La violencia peruana ante la violencia política* (Lima: Instituto de Estudios Peruanos, 2018); María Eugenia Ulfe, *Cajones de la memoria: La historia reciente del Perú a través de los retablos andinos* (Lima: Pontificia Universidad Católica del Perú, 2011).

11. See, for example, Kimberly Theidon, *Intimate Enemies: Violence and Reconciliation in Peru* (Philadelphia: University of Pennsylvania Press, 2013); Olga M. González, *Unveiling Secrets of War in the Peruvian Andes* (Chicago: University of Chicago Press, 2011); Carlos Iván Degregori, Tamia Portugal Teillier, Gabriel Salazar Borja, and Renzo Aroni Sulca, *No hay mañana sin ayer: Batallas por la memoria y consolidación democrática en el Perú* (Lima: Instituto de Estudios Peruanos, 2015); William P. Mitchell, *Voices from the Global Margin: Confronting Poverty and Inventing New Lives in the Andes* (Austin: University of Texas Press, 2006); and Hillel David Soifer and Alberto Vergara, eds., *Politics after Violence: Legacies of the Shining Path Conflict in Peru* (Austin: University of Texas Press, 2019).

12. Stern, *Shining and Other Paths*.

13. Cecilia Méndez, *The Plebeian Republic: The Huanta Rebellion and the Making of the Peruvian State, 1820–1850* (Durham: Duke University Press, 2005); Jaymie Patricia Heilman, *Before the Shining Path: Politics in Rural Ayacucho, 1895–1980* (Stanford: Stanford University Press, 2010); Ponciano Del Pino, *En nombre del gobierno: El Perú y Uchuraccay: Un siglo de política campesina* (Juliaca: La Siniestra, 2017); Ponciano Del Pino and Caroline Yezer, eds.,

Las formas del recuerdo: Etnografías de la violencia política en el Perú (Lima: Instituto de Estudios Peruanos, 2013); Lewis Taylor, *Shining Path: Guerrilla War in Peru's Northern Highlands, 1980–1997* (Liverpool: Liverpool University Press, 2006); José Luis Rénique, *Incendiar la pradera: Un ensayo sobre la revolución en el Perú* (Juliaca: La Sieniestra, 2015); Miguel La Serna, *The Corner of the Living: Ayacucho on the Eve of the Shining Path Insurgency* (Chapel Hill: University of North Carolina Press, 2012); Nelson Manrique, *El tiempo del miedo: La violencia política en el Perú, 1980–1996* (Lima: Fondo Editorial del Congreso del Perú, 2002); Ricardo Caro Cárdenas, "'La comunidad es base, trinchera de la guerra popular': Izquierda, campesinismo y lucha armada Huancavelica, 1974–1982," *Bulletin de L'Institut francais d'Etudes Andines* 43, no. 2 (2014): 265–83.

14. Cynthia E. Milton, *Conflicted Memory: Military Cultural Interventions and the Human Rights Era in Peru* (Madison: University of Wisconsin Press, 2018); Paulo Drinot, "Contested Memories of the Peruvian Internal Armed Conflict," in Soifer and Vergara, *Politics after Violence*; Carlos Aguirre, "Terruco de m . . . Insulto y stigma en la guerra sucia peruana," *Histórica* 35, no. 1 (2011): 103–39.

15. Abimael Guzmán, *De puño y letra* (Los Olivos: Manoalzada, 2009); Abimael Guzmán and Elena Yparraguirre, *Memorias desde Némesis* (self-published, 2015).

16. Gonzalo Portocarrero, *Profetas del odio: Raíces culturales y líderes de Sendero Luminoso* (Lima: Pontificia Universidad Católica del Perú, 2012); Santiago Roncagliolo, *La cuarta espada: La historia de Abimael Guzmán y Sendero Luminoso* (Buenos Aires: Debate, 2007); Umberto Jara, *Abimael: El Sendero del terror* (Lima: Planeta, 2017).

17. For succinct syntheses of the Shining Path war, see, for example, José Luis Rénique and Adrián Lerner, "Shining Path: The Last Peasant War in the Andes," in Soifer and Vergara, *Politics after Violence*, and Miguel La Serna, "Revolutions and Violence," in *The Andean World*, ed. Linda J. Seligmann and Kathleen Fine-Dare (London: Routledge, 2019). For more comprehensive narrative histories, see Antonio Zapata, *La guerra senderista: Hablan los enemigos* (Lima: Taurus, 2017); Orin Starn and Miguel La Serna, *The Shining Path: Love, Madness, and Revolution in the Andes* (New York: Norton, 2019); and Renzo Aroní, "Beyond Ideology: The Senderistas' Memories about the 1992 Huamanquiquia Massacre" (paper presented at the Latin American Studies Association Congress, Boston, 24–27 May 2019).

18. Carlos Iván Degregori, *How Difficult It Is to Be God: Shining Path's Politics of War in Peru, 1980–1999* (Madison: University of Wisconsin Press, 2012), 87.

19. See, for example, Kirk, *Monkey's Paw*; Theidon, *Intimate Enemies*, esp. chaps. 5–6; Ponciano Del Pino, "Family, Culture, and 'Revolution': Everyday Life with Sendero Luminoso," in Stern, *Shining and Other Paths*; Isabel Coral Cordero, "Women in War: Impact and Responses," in Stern, *Shining and Other Paths*; and Ponciano Del Pino and Kimberly Theidon, "Las políticas de identidad: Narrativas de guerra y la construcción de ciudadanía en Ayacucho," "Hacerse macho: La participación de la mujer campesina en los Comités de Autodefensa durante la guerra contraterrorista (Perú, 1980–2000)" (paper presented at the Latin American Studies Association Congress, Boston, 24–27 May 2019).

20. Robin Kirk, *Grabado en piedra: Las mujeres de Sendero Luminoso* (Lima: Instituto de Estudios Peruanos, 1993).

21. Zapata, *La guerra senderista*; Starn and La Serna, *The Shining Path*; Jaymie Patricia Heilman, "Family Ties: The Political Genealogy of Shining Path's Comrade Norah," *Bulletin of Latin American Research* 29, no. 2 (2010): 155–69.

22. A notable exception is the Ph.D. dissertation by historian Mario Miguel Meza, "El Movimiento Revolucionario Túpac Amaru (MRTA) y las fuentes de la revolución en América Latina" (El Colegio de México, 2012), which situates the rise of the MRTA within a deeper history of the Peruvian left.

23. Degregori, *How Difficult*, 87–89.

24. Portocarrero, *Profetas del odio*, 157–59.

25. José Carlos Agüero, *Los rendidos: Sobre el don de perdonar* (Lima: Instituto de Estudios Peruanos, 2015); Lurgio Gavilán Sánchez, *When Rains Became Floods: A Child Soldier's Story*, trans. Margaret Randall (Durham: Duke University Press, 2015).

26. Some of this work is under way for Shining Path. See, for example, Aroní, "Beyond Ideology," and Charles F. Walker, "Inocencia: Los menores de edad, El Juzgado de Menores, y Sendero Luminoso, Huamanga, 1980–1986" (paper presented at the Latin American Studies Association Congress, Boston, 24–27 May 2019).

27. Michelle Chase, *Revolution within the Revolution: Women and Gender Politics in Cuba, 1952–1962* (Chapel Hill: University of North Carolina Press, 2015).

28. Gilbert M. Joseph, "What We Know and Should Know: Bringing Latin America More Meaningfully into Cold War Studies," in *In from the Cold: Latin America's New Encounter with the Cold War*, ed. Gilbert M. Joseph and Daniela Spenser (Durham: Duke University Press, 2008), 17.

29. Daniela Spenser, "Standing Conventional Cold War History on Its Head," in Joseph and Spenser, *In from the Cold*, 381.

30. See, for example, Elizabeth Jelin, *State Repression and the Labors of Memory* (Minneapolis: University of Minnesota Press, 2003); Peter Winn et al., eds., *No hay mañana sin ayer: Batallas por la memoria histórica en el Cono Sur* (Lima: Instituto de Estudios Peruanos, 2013); and Steve J. Stern, *The Memory Box of Pinochet's Chile*, 3 vols. (Durham: Duke University Press, 2006, 2010).

31. Anthony D. Smith, *The Ethnic Origins of Nations* (Oxford: Basil Blackwell, 1988), 15.

32. Pierre Nora, ed., *Realms of Memory: The Construction of the French Past*, 3 vols. (New York: Columbia University Press, 1996).

33. For a critique of press coverage of Shining Path, Peru's other major guerrilla group, see Víctor Peralta, *Sendero Luminoso y la prensa, 1980–1994* (Lima: Sur, 2000).

34. Shane Greene, *Punk and Revolution: Seven More Interpretations of Peruvian Reality* (Durham: Duke University Press, 2016), 123–24.

CHAPTER 1

1. "Asaltan banco y se llevan metralleta y diez millones," *La República*, 1 June 1982, 10; CVR, *Informe Final*, 9 vols. (Lima: CVR, 2003), 2:385.

2. Mario Miguel Meza, "El Movimiento Revolucionario Túpac Amaru (MRTA) y las fuentes de la revolución en América Latina" (Ph.D. diss., El Colegio de México, 2012), 15–16.

3. See Peter F. Klarén, *Modernization, Dislocation, and Aprismo: Origins of the Peruvian Aprista Party, 1860–1932* (Austin: University of Texas Press, 1973), and Iñigo García-Bryce, *Haya de la Torre and the Pursuit of Power in Twentieth-Century Peru and Latin America* (Chapel Hill: University of North Carolina Press, 2018).

4. García-Bryce, *Haya de la Torre*, 43.

5. García-Bryce, *Haya de la Torre*, 43–44, 60–66.

6. García-Bryce, *Haya de la Torre*, 70–73.

7. García-Bryce, *Haya de la Torre*, 80.

8. Interview with Otilia Campos, Miraflores, 13 March 2018.

9. Francisco Matos, "Lazos de sangre," *La República*, 23 February 1997, 14–15.

10. Víctor Polay Campos, "Desde la prisión, Polay responde: Un balance del MRTA" (unpublished manuscript, 2017), "Mis origenes familiares y el APRA," point 5.

11. Interview with Otilia Campos.

12. Interview with Otilia Campos.

13. Interview with Otilia Campos.

14. Campos, "Desde la prisión," "Mis orígenes," point 5.

15. Interview with Otilia Campos.

16. Campos, "Desde la prisión," "Mis orígenes," point 4.

17. Campos, "Desde la prisión," "Mis orígenes," point 5.

18. Interview with Otilia Campos.

19. Campos, "Desde la prisión," "Mis orígenes," point 6.

20. Interview with Otilia Campos.

21. Interview with Marco Miyashiro, Miraflores, 30 May 2015; Campos, "Desde la prisión," "Mis orígenes," point 8.

22. Campos, "Desde la prisión," "Mis orígenes," point 14; interview with Otilia Campos.

23. Campos, "Desde la prisión," "Mis orígenes," point 15.

24. Ernesto Che Guevara, *Guerrilla Warfare* (Melbourne: Ocean Press, 2006).

25. For more on the military regime and its policies, see Cynthia McClintock, *Peasant Cooperatives and Political Change in Peru* (Princeton: Princeton University Press, 1982); Abraham F. Lowenthal, ed., *The Peruvian Experiment: Continuity and Change under Military Rule* (Princeton: University of Princeton Press, 1975); Cynthia McClintock and Abraham F. Lowenthal, eds., *The Peruvian Experiment Reconsidered* (Princeton: Princeton University Press, 1983); Enrique Mayer, *Ugly Stories of the Peruvian Agrarian Reform* (Durham: Duke University Press, 2009); and Carlos Aguirre and Paulo Drinot, eds., *The Peculiar Revolution: Rethinking the Peruvian Experiment under Military Rule* (Austin: University of Texas Press, 2017).

26. Campos, "Desde la prisión," "Mis orígenes," point 16.

27. Campos, "Desde la prisión," "Mis orígenes," point 17; interview with Otilia Campos.

28. Interview with Otilia Campos.

29. Campos, "Desde la prisión," "Mis orígenes," point 17; "Polay Confiesa," *Caretas* 1044 (13 February 1989): 80.

30. Interview with Otilia Campos.

31. Interview with Otilia Campos.

32. Interview with Otilia Campos.

33. Meza, "El Movimiento Revolucionario Túpac Amaru," 135.

34. See Jan Lust, *Lucha revolucionaria Perú, 1958–1967* (Barcelona: RBA Libros, 2013).

35. See José Luis Rénique, "De la traición aprista al gesto heroico: Luis de la Puente y la guerrilla del MIR," *Ecuador Debate* 67, no. 7 (April 2006): 77–97.

36. Campos, "Desde la prisión," "Mis orígenes," point 17, and "Mi militancia en el MIR," points 24–25.

37. Interview with Otilia Campos; "Polay confiesa," 80.

38. Campos, "Desde la prisión," "Mis orígenes," point 22.

39. Campos, "Desde la prisión," "Mi militancia," point 30.

40. Campos, "Desde la prisión," "Mi militancia," point 32.

41. See Tamara Feinstein, "How the Left Was Lost: Remembering *Izquierda Unida* and the Legacies of Political Violence in Peru" (Ph.D. diss., University of Wisconsin, Madison, 2013).

42. See Gustavo Gorriti, *The Shining Path: A History of the Millenarian War in Peru*, trans. Robin Kirk (Chapel Hill: University of North Carolina Press, 1999).

43. See Miguel La Serna, *The Corner of the Living: Ayacucho on the Eve of the Shining Path Insurgency* (Chapel Hill: University of North Carolina Press, 2012), chap. 4.

44. Orin Starn and Miguel La Serna, *The Shining Path: Love, Madness, and Revolution in the Andes* (New York: Norton, 2019), 84–102.

45. La Serna, *Corner of the Living*, chap. 5.

46. Starn and La Serna, *The Shining Path*, 148–53.

47. See Carlos Iván Degregori, *How Difficult It Is to Be God: Shining Path's Politics of War in Peru, 1980–1999* (Madison: University of Wisconsin Press, 2012).

48. Campos, "Desde la prisión," "La fundación del MRTA," point 40.

49. Aldo Marchesi, *Latin America's Radical Left: Rebellion and Cold War in the Global 1960s* (Cambridge: Cambridge University Press, 2017), 23–59.

50. MRTA, "Diles que no hemos muerto," in MRTA, *Conquistando el porvenir: Con las masas y las armas. Notas sobre la historia del MRTA* (Lima: MRTA, 1990), 198.

51. See Charles F. Walker, *The Tupac Amaru Rebellion* (Cambridge: Harvard University Press, 2014).

52. Chilip Corrigan and Derek Sayer, *The Great Arch: English State Formation as Cultural Revolution* (Oxford: Basil Blackwell, 1985).

53. Charles F. Walker, "The General and His Rebel: Juan Velasco Alvarado and the Reinvention of Túpac Amaru II," in Aguirre and Drinot, *Peculiar Revolution*; Raúl H. Asensio, *El Apóstol de los andes: El culto a Túpac Amaru en Cusco durante la rebolución velasquista (1968–1975)* (Lima: Instituto de Estudios Peruanos, 2017); Christabelle Roca-Rey, *La propaganda*

visual durante el gobierno de Juan Velasco Alvarado (1968–1975) (Lima: Instituto de Estudios Peruanos, 2016).

54. Mayer, *Ugly Stories*, 43.

CHAPTER 2

1. See Cecilia Blondet, *Las mujeres y el poder: Una historia de Villa El Salvador* (Lima: Instituto de Estudios Peruanos, 1991); Antonio Zapata Velasco, *Sociedad y poder local: La comunidad de Villa El Salvador* (DESCO: Lima, 1976); and Jürgen Golte and Norma Adams, *Los caballos de Troya de los invasores: Estrategias campesinas en la conquista de la gran Lima* (Lima: Instituto de Estudios Peruanos, 1990).

2. "50 terroristas atacan comisaría de Villa El Salvador y hieren policía," *La República*, 23 January 1984, 6; MRTA, *Conquistando el porvenir: Con las masas y las armas. Notas sobre la historia del MRTA* (Lima: MRTA, 1990), 43.

3. See, for example, *Documenting the Peruvian Insurrection*, group A, box 1, folder 2, Movimiento Revolucionario Túpac Amaru, "Ataque simultáneo a siete comisarías contra los excesos policiales," *Venceremos* 4 (July 1984) (archival collection, Davis Library, University of North Carolina, Chapel Hill), and MRTA, *Conquistando el porvenir*, 43.

4. *Documenting the Peruvian Insurrection*, "Ataque simultáneo a siete comisarías contra los excesos policiales."

5. Roberto Mejía, "Ulloa y Rodríguez Pastor trajeron modelo antinacional y antipopular," *La República*, 25 March 1984, 17.

6. MRTA, *Conquistando el porvenir*, 43; "La situación actual y las tareas en el proceso de la guerra revolucionaria del pueblo" (1984), in MRTA, *Conquistando el porvenir*, 58–59.

7. MRTA, *Conquistando el porvenir*, 43; "La situación actual y las tareas en el proceso de la guerra revolucionaria del pueblo," 58–59; Humberto Castillo A., "32 balas del FAL dispararon contra la residencia de Rodríguez Pastor," *La República*, 27 March 1984, 3; "Diez minutos duró violento ataque a residencia de Rodríguez Pastor," *La República*, 28 March 1984, 34.

8. "La situación actual y las tareas en el proceso de la guerra revolucionaria del pueblo," 58.

9. *Documenting the Peruvian Insurrection*, group A, box 1, folder 2, Movimiento Revolucionario Túpac Amaru, "La espada y la bandera de San Martín en manos del pueblo," *Venceremos* 4 (July 1984): 15–18.

10. Kim MacQuarrie, *The Last Days of the Incas* (New York: Simon and Schuster, 2007); John Hemmings, *The Conquest of the Incas* (San Diego: Harcourt, 1970).

11. Howard Handelman, *Struggle in the Andes: Peasant Political Mobilization in Peru* (Austin: University of Texas Press, 1975); Rodrigo Monyota, *Lucha por la tierra, reformas agrarias, y capitalismo en el Perú del siglo XX* (Lima: Mozca Azul Editores, 1989).

12. See Alberto Flores Galindo, *In Search of an Inca: Identity and Utopia in the Andes*, trans. Charles F. Walker, ed. Charles F. Walker and Carlos Aguirre (Cambridge: Cambridge University Press, 2010).

13. "El caso Varese," *La República*, 16 November 1986, 21; "Cerpa Cartolini: Experto en toma de locales," *Caretas* 1446 (26 December 1996).

14. MRTA, *Conquistando el porvenir*, 43.

15. MRTA, *Conquistando el porvenir*, 43.

16. "PIP capture a 9 miembros de MRTA," *La República*, 9 December 1984, 12.

17. *Documenting the Peruvian Insurrection*, group A, reel 4, box 4, folder 3, "Notas policiales sobre MRTA."

18. MRTA, *Conquistando el porvenir*, 44.

19. ADP, "Manifestación de Félix Rodríguez" (n.d.), Secretaria Ejecutiva 30115, Documentos Reservados, Documentos sobre personas secuestradas por el MRTA, SC010101.

20. MRTA, *Conquistando el porvenir*, 45.

21. ADP, "Manifestación de Virginia Peláez Ocampo" (10 December 1984), Secretaria Ejecutiva 30115, Documentos reservados DIRCOTE, Documentos sobre personas secuestradas por el MRTA, SC010102.

22. ADP, "Manifestación de Virginia Peláez Ocampo."

23. ADP, "Manifestación de Virginia Peláez Ocampo."

24. ADP, "Manifestación de Virginia Peláez Ocampo."

25. "Vuelve al país reportera de televisión que fue secuestrada por el MRTA el '84," *La República*, 22 January 1997, 8.

26. "Cerpa es el 'comandante Huertas,'" *La República*, 22 December 1996, 10.

27. Interview with Alberto Gálvez Olaechea, Chorrillos, 13 March 2018.

28. ADP, "Manifestación de Virginia Peláez Ocampo"; MRTA, *Conquistando el porvenir*, 45

29. ADP, "Manifestación de Virginia Peláez Ocampo"; MRTA, *Conquistando el porvenir*, 45; "La entrevista de Vicky Peláez," in MRTA, *Conquistando el porvenir*, 63–65.

30. "La entrevista de Vicky Peláez," 63–65.

31. "La entrevista de Vicky Peláez," 63–65.

32. "Vuelve al país reportera de televisión que fue secuestrada por el MRTA el '84."

CHAPTER 3

1. "Cerpa es el 'comandante Huertas,'" *La República*, 22 December 1996, 10; "Comando terrorista incendia tres locales del Kentucky Fried Chicken," *La Republica*, 21 March 1985, 8.

2. MRTA, *Conquistando el porvenir: Con las masas y las armas. Notas sobre la historia del MRTA* (Lima: MRTA, 1990), 83; *Documenting the Peruvian Insurrection*, group A, reel 1, box 1, folder 2, Movimiento Revolucionario Tupac Amaru, "El MRTA y la situación actual (Declaración)," August 1985.

3. *Documenting the Peruvian Insurrection*, group A, reel 1, box 1, folder 2, Movimiento Revolucionario Tupac Amaru, "Con las armas," *Venceremos*, issue and page number illegible, 1985 (archival collection, Davis Library, University of North Carolina, Chapel Hill).

4. *Documenting the Peruvian Insurrection*, group A, reel 4, box 4, folder 3, "Notas policiales sobre MRTA Comunicado de la Dirección Nacional del MRTA," ca. 11 April 1985.

5. For more on this fascinating story of conquest and resistance, see Kim MacQuarrie, *The Last Days of the Incas* (New York: Simon & Schuster, 2007).

6. Manifiesto del MRTA (1984), in MRTA, *Conquistando el porvenir*, 51

7. Conferencia de Prensa clandestina (August 1985), in MRTA, *Conquistando el porvenir*, 99.

8. Manifiesto del MRTA (1984), 51.

9. Conferencia de Prensa clandestina (August 1985), 99.

10. Conferencia de Prensa clandestina (August 1985), 99.

11. *Documenting the Peruvian Insurrection*, group A, box 1, folder 2, Movimiento Revolucionario Túpac Amaru, "Ataque simultáneo a siete comisarías contra los excesos policiales," *Venceremos* 4 (July 1984).

12. Interview with Lucero Cumpa, Chorrillos, 24 July 2016.

13. Interview with Lucero Cumpa, Chorrillos, 31 July 2016.

14. APJP, Juicio contra Víctor Polay Campos y otros, Exp. 01-93, Acta de la decimonovena sesión, Interrogatorio de la acusada María Lucero Cumpa Miranda, 28 March 2005.

15. APJP, Juicio contra Víctor Polay Campos y otros, Interrogatorio de Lucero Cumpa.

16. APJP, Juicio contra Víctor Polay Campos y otros, Interrogatorio de Lucero Cumpa.

17. Interview with Lucero Cumpa, Chorrillos, 18 March 2019.

18. Interview with Lucero Cumpa, 18 March 2019.

19. Interview with Lucero Cumpa, 18 March 2019.

20. Interview with Gladys (pseud.), Lima, 5 January 2017.

21. Interview with Gladys.

22. Interview with Lucero Cumpa, 18 March 2019.

23. CVR, Testimonio 162117233, Entrevista a Lucero Cumpa, [n.d., ca. 2002], ADP.

24. Cumpa has given details of this traumatic event in CVR, Testimonio 162117233, but I have elected not to repeat them here.

25. CVR, Testimonio 162117233.

26. CVR, Testimonio 162117233.

27. Interview with Lucero Cumpa, 18 March 2019.

28. Interview with Lucero Cumpa, 24 July 2016.

29. Interview with Lucero Cumpa, 24 July 2016.

30. Focus group with MRTA women, Lima, 5 January 2017.

CHAPTER 4

1. Interview with Penelope (pseud.), Lima, 6 January 2017.

2. Mario Campos, "MRTA pide amnistía al gobierno de Alan García," *La República*, 17 August 1985, 4–8.

3. "Interrogatorio a Víctor Polay, Trigésima Quinta Sesión," 11 June 2005, in *En el banquillo: ¿Terrorista o rebelde?*, ed. Víctor Polay Campos (Lima: Canta Editores, 2007), 303.

4. Campos, "MRTA pide amnistía al gobierno de Alan García," 4–8.

5. *Documenting the Peruvian Insurrection*, group B, reel 10, box 2, folder 1, DIGIMIN, Situación Subversiva en el País, "Movimiento Revolucionario Tupac Amaru: Principales Dirigentes," 7 May 1986, 11 (archival collection, Davis Library, University of North Carolina, Chapel Hill).

6. "Conferencia de Prensa," August 1985, in MRTA, *Conquistando el porvenir: Con las masas y las armas. Notas sobre la historia del MRTA* (Lima: MRTA, 1990), 99–100.

7. John Charles Chasteen, *Americanos: Latin America's Struggle for Independence* (Oxford: Oxford University Press, 2008), 148–50.

8. "Réplica del sable de San Martín entregan al museo de Real Felipe," *La República*, 17 August 1985, 10.

9. "Aniversario con bombas," *Cambio* 37 (10 November 1988): 2.

10. Interview with Alberto Aguilar, Lima, 6 January 2017; "Allanan radio clandestina del MRTA," *La República*, 6 November 1986, 17.

11. "Texto de la introducción del mensaje propolado de la Radio 4 de Noviembre," in MRTA, *Conquistando el porvenir*, 46.

12. *Documenting the Peruvian Insurrection*, group A, reel 1, box 1, folder 2, Movimiento Revolucionario Tupac Amaru, "¡Es hora de recuperar lo que es nuestro!," *Venceremos* 3 (June 1985): 7.

13. *Documenting the Peruvian Insurreciton*, group B, reel 10, box 2, folder 1, Hechos subversivos, Documentos policiales sobre los atentados del MRTA, 16.

14. *Documenting the Peruvian Insurrection*, "¡Es hora de recuperar lo que es nuestro!," 7; "Terroristas toman mercado," *La República*, 23 April 1985, 20–21; "MRTA asaltó un camión que llevaba leche y la repartió," *Cambio*, 18 June 1987, 3; "MRTA asalta camión frigorífico y repartee 4 kilos de pollo," *La República*, 7 September 1988, 15.

15. "Cuantiosos daños deja cadena de atentados en otra noche de terror," *La República*, 4 April 1986, 12.

16. "Las acciones de abril: MRTA reivindica acciones realizadas el mes pasado," *Cambio*, 4 May 1986, 6.

17. Phone interview with Alexander Watson, 2 March 2015.

18. Phone interview with Alexander Watson, 27 February 2015.

19. Phone interview with Alexander Watson, 27 February 2015; phone interview with Alexander Watson, 4 February 2013.

20. Phone interview with Alexander Watson, 27 February 2015; phone interview with Alexander Watson, 4 February 2013.

21. Phone interview with Alexander Watson, 4 February 2013.

22. Phone interview with Alexander Watson, 2 March 2015.

23. Phone interview with Alexander Watson, 2 March 2015.

24. *Documenting the Peruvian Insurrection*, "¡Es hora de recuperar lo que es nuestro!," 7; "Libia: Criminal ataque yanki," *Venceremos* 13 (April 1986): 12; "¡Basta de demagogia! ¡Ruptura de relaciones con Reagan ahora! ¡Nicaragua vencerá!," *Venceremos*, date and page illegible, 1986.

25. *Documenting the Peruvian Insurrection*, group A, reel 4, box 4, folder 3, Notas policiales sobre MRTA, Carta de la Dirección Nacional del MRTA al Sr. Embajador de los EE.UU., 21 April 1986.

26. Personal correspondence with Alexander Watson, 4 February 2013.

27. "Reivindican atentados," *Cambio* 37 (23 December 1986): 3.

28. *Documenting the Peruvian Insurrection*, "¡Es hora de recuperar lo que es nuestro!," 7; "Alan García, 'Basta de marchas, basta de paros . . . se me acabó la paciencia,'" *Venceremos* 14 (May 1986): 3.

CHAPTER 5

1. "Bienvenida al '87 fue ruidosa y alegre," *La República*, 2 January 1987, 12.

2. "Alan recibió el año cantando y tocando guitarra en local PAP," *La República*, 2 January 1987, 2.

3. "Bienvenida al '87 fue ruidosa y alegre," 12–13.

4. "Dinamitazos y balaceras en todo Lima," *La República*, 1 January 1987, 18.

5. "Dinamitazos y balaceras en todo Lima," 18–20.

6. Tupac Amaristas rebels also attacked the Ministries of the Interior, Economy, Labor, and Energy and Mining. See "¡Alerta total en el país!," *La República*, 16 July 1985, 2–3; Inés Flores y Luis Castro, "¡Qué indefensos estamos!," *La República*, 26 July 1985, 17–21; and *La República*, 28 August 1986, 17.

7. MRTA, *Conquistando el porvenir: Con las masas y las armas. Notas sobre la historia del MRTA* (Lima: MRTA, 1990), 87.

8. "MRTA atacó Palacio con lanzacohetes," *Cambio* 99 (7 August 1987): 1–2; César Terán Vega, "Atacaron Palacio y al asesor de Alan," *La República*, 7 August 1987, 9–12.

9. "Presentan a presuntos miembros de MRTA," *Cambio* 110 (18 August 1987): 5.

10. Interview with Alberto Gálvez, Chorrillos, 13 March 2018.

11. Interview with Alberto Gálvez, 13 March 2018.

12. Interview with Alberto Gálvez, 13 March 2018.

13. For more on Gálvez's years of militancy, see Alberto Gálvez Olaechea, *Con la palabra desarmada: Ensayos sobre el (pos)conflict* (Lima: Fauno Ediciones, 2015); Alberto Gálvez Olaechea, *Desde el país de las sombras* (Lima: Sur, 2009).

14. Interview with Alberto Gálvez, 13 March 2018.

15. Interview with Alberto Gálvez, 13 March 2018.

16. Interview with Alberto Gálvez, 13 March 2018.

17. Interview with Alberto Gálvez, Chorrillos, 15 March 2018.

18. Interview with Alberto Gálvez, 15 March 2018.

19. Interview with Alberto Gálvez, 15 March 2018.

20. Cromotex was not the only target. See, for example, "Comando del MRTA toma fábrica y dicta charla a trabajadores," *La República*, 5 March 1987, 18.

21. "MIR-MRTA Toman Cromotex," *Cambio* 43 (12 February 1987): 3.

22. "MIR-MRTA Toman Cromotex," 3.

23. "Asaltan y dinamitan la fábrica Cromotex," *La República*, 6 February 1987, 16; "MIR-MRTA Toman Cromotex," 3.

24. "Asaltan y dinamitan la fábrica Cromotex," 16.

25. "MIR-MRTA Toman Cromotex," 3.

26. "MIR-MRTA Toman Cromotex," 3; "Asaltan y dinamitan la fábrica Cromotex," 16.

27. The guerrillas returned to Cromotex the following year. See "Terroristas del MRTA intentan dinamitar la fábrica Cromotex," *La República*, 7 February 1988, 18.

28. "Queman seis omnibus en plena calle," *La República*, 8 January 1987, 15–19; "MRTA-MIR ataca agencias bancarias," *Cambio* 45 (27 February 1987): 3; "Dinamitan 16 agencias del Banco de Crédito," *La República*, 25 February 1987, 4; "Sediciosos dinamitan otras 15 agencias del Banco de Crédito," *La República*, 28 February 1987, 16; "Detonan trece dinamitazos ante miles de aficionados," *La República*, 6 April 1987, 16–17.

CHAPTER 6

1. Interview with Lucero Cumpa, Chorrillos, 24 July 2016.
2. Interview with Penelope, Lima, 23 December 2016.
3. Interview with Leo (pseud.), Lima, 18 July 2016.
4. Interview with Lucero Cumpa, 24 July 2016.
5. Interview with Lucero Cumpa, Chorrillos, 18 March 2018.
6. Interview with Lucero Cumpa, 24 July 2016; interview with Lucero Cumpa, 18 March 2018.
7. Interview with Lucero Cumpa, 24 July 2016.
8. Garry Leech, *The FARC: The Longest Insurgency* (London: Zed Books, 2011), 109–19.
9. Nelson Manrique, *El tiempo del miedo: La violencia política en el Perú, 1980–1996* (Lima: Fondo Editorial del Congreso del Perú, 2002), 121.
10. "Violento secuestro de empresario," *La República*, 27 September 1987, 20–21.
11. "Violento secuestro de empresario," 20–21.
12. "Exigen 45 millones por rescate de industrial," *La República*, 28 September 1987, 17.
13. Interview with Lucero Cumpa, 24 July 2016; "Sano y salvo liberan a Julio Ikeda," *La República*, 30 October 1987, 20–21; APJP, Juicio contra Víctor Polay Campos y otros, Exp. 01-93, Acta de la decimonovena sesión, Interrogatorio de la acusada María Lucero Cumpa Miranda, 28 March 2005.
14. "Sano y salvo liberan a Julio Ikeda," 20–21.
15. APJP, Juicio contra Víctor Polay Campos y otros, Interrogatorio de Lucero Cumpa.
16. APJP, Juicio contra Víctor Polay Campos y otros, Interrogatorio de Lucero Cumpa; interview with Lucero Cumpa, 24 July 2016.
17. "Sano y salvo liberan a Julio Ikeda," 20–21.
18. APJP, Juicio contra Víctor Polay Campos y otros, Interrogatorio de Lucero Cumpa.
19. APJP, Juicio contra Víctor Polay Campos y otros, Interrogatorio de Lucero Cumpa.
20. APJP, Juicio contra Víctor Polay Campos y otros, Interrogatorio de Lucero Cumpa.
21. APJP, Juicio contra Víctor Polay Campos y otros, Acta de la vigésima sesión, Interrogatorio de Lucero Cumpa, 8 April 2005.
22. Interview with Lucero Cumpa, 24 July 2016.
23. "Recuperan bandera de San Martín," *La República*, 25 October 1985, 20–21.
24. "Ni concesiones ni diálogo con los grupos terroristas," *La República*, 31 October 1987, 2.
25. "Ni concesiones ni diálogo con los grupos terroristas."
26. "Banderas y petardos del MRTA," *Cambio* 30 (6 November 1986): 3; "Paralizan carretera central para desactivar un explosivo," *La República*, 6 October 1986, 16.
27. "Asaltan 2 camiones con pollos y viveres e izan banderas del MRTA," *La República*, 5 November 1987, 18.
28. Interview with Luis Giampietri, Callao, 24 July 2012.
29. Interview with Marco Miyashiro, Miraflores, 30 May 2015.
30. "Presentan a presuntos miembros de MRTA," *Cambio* 110 (18 August 1987): 5.
31. Marco Miyashiro, "Reflexiones sobre el MRTA" (unpublished manuscript, n.d.), 2.
32. Miyashiro, "Reflexiones," 2.
33. "Presentan a presuntos miembros de MRTA," 5.
34. "Interrogatorio a Víctor Polay, Trigésima Quinta Sesión," 11 June 2005, in *En el banquillo: ¿Terrorista o rebelde?*, ed. Víctor Polay Campos (Lima: Canta Editores, 2007), 205–6.
35. Interview with Alberto Gálvez, Chorrillos, 15 March 2018.
36. Anahí Durand Guevara, *Donde habita el olvido: Los (h)usos de la memoria y la crisis del movimiento social en San Martín* (Lima: Universidad Nacional Mayor de San Marcos, 2005). For more on the *rondas campesinas* in the north, see Orin Starn, *Nightwatch: The Politics of Protest in the Andes* (Durham: Duke University Press, 1999).
37. "Interrogatorio a Víctor Polay," 247.

CHAPTER 7

1. Interview with Daniel Bravo (pseud.), Tarapoto, 22 May 2015.

2. "Interrogatorio a Víctor Polay, Trigésima Quinta Sesión," 11 June 2005, in *En el banquillo: ¿Terrorista o rebelde?*, ed. Víctor Polay Campos (Lima: Canta Editores, 2007), 248.

3. MRTA, *Conquistando el porvenir: Con las masas y las armas. Notas sobre la historia del MRTA* (Lima: MRTA, 1990), 123; "Interrogatorio a Víctor Polay," 248–49

4. "Interrogatorio a Víctor Polay," 248–49.

5. Luis Castro Gavelán, "Entrevista en la selva al 'Comandante Rolando,'" *La República*, 11 November 1987, 9–11.

6. "Interrogatorio a Víctor Polay," 253–54.

7. "Interrogatorio a Víctor Polay," 253–55.

8. "Interrogatorio a Víctor Polay," 254–55.

9. "Interrogatorio a Víctor Polay," 255.

10. Interview with Bronco (pseud.), Juanjuí, 11 August 2014.

11. "Interrogatorio a Víctor Polay," 240, 257–58.

12. "Declaración de James John Trisolini," in *En el banquillo: ¿Terrorista o rebelde?*, ed. Víctor Polay Campos (Lima: Canta Editores, 2007), 383–85.

13. "Interrogatorio a Víctor Polay," 256, 260; "Ejército y FF.PP. a la contraofensiva en Juanjuí," *La República*, 7 November 1987, 18–21.

14. "Interrogatorio a Víctor Polay," 262–63; "Terroristas toman San José de Sisa," *La República*, 9 November 1987, 19–22.

15. "Hay que reorganizar servicios de inteligencia de la policía," *La República*, 10 November 1987, 14; "Gobierno debe escuchar al pueblo de San Martín y attender sus demandas," *La República*, 20 November 1987, 8; "Bernales pide diálogo con alzados en armas," *La República*, 16 November 1987, 3.

16. "Si se da amnistía el MRTA podría acogerse a ella deponiendo armas," *La República*, 24 November 1987, 8.

17. Réger Rumrrill, "¿Una nueva Ayacucho?," *La República*, 11 December 1987, 23.

18. "Alan García pide a MRTA que deponga las armas," *La República*, 12 November 1987, 2.

19. "Alan García pide a MRTA que deponga las armas," 2.

20. "Barsallo culpa al periodismo de estar coludido con MRTA," *La República*, 13 November 1987, 2–3.

21. "Larco Cox asegura que n ohabrá diálogo con el MRTA," *La República*, 14 November 1987, 2.

22. "Ejército y FF.PP. a la contraofensiva en Juanjuí," 18–21; "FF.AA. salen a combater a subversivos en San Martín," *La República*, 11 November 1987, 2–3; "Toque de queda empieza a regir desde la 11 p.m. en San Martín," *La República*, 17 December 1987, 33.

23. "Capturar 'vivo o muerto' al jefe del MRTA es la consigna," *La República*, 17 November 1987, 2–3.

24. "Ministro de Defensa: 'Ninguna Justificación para que las FF.AA. intervengan,'" *Quehacer*, February–March 1989, 6–12.

25. "Tengan confianza plena en FF.AA.," *La República*, 17 November 1987, 3.

26. "Ejército y FF.PP. a la contraofensiva en Juanjuí," 18–21; "FF.AA. salen a combater a subversivos en San Martín," 2–3; "Toque de queda empieza a regir desde la 11 p.m. en San Martín," 33.

27. "4 muertos deja violento choque ante subversivos y soldados," *La República*, 18 November 1987, 4.

28. "Intentan secuestrar restos de subversivos en cementerio," *La República*, 20 November 1987, 17.

29. "Cae arsenal del MRTA en plena selva," *La República*, 6 December 1987, 20–21.

30. "Todos los peruanos debemos cerrar filas contra agresión subversive," *La República*, 7 December 1987, 3.

31. Interview with Daniel Bravo.

32. MRTA, *Conquistando el porvenir*, 124.

33. Castro Gavelán, "Entrevista en la selva," 9–11.

34. Castro Gavelán, "Entrevista en la selva," 9–11.

35. Castro Gavelán, "Entrevista en la selva," 9–11.

36. Castro Gavelán, "Entrevista en la selva," 9–11.

37. "El Comando MRTA y el estado de emergencia," *Cambio*, 30 December 1987, 23–25.

38. GlobalSecurity.org, "Tupac Amaru Revolutionary Movement," https://www.global security.org/military/world/para/tupac_amaru.htm (accessed 1 September 2019).

39. Interview with Carlos Peña (pseud.), Lima, 6 January 2017.

40. Nelson Manrique, *El tiempo del miedo: La violencia política en el Perú, 1980–1996* (Lima: Fondo Editorial del Congreso del Perú, 2002), 122.

CHAPTER 8

1. Interview with Franco Gálvez, Tarapoto, 23 May 2015; MRTA, *Conquistando el porvenir: Con las masas y las armas. Notas sobre la historia del MRTA* (Lima: MRTA, 1990), 164.

2. "Despedida de Rodrigo Gálvez," 2 October 1984 (audio recording, personal archive of Franco Gálvez, Tarapoto, San Martín, Peru).

3. "Despedida de Rodrigo Gálvez."

4. MRTA, *Conquistando el porvenir*, 164.

5. MRTA, *Conquistando el porvenir*, 164.

6. Interview with Franco Gálvez; MRTA, *Conquistando el porvenir*, 164.

7. Interview with Franco Gálvez; MRTA, *Conquistando el porvenir*, 164.

CHAPTER 9

1. CVR, interview with Peter Cárdenas Shulte, 17 September 2002, ADP.

2. "MRTA: Capturan al No. 2," *Caretas* 994 (22 February 1988): 18.

3. "MRTA: Capturan al No. 2," 18.

4. "Destacado dirigente de grupo MRTA capturan en Tarapoto," *La República*, 26 January 1988, 2; "Cargado de armas cayó en Tarapoto número 3 del MRTA," *La República*, 2 February 1988, 25.

5. Interview with Leo, Lima, 18 July 2016.

6. MRTA, "El camino de la revolución peruana: Documentos del II C.C. del MRTA," *Cambio*, edición especial, August 1988, 4.

7. MRTA, "El camino," 5.

8. MRTA, "El camino," 4.

9. MRTA, "El camino," 5.

10. MRTA, "El camino," 5–19.

11. MRTA, "El camino," 32.

12. MRTA, "El camino," 36.

13. MRTA, "El camino," 37.

14. MRTA, "El camino," 37.

15. MRTA, "El camino," 63.

16. MRTA, *Conquistando el porvenir: Con las masas y las armas. Notas sobre la historia del MRTA* (Lima: MRTA, 1990), 152.

17. Oscar Chumpitaz, "Matan a balazos a Rosa Cusquén en su cama del hospital Loayza," *La República*, 2 June 1988, 16; "Dos feroces asesinos en la lista," *La República*, 11 July 1990, 14.

18. "Toda la verdad sobre el secuestro del General Jerí," *Cambio* 35 (6 October 1988): 7.

19. CVR, Testimonio 100204, ADP; "Toda la verdad sobre el secuestro del General Jerí," 7.

20. CVR, Testimonio 100204; ADP, "Informe de la Comisión Investigadora de los ilícitos cometidos por el Comando Rodrigo Franco"; "Toda la verdad sobre el secuestro del General Jerí," 7.

21. "Toda la verdad sobre el secuestro del General Jerí," 7; "Habla el General Jerí y sus familiares," *Cambio* 35 (6 October 1988): 8.

22. MRTA, *Conquistando el porvenir*, 147.

23. "Secuestro equivocado," *Caretas* 1044 (13 February 1989): 84–85.

24. "MRTA mata empresario," *Cambio* 47 (13 February 1989).

25. Laura Puertas, Abilio Arroyo, and Jimmy Torres, "Víctimas inocentes de los que dicen ser respetuosos de la vida humana," *Caretas* 1044 (13 February 1989): 76–77.

26. "Aves de rapiña devoran cadavers de 50 subversivos en valles de Sisa," *La República*, 7 January 1988, 17.

27. "Jefe militar del MRTA cayó con su amante en un hotel," *La República*, 4 February 1989, 2–4.

28. "Interrogatorio a Víctor Polay, Trigésima Quinta Sesión," 11 June 2005, in *En el banquillo: ¿Terrorista o rebelde?*, ed. Víctor Polay Campos (Lima: Canta Editores, 2007), 241–42; "Un cordon de acero protégé a Víctor Polay," *La República*, 5 February 1989, 20.

29. "La novicia roja," *Caretas* 1044 (13 February 1989): 82–83.

30. "Interrogatorio a Víctor Polay," 305–6. Padilla has never publicly divulged the reason for her abrupt departure from the hotel.

31. Archivo del Cuartel General del Ejército, Lima, Peru, Comisión Permanente de la Historia del Ejército del Perú (Comisión Permanente), Documentos sobre la captura de Víctor Polay Campos, Testimonio del Comandante Miguel Amoretti, n.d., 6 pp.

32. Archivo del Cuartel General del Ejército, Testimonio del Comandante Miguel Amoretti, n.d., 6 pp.

33. Archivo del Cuartel General del Ejército, Testimonio del Comandante Miguel Amoretti, n.d., 6 pp., and Informe del Cptn. Fernando Bolívar Navarro sobre el Plan de Operaciones "Visita," 3 February 1989, 4 pp.; *La República*, 5 February 1989, 20; "Jóvenes, no tomen el amino de mi hijo," *La República*, 6 February 1989, 17.

34. "Alan afirma que se ha dado un golpe decisivo a la subversión," *La República*, 5 February 1989, 2.

35. "No habrá concesiones ni status especial para terrorista Polay," *La República*, 6 February 1989, 2.

36. "Alan afirma que se ha dado un golpe decisivo a la subversión," 2.

37. "Un cordón de acero protégé a Víctor Polay," 20; "Jóvenes, no tomen el amino de mi hijo," 17.

38. Víctor Polay Campos, "Desde la prisión, Polay responde: Un balance del MRTA" (unpublished manuscript, 2017), 5.

39. Interview with Marco Miyashiro, Miraflores, 30 May 2015.

40. "Polay dice que no es delincuente," *La República*, 7 February 1989, 15–17.

41. "Polay dice que no es delincuente," 15; "García . . . no tiene calidad moral . . . ," *Cambio* 50 (9 February 1989): 10.

42. "Polay dice que no es delincuente," 15.

43. "Cae guerrillero colombiano del M-19 con miembro del MRTA," *La República*, 17 April 1989, 15; "Colombiano abastecíaarmas al MRTA," *La República*, 18 April 1989, 16–17.

CHAPTER 10

1. "¿Quiénes eran?," *Sí*, 8 May 1989, 14–16.

2. "¿Quiénes eran?," 4–16; MRTA, *Conquistando el porvenir: Con las masas y las armas. Notas sobre la historia del MRTA* (Lima: MRTA, 1990), 158.

3. MRTA, *Conquistando el porvenir*, 160.

4. MRTA, *Conquistando el porvenir*, 158.

5. ADP, 100320, "Molinos," Interrogatorio de Abel Aquino Quito, 14 July 1989.

6. "Revés rojo," *Caretas* 1055 (2 May 1989): 3–6.

7. Liz Mineo, "Descalabro de MRTA," *Sí*, 2 May 1989.

8. Mineo, "Descalabro de MRTA."

9. "Revés rojo," 5; MRTA, *Conquistando el porvenir*, 159; ADP, 100320-Molinos, Comunicado Oficial N. 008 DIR/ZSNC, 28 April 1989.

10. MRTA, *Conquistando el porvenir*, 159.

11. ADP, 100320-Molinos, Pronunciamiento de la Dirección Nacional del MRTA sobre los sucesos de Molinos, 3 May 1989.

12. ADP, 100320-Molinos, Pronunciamiento de la Dirección Nacional del MRTA.

13. MRTA, *Conquistando el porvenir*, 159.

14. CVR, Testimonio 100092, ADP.

15. MRTA, *Conquistando el porvenir*, 164; "Secuestran al president de la Corporación de San Martín," *La República*, 27 June 1989, 13.

16. Interview with Daniel Bravo (pseud.), Tarapoto, 22 May 2015.

17. Interview with Daniel.

18. "Revés rojo," 6.

CHAPTER 11

1. There was, nevertheless, an indigenous presence in the San Martín Amazon. See Bartholomew Dean, *Urarina Society, Cosmology, and History in Peruvian Amazonia* (Gainesville: University Press of Florida, 2009).

2. Stefano Varese, *Salt of the Mountain: Campa Asháninka History and Resistance in the Peruvian Jungle*, trans. Susan Giershbach Rascón (Norman: University of Oklahoma Press, 2002).

3. CVR, Testimonio 314121, ADP.

4. "Yo fui un terrorista y ahora me arrepiento," *La República*, 14 January 1990, 21.

5. CVR, Testimonio 734001, ADP.

6. Interview with Tigre, San Agustino, 6 August 2016.

7. For more on the guerrilla encounters with the Asháninka, see Michael F. Brown and Eduardo Fernández, *War of Shadows: The Struggle for Utopia in the Peruvian Amazon* (Berkeley: University of California Press, 1993).

8. Interview with Tigre.

9. Interview with Tigre.

10. "Yo fui un terrorista y ahora me arrepiento," 20–22; "Comandantes ashaninkas son universitarios," *La República*, 14 January 1990, 22–23.

11. Lugar de la Memoria, "Asháninkas," http://www.lum.cultura.pe/visita360 (accessed 25 October 2017); Armando Campo Linares y Jesús Abad Luján, "Cuatro mil nativos marchan hacia el fortín del MRTA," *La República*, 15 January 1990, 11–13; Armando Campos and Jesús Abad, "Asháninkas van ganando la guerra a terroristas," *La República*, 13 January 1990, 13.

12. Armando Campos and Jesús Abad, "Asháninkas van ganando la guerra a terroristas," 13.

13. "Yo les conozco, ¡ustedes son terroristas!," *La República*, 15 January 1990, 13–14.

14. "Yo les conozco," 14.

15. Armando Campos Linares and Jesús Abad Luján, "Asháninkas condenan a muerte a 27 detenidos," *La República*, 16 January 1990, 21.

16. CVR, Testimonio 100092, ADP.

17. MRTA, *Conquistando el porvenir: Con las masas y las armas. Notas sobre la historia del MRTA* (Lima: MRTA, 1990), 164; interview with Franco Gálvez, Tarapoto, 23 May 2015.

18. "MRTA: Por mano propia," *Caretas* 1060 (5 June 1989): 38–39.

19. Lugar de la Memoria, "Una persona 2," Testimonio de Roger Pinchi Vásquez, http://www.lum.cultura.pe/visita360.

20. "Será recordado como primer ministro de Defensa del Perú," *La República*, 10 January 1990, 8.

21. "MRTA: Nuevo azote," *Caretas* 1092 (15 January 1990): 12.

22. "Lo emboscaron y asesinaron con ráfagas de metralleta," *La República*, 10 January 1990, 2–3.

23. "MRTA: Nuevo azote," 13.

24. "Quién es quién," *Caretas*, 22 January 1990, 34–35; "Identificaron a dos de los asesinos de López Albújar," *Caretas*, 19 January 1990, 2.

25. ADP, Unidad de Investigaciones Especiales y Antropológicas Forenses, Equipos de Investigaciones, 100320—Molinos, folder 2, Atestado Ampliatorio 153-D1-DIRCOTE, 5 September 1990.

26. "La 'senderización' del MRTA," *La República*, 17 January 1990, 18.

27. "MRTA: Nuevo Azote," 14.

CHAPTER 12

1. "Polay no da tregua," *Caretas* 1114 (25 June 1990): 31–33.

2. Víctor Polay Campos, "Desde la prisión, Polay responde: Un balance del MRTA" (unpublished manuscript, 2017), point 80.

3. Claribel Alegría and Darwin Flakoll, *Tunnel to Canto Grande: The Story of the Most Daring Prison Escape in Latin American History* (Willimantic, Conn.: Curbstone, 1996), 15.

4. *Documenting the Peruvian Insurrection*, Informe No. 05-35-CGC, al Tnte. Crnl. GC sobre intervención Policial a Personas presuntamento terroristas, 15 January 1986 (archival collection, Davis Library, University of North Carolina, Chapel Hill). For more on the experience of Shining Path in the prisons, see Juan Luis Rénique, *La voluntad encarcelada: Las 'luminosas trincheras de combate' de Sendero Luminoso del Perú* (Lima: Instituto de Estudios Peruanos, 2003), and Carlos Aguirre, "Punishment and Extermination: The Massacre of Political Prisoners in Lima, Peru, June 1986," in *Murder and Violence in Modern Latin America*, ed. E. A. Johnson, R. D. Salvatore, and P. Spierenburg (West Sussex: Wiley-Blackwell, 2013).

5. Campos, "Desde la prisión," "Cuándo supiste que se estaba construyendo un túnel para sacarlos de la cárcel?," point 79.

6. Pablo Brum, *The Robin Hood Guerrillas: The Epic Journey of Uruguay's Tupamaros* (self-published, 2014), 208–21.

7. Campos, "Desde la prisión," "79."

8. Campos, "Desde la prisión," "79."

9. "Frustran gran escape de 300 acusados de terrorismo," *La República*, 19 July 1987, 19.

10. Campos, "Desde la prisión," "79."

11. "Los Planes de fuga de Polay," *Caretas* 1157 (29 April 1990): 30–32.

12. "Roca a roca," *Caretas* 1117 (16 July 1990): 31–32.

13. "Roca a roca," 31.

14. Alegría and Flakoll, *Tunnel*, 52.

15. Alegría and Flakoll, *Tunnel*, 53.

16. Alegría and Flakoll, *Tunnel*, 53.

17. "Roca a roca," 31–32.

18. "Roca a roca," 31–32; Alegría and Flakoll, *Tunnel*, 58–59.

19. "Roca a roca," 31–32; Alegría and Flakoll, *Tunnel*, 58–59.

20. "Roca a roca," 31–32; Alegría and Flakoll, *Tunnel*, 58–59, 1–2, 45–47.

21. Alegría and Flakoll, *Tunnel*, 87, 146.

22. Quoted in Alegría and Flakoll, *Tunnel*, 148.

23. Quoted in Alegría and Flakoll, *Tunnel*, 149.

24. Alegría and Flakoll, *Tunnel*, 149–50.

25. Quoted in Alegría and Flakoll, *Tunnel*, 150.

26. Quoted in Alegría and Flakoll, *Tunnel*, 152.

27. Alegría and Flakoll, *Tunnel*, 153

28. Alegría and Flakoll, *Tunnel*, 154.

29. "El show de Polay," *Caretas* 1116 (9 July 1990): 20.

30. Alegría and Flakoll, *Tunnel*, 157.

31. Quoted in Alegría and Flakoll, *Tunnel*, 161.

32. Interview with Alberto Gálvez, Chorrillos, 15 March 2018.

33. Quoted in Alegría and Flakoll, *Tunnel*, 161.

34. Quoted in Alegría and Flakoll, *Tunnel*, 161.

35. Interview with Alberto Gálvez.

36. Alegría and Flakoll, *Tunnel*, 164–67; Campos, "Desde la prisión," question 80.

37. CVR, Testimonio 700570, ADP.

38. Interview with Lucero Cumpa, Chorrillos, 18 March 2018.

39. Interview with Alberto Gálvez.

40. CVR, Testimonio 700570.

41. Alegría and Flakoll, *Tunnel*, 174–76.

42. ADP, Secretaria Ejecutiva, SC016105, Documentos sobre personas secuestradas por el MRTA, Atestado 119-D1-DINCOTE, Contra Alberto Gálvez Olaechea y otros por delito de terrorismo.

43. Alegría and Flakoll, *Tunnel*, 178–79; "El túnel," *Caretas* 1117 (16 July 1990): 26–30.

44. Interview with Lucero Cumpa.

45. ADP, Secretaria Ejecutiva, SC016105; interview with Lucero Cumpa.

46. Interview with Lucero Cumpa; Alegría and Flakoll, *Tunnel*, 179–80.

47. Interview with Lucero Cumpa.

48. APJP, Expediente N. 01-93, Contra Víctor Polay Campos y otros, Acta de la vigésima sesión, Interrogatorio a Lucero Cumpa Miranda, 8 April 2005; "MRTA se burló del gobierno y de carceleros!," *La República*, 16 July 1990, 13–16; ADP, Secretaria Ejecutiva, SC016105; interview with Lucero Cumpa.

49. "Los Planes de fuga de Polay," 32.

CHAPTER 13

1. Víctor Polay Campos, "Desde la prisión, Polay responde: Un balance del MRTA" (unpublished manuscript, 2017), point 81.

2. "Mantilla no puede ser juez y parte en investigación de fuga de Polay," *La República*, 15 July 1990, 4.

3. "Recapturan dos prófugos del MRTA," *La República*, 12 July 1990, 16–17.

4. "MRTA asalta Yurimaguas y mata 10 policías," *La República*, 26 July 1990, 12–13; "Yurimaguas: Pueblo inerme," *Caretas* 1119 (30 July 1990): 35–37.

5. "No descartan a Polay como líder del ataque," *La República*, 26 July 1990, 13.

6. Interview with Alberto Gálvez, Chorrillos, 15 March 2018.

7. Interview with Alberto Gálvez.

8. "Germán denuncia: Un miembro del Comité Central y 'Mando del frente norteno' acusa a Polay de delación, autoritarismo y manipulación," *Caretas* 1175 (15 July 1991): 44.

9. Campos, "Desde la prisión," point 81.

10. "Germán denuncia," 44.

11. For more on Rodolfo Klien, see Nelson Manrique, "La verdadera identidad de Rodolfo Klien," http://www.desco.org.pe/recursos/sites/indice/293/977.pdf (accessed 1 September 2019).

12. Campos, "Desde la prisión," point 81.

13. Campos, "Desde la prisión," point 81.

14. "Malas compañías," *Caretas* 1128 (1 October 1990): 30–35.

15. "Terroristas dicen que quieren diálogo pero sin deponer armas," *La República*, 1 October 1990, 2–3.

16. "Terroristas dicen que quieren diálogo pero sin deponer armas," 2–3.

17. "Terroristas dicen que quieren diálogo pero sin deponer armas," 2–3.

18. "Fujimori no recibió al liberado Gerardo López," *La República*, 2 October 1990, 2.

19. Ismael León, "No puede haber diálogo con quienes practican la violencia," *La República*, 5 October 1990, 2–3.

20. Campos, "Desde la prisión," point 81.

21. Campos, "Desde la prisión," point 81.

22. APJP, Juicio contra Víctor Polay y otros, Exp. 01-93, Acta de la decimonovena sesión, Interrogatorio de la acusada María Lucero Cumpa Miranda, 28 March 2005.

23. APJP, Juicio contra Víctor Polay y otros, Interrogatorio de Lucero Cumpa, 28 March 2005.

24. Interview with Lucero Cumpa, Chorrillos, 31 July 2016.

25. APJP, Juicio contra Víctor Polay y otros, Interrogatorio de Lucero Cumpa, 28 March 2005.

26. APJP, Juicio contra Víctor Polay y otros, Exp. 01-93, Acta de la decimonovena sesión, Interrogatorio de la acusada María Lucero Cumpa Miranda, 14 April 2005.

27. "Opaco fulgor," *Caretas* 1150 (11 March 1991): 26–27; interview with Lucero Cumpa, 31 July 2016.

28. "Opaco fulgor," 26–27.

29. Interview with Lucero Cumpa, 31 July 2016.

30. "Lucero Fugaz," *Caretas* 1151 (18 March 1991): 30–35; Jaime Díaz and Willy Banda, "A balazos liberan lideresa del MRTA," *La República*, 12 March 1991, 13–15.

31. Abilio Arroyo, "Habla la Cumpa," *Caretas* 1152 (25 March 1991): 34.

32. Interview with Lucero Cumpa, Chorrillos, 24 July 2016.

33. "Primeras pistas," *Caretas* 1154 (8 April 1991): 36–37.

34. Interview with Lucero Cumpa, 31 July 2016.

35. APJP, Juicio contra Víctor Polay y otros, Interrogatorio de Lucero Cumpa, 14 April 2005.

36. "Lucero Cumpa habría sido recatada por MRTA porque está embarazada," *La República*, 15 March 1991, 25; "Rango en el MRTA," *Caretas* 1151 (18 March 1991): 32–33.

37. Interview with Lucero Cumpa, 31 July 2016.

38. Interview with Lucero Cumpa, 31 July 2016.

39. Arroyo, "Habla la Cumpa," 32–37.

40. Arroyo, "Habla la Cumpa," 36.

41. Eduardo Torrejón, "MRTA depondría las armas para insertarse en vida democrática," *La República*, 6 March 1991, 2–3.

42. "No podemos condicionarnos a lo que pidan delincuentes subversivos," *La República*, 15 May 1991, 7.

43. "Ligaduras," *Caretas* 1160 (20 May 1991):, 10–14, 76.

44. "Ligaduras," 12.

45. "Fin del infierno," *Caretas* 1163 (10 June 1991): 26–27.

46. Interview with Alberto Gálvez.

47. ADP, Secretaria Ejecutiva, SC016105, Documentos sobre personas secuestradas por el MRTA, Atestado 119-D1-DINCOTE, Contra Alberto Gálvez Olaechea y otros por delito de terrorismo, Manifestación de rosa Luz Padilla Baca, 10 June 1991.

48. "Nido en Marbella," *Caretas* 1163 (10 June 1991): 34–36, 38–39.

49. ADP, Secretaria Ejecutiva, SC016105.

50. Interview with Marco Miyashiro, Lima, 8 August 2014; interview with Alberto Gálvez.

51. "Nido en Marbello," 35–36; ADP, Secretaria Ejecutiva, SC016105.

52. "Germán denuncia," 45.

53. "Purga sangrienta," *Caretas* 1175 (2 September 1991): 40–42.

CHAPTER 14

1. APJP, Juicio contra Víctor Polay y otros, Exp. 01-93, Acta de la decimonovena sesión, Interrogatorio de la acusada María Lucero Cumpa Miranda, 28 March 2005.

2. APJP, Juicio contra Víctor Polay y otros, Exp. 01-93, Acta de la decimonovena sesión, Interrogatorio de la acusada María Lucero Cumpa Miranda, 14 April 2005.

3. Interview with Lucero Cumpa, Chorrillos, 24 July 2016.

4. APJP, Juicio contra Víctor Polay y otros, Interrogatorio de Lucero Cumpa, 14 April 2005.

5. APJP, Juicio contra Víctor Polay y otros, Interrogatorio de Lucero Cumpa, 14 April 2005.

6. APJP, Juicio contra Víctor Polay y otros, Interrogatorio de Lucero Cumpa, 14 April 2005.

7. APJP, Juicio contra Víctor Polay y otros, Interrogatorio de Lucero Cumpa, 14 April 2005.

8. Interview with Lucero Cumpa, Chorrillos, 31 July 2016.

9. For more on Fujimori's descent into authoritarianism, see Julio Cotler and Romeo Grompone, *El fujimorismo: Ascenso y caída de un regimen autoritario* (Lima: Instituto de Estudios Peruanos, 2001); Carlos Iván Degregori, *La década de la antipolítica: Auge y huida de Alberto Fujimori y Vladimiro Montesinos* (Lima: Instituto de Estudios Peruanos, 2001); Catherine M. Conaghan, *Fujimori's Peru: Deception in the Public Sphere* (Pittsburgh: University of Pittsburgh Press, 2005); and Jo-Marie Burt, *Political Violence and the Authoritarian State in Peru: Silencing Civil Society* (New York: Palgrave Macmillan, 2007).

10. CVR, Testimonio 700472, ADP.

11. CVR, Testimonio 700472.

12. Interview with Clara (pseud.), Lima, 30 July 2016.

13. Interview with Clara.

14. Interview with Clara.

15. Francisco Reyes, "MRTA admite que vive de extorsiones (Entrevista Exclusiva)," *La República*, 17 June 1992, I, IV.

16. Víctor Polay Campos, "Desde la prisión, Polay responde: Un balance del MRTA" (unpublished manuscript, 2017), point 89.

17. ADP, Secretaria Ejecutiva, SC016105, Documentos sobre personas secuestradas por el MRTA, Atestado 121-D3-DINCOTE, Contra Víctor Polay Campos y Gabriel Antonio Vásquez por delito de terrorismo.

18. Campos, "Desde la prisión," point 90.

19. Campos, "Desde la prisión," point 90.

20. Campos, "Desde la prisión," point 89.

21. "'La Dincote¡, ya me jodí¡,' exclamó Polay y se entregó a la policía," *La República*, 11 June 1992, 2–3.

22. "'La Dincote¡, ya me jodí¡,'" 2–3.

23. "Captura de Polay es paso decisive para derrotar a MRTA, dice general Briones," *La República*, 11 June 1992, 4–5.

24. "Recapturan a Polay a casi dos años de su escandalosa fuga del Castro," *La República*, 10 June 1992, 13; "Polay será uno de los primeros en ser juzgado por 'jueces sin rostro,'" *La República*, 18 June 1992, 14.

25. Interview with Lucero Cumpa, 31 July 2016.

26. Interview with Lucero Cumpa, 31 July 2016.

CHAPTER 15

1. Interview with Daniel Bravo (pseud.), Tarapoto, 22 May 2015. The entire chapter is based on this interview.

CHAPTER 16

1. Interview with Esperanza Tapia (pseud.), Chorrillos, 24 July 2016.

2. Interview with Esperanza Tapia (pseud.), Chorrillos, 31 July 2016.

3. Focus group with MRTA women, Lima, 5 January 2017. "Veronica" is a pseudonym.

4. Interview with Esperanza Tapia, 24 July 2016.

5. See Timothy P. Wickham-Crowley, *Guerrillas and Revolution in Latin America: A Comparative Study of Insurgents and Regimes since 1956* (Princeton: Princeton University Press, 1993).

6. Interview with Lucero Cumpa, Chorrillos, 31 July 2016.

7. Interview with Lucero Cumpa, Chorrillos, 18 March 2018.

8. APJP, Juicio contra Víctor Polay y otros, Exp. 01-93, Acta de la decimonovena sesión, Interrogatorio de la acusada María Lucero Cumpa Miranda, 14 April 2005.

CHAPTER 17

1. Interview with Lucero Cumpa, Chorrillos, 31 July 2016.

2. Interview with Esperanza Tapia (pseud.), Chorrillos, 31 July 2016.

3. Interview with Esperanza Tapia (pseud.), Chorrillos, 24 July 2016.

4. APJP, Caso contra Víctor Polay y otros, Acta de la vigésima sesión, 14 April 2005; interview with Lucero Cumpa.

5. See Fernando Rospigliosi, *Montesinos y las fuerzas armadas: Cómo control durante una década las instituciones militares* (Lima: Instituto de Estudios Peruanos, 2000); Sally Bowen and Jane Holligan, *The Imperfect Spy: The Many Lives of Vladimiro Montesinos* (Lima: Peisa, 2003).

6. APJP, Caso contra Víctor Polay y otros; interview with Lucero Cumpa.

7. Interview with Lucero Cumpa.

8. Interview with Daniel Bravo (pseud.) Tarapoto, 22 May 2015.

9. Interview with Daniel Bravo (pseud.), San Martín, 19 July 2016.

10. Interview with Daniel Bravo, 19 July 2016.

CHAPTER 18

1. Interview with Esperanza Tapia (pseud.), Chorrillos, 24 July 2016.

2. Interview with Esperanza Tapia (pseud.), Chorrillos, 31 July 2016.

3. Interview with Daniel Bravo (pseud.), San Martín, 19 July 2016.

4. Interview with Daniel Bravo (pseud.), Tarapoto, 22 May 2015. The details of the training are corroborated in CVR, Testimonio 736003, ADP.

5. CVR, Testimonio 736005, Testimonio 736003, Testimonio 736004, ADP.

6. "Son 458 los emerretistas presos en todo el país que pretenden liberar," *La República*, 18 December 1996, 8.

7. Interview with Daniel Bravo, 22 May 2015.

8. Interview with Javier (pseud.) Cuzco, 30 December 2016.

9. Interview with Marc Berenson, Manhattan, N.Y., 13 October 2012.

10. "MIT Anthropology Prof. Martin Diskin Dies at 62; was expert on Latin America," *MIT Bulletin*, 4 August 1997, http://news.mit.edu/1997/diskin-new.

11. Interview with Marc Berenson.

12. Interview with Marc Berenson.

13. Interview with Marc Berenson.

14. Interview with Marc Berenson.

15. Interview with Lori Berenson, Pueblo Libre, 8 August 2012.

16. Interview with Lori Berenson.

17. Interview with Marc Berenson.

18. Interview with Lori Berenson; CVR, Testimonio 700585, ADP.

19. CVR, interview with Víctor Polay Campos and Miguel Rincón Rincón, 8 April 2003, ADP.

20. CVR, Testimonio 736005.

21. CVR, interview with Víctor Polay Campos and Miguel Rincón Rincón; CVR, Testimonio 736003.

22. CVR, Testimonio 736003.

23. "Quimera de sangre," *Caretas* 1392 (7 December 1995): 14–17, 80.

24. "Quimera de sangre."

25. "Quimera de sangre," 14.

26. "Quimera de sangre," 17, 80.

27. CVR, interview with Víctor Polay Campos and Miguel Rincón Rincón; CVR, Testimonio 736003.

28. CVR, interview with Víctor Polay Campos and Miguel Rincón Rincón; "Quimera de sangre," 80.

29. CVR, interview with Víctor Polay Campos and Miguel Rincón Rincón; "Quimera de sangre," 80.

30. "Quimera de sangre," 80.

31. "Rincón se rinde tras 10 horas de pesadilla," *La República*, 2 December 1995, 3.

32. "Rincón se rinde tras 10 horas de pesadilla," 3.

33. CVR, interview with Víctor Polay Campos and Miguel Rincón Rincón.

34. "Quimera de sangre"; "Rincón se rinde tras 10 horas de pesadilla," 3.

35. "Se acabó el MRTA," *La República*, 3 December 1995, 1.

36. "Cerpa Cartolini tiene su fortín en La Paz," *La República*, 4 December 1995, 5; "Liberan en Bolivia a Samuel Doria," *La República*, 18 December 1995, 3; "Cerpa Cartolini habría caído con diez emerretistas en frontera boliviana," *La República*, 17 December 1995, 4.

37. "¡Están con los días contados!," *La República*, 3 December 1995, 8.

CHAPTER 19

1. Fernando Rospigliosi and Jimmy Torres, "La toma de la embajada," *Caretas* 1445 (19 December 1996): 14–23.

2. "De película: La historia de la casa," *Caretas* 1446 (26 December 1996): 26.

3. Luis Giampietri, *Rehén por siempre: Operación Chavín de Huántar* (Lima: Fondo Editorial del Congreso del Perú, 2011), 26–27.

4. Interview with Luis Giampietri, Callao, 24 July 2012.

5. Giampietri, *Rehén por siempre*, 27.

6. Giampietri, *Rehén por siempre*, 28.

7. Giampietri, *Rehén por siempre*, 28.

8. ADP, Tomo 1.1, SC049501, Unidad Investigaciones 100337, Chavín de Huántar, Manifestación de Marco Miyashiro, 16 April 2001; Francisco Sagasti, "Diario de un rehén," *Caretas* 1446 (26 December 1996): 32.

9. "Testigo con filo," *Caretas* 1448 (15 January 1997): 35.

10. Sagasti, "Diario de un rehén," 32.

11. Sagasti, "Diario de un rehén," 38.

12. Sagasti, "Diario de un rehén," 32.

13. "El Asedio," *Caretas* 1446 (26 December 1996): 26.

14. Rospigliosi and Torres, "La toma," 20.

15. Interview with Luis Giampietri.

16. Interview with Luis Giampietri; Giampietri, *Rehén por siempre*, 28–29.

17. ADP, Tomo 1.2, SC049502, Unidad Forénsica, Chavín de Huántar, Manifestación de Samuel Matsuda Nishimura, 2 April 2001.

18. ADP, Tomo 1.1, SC049501, Unidad Investigaciones 100337, Chavín de Huántar, Manifestación de Francisco Tudela, 3 August 2003.

19. Quoted in Giampietri, *Rehén por siempre*, 29.

20. Sagasti, "Diario de un rehén," 32.

21. Interview with Luis Giampietri.

22. Giampietri, *Rehén por siempre*, 29.

23. Sagasti, "Diario de un rehén," 32.

24. "La táctica de los regalitos de Navidad," *Caretas* 1446 (26 December 1996): 16.

25. "La táctica de los regalitos de Navidad," 16.

26. ADP, Tomo 1.1 SC049501, Unidad Investigaciones 100337, Chavín de Huántar, Manifestación de Carlos Domínguez Solis, 21 March 2001.

27. "Michel Minning seguirá siendo pieza clave para liberar resto de rehenes," *La República*, 25 December 1996, 4.

28. Quoted in Giampietri, *Rehén por siempre*, 30.

29. Giampietri, *Rehén por siempre*, 30.

30. "¡450 rehenes!," *La República*, 18 December 1996, 2–3.

31. "¡450 rehenes!," 3.

32. Sagasti, "Diario de un rehén," 32.

33. Marco Miyashiro, "Juan Julio Wicht, un sacerdote ejemplar" (unpublished manuscript, March 2010).

34. Miyashiro, "Juan Julio Wicht."

35. Miyashiro, "Juan Julio Wicht."

36. Giampietri, *Rehén por siempre*, 33.

37. Giampietri, *Rehén por siempre*, 43–44.

38. Sagasti, "Diario de un rehén," 34.

39. Sagasti, "Diario de un rehén," 37.

40. "El drama continúa," *La República*, 21 December 1996, 17; Sagasti, "Diario de un rehén," 36–37.

41. "Explosión de júbilo en reencuentro de los 38 liberados con sus familiares," *La República*, 21 December 1996, 2.

42. Sagasti, "Diario de un rehén," 39.

43. "Explosión de júbilo en reencuentro de los 38 liberados con sus familiares," 2.

44. "La noticia no da tregua," *La República*, 21 December 1996, 15; "Extramuras de la noticia," *Caretas* 1446 (26 December 1996): 28–29.

45. "Miles rezan por una solución pacífica para crisis de los rehenes en embajada," *La República*, 22 December 1996, 14; Patricia Kadena, "Un canto por la paz y la libertad," *La República*, 23 December, 1996, 11–13; Esther Vargas, "Una luz de esperanza," *La República*, 20 December 1996, 24–25.

46. "Fujimori agradece a Bill Clinton," *La República*, 20 December 1996, 3.

47. "Los rehenes ligados al gobierno sólo saldrán si se aceptan las demandas," *La República*, 22 December 1996, 4.

48. "Fujimori exige a MRTA deponer armas y liberar a los rehenes," *La República*, 22 December 1996, 2–3.

49. "Gobierno ha descartado acción militar," *La República*, 22 December 1996, 12.

CHAPTER 20

1. "¡Al fin libres!," *La República*, 23 December 1996, 2–3.

2. "¡Al fin libres!," 3.

3. "Washington hace llamado para que sean liberados todos los rehenes," *La República*, 24 December 1996, 3.

4. "Uruguay libera a dos del MRTA que secuestraron empresario boliviano," *La República*, 25 December 1996, 2.

5. "Cuba dispuesta a dar asilo a los rebeldes," *La República*, 25 December 1996, 3.

6. Marco Miyashiro, "Anécdotas de un policía" (unpublished manuscript, n.d.).

7. "El duro representante del Opus Dei," *La República*, 26 December 1996, 2.

8. "Fujimori juega nueva carta para obtener libertad de 104 rehenes," *La República*, 26 December 1996, 2–3.

9. "El diálogo entre el vocero del gobierno y el jefe emerretista," *La República*, 11 January 1997, 3.

10. "Cipriani volvió a la residencia pero negó papel de mediador," *La República*, 27 December 1996, 3.

11. "Presidente Fujimori estudia propuestas de emerretistas," *La República*, 30 December 1996, 3; "MRTA libera a siete rehenes pero quedan todavía 74 en cautiverio," *La República*, 2 January 1996, 2.

12. "El diálogo entre el vocero del gobierno y el jefe emerretista," 3.

13. "Gobierno dispuesto a discutir con MRTA sus demandas para liberar a los rehenes," *La República*, 13 January 1997, 2–3.

14. "MRTA acusa a policía de provocación y lanza 12 disparos desde la residencia," *La República*, 14 January 1997, 8–9.

15. "Militante del MRTA lanza ráfaga de disparos contra camión antiminas," *La República*, 28 January 1997, 2–3.

16. "Néstor Cerpa acepta la propuesta para formar comisión de garantes," *La República*, 16 January 1997, 4.

17. "MRTA libera a jefe de la policía antiterrorista," *La República*, 18 January 1997, 7;

"Evacúan de la residencia en camilla al general PNP José Rivas Ridríguez," *La República*, 26 January 1997, 4; Luis Giampietri, *Rehén por siempre: Operación Chavín de Huántar* (Lima: Fondo Editorial del Congreso del Perú, 2011), 69.

18. Quoted in Giampietri, *Rehén por siempre*, 69.

19. "El Papa respalda a Mons. Cipriani y reclama liberación de los rehenes," *La República*, 31 March 1997, 2.

20. "Madre de Polay se ofrece a mediar," *La República*, 23 March 1997, 3; "Madres de Plaza de Mayo piden mediar en crisis de los rehenes," *La República*, 22 February 1997, 3; Doris Hinojosa, "Cuba acepta otorgar asilo si hay pedido formal de los involucrados en la crisis," *La República*, 4 March 1997, 2; "Mandela mediaría en crisis de rehenes," *La República*, 17 April 1997, 7.

21. "Cerpa-Marcos se verían en la selva de Chiapas," *La República*, 10 January 1997, 16–17.

22. "Vuelve al país reportera de televisión que fue secuestrada por el MRTA el '84," *La República*, 22 January 1997, 8.

23. Miyashiro, "Anécdotas de un policía."

24. Miyashiro, "Anécdotas de un policía."

25. ADP, Tomo 1.1, SC049501, Unidad Investigaciones 100337, Chavín de Huántar, Manifestación de Marco Miyashiro, 16 April 2001.

26. Marco Miyashiro, "Carta despidiendo al Ingeniero Rodolfo Masuda" (unpublished manuscript, ca. 2010).

27. Marco Miyashiro, "Juan Julio Wicht, un sacerdote ejemplar" (unpublished manuscript, March 2010).

28. Miyashiro, "Juan Julio Wicht."

29. Miyashiro, "Anécdotas de un policía."

30. Interview with Luis Giampietri, Callao, 24 July 2012.

31. Giampietri, *Rehén por siempre*, 80.

32. Giampietri, *Rehén por siempre*, 83–84.

33. Interview with Luis Giampietri.

34. Interview with Luis Giampietri.

35. See, for example, ADP, Tomo 1.1, SC049501, Unidad Investigaciones 100337, Chavín de Huántar, Manifestación de Máximo Rivera Díaz, 19 March 2001.

36. Quoted in Giampietri, *Rehén por siempre*, 91–92.

37. CVR, Testimonio 320087, ADP.

38. ADP, Tomo 1.1, SC049501, Unidad Investigaciones 100337, Chavín de Huántar, Manifestación de Carlos Rosas Domínguez, 21 March 2001.

39. ADP, Tomo 1.1, SC049501, Unidad Investigaciones 100337, Chavín de Huántar, Manifestación de Félix Rivera, 19 March 2001, and Manifestación de Carlos Rosas Domínguez, 21 March 2001.

40. ADP, Tomo 1.1, SC049501, Unidad Investigaciones 100337, Chavín de Huántar, Manifestación de Francisco Tudela, 3 August 2003.

41. ADP, Tomo 1.2, SC049502, Unidad Forénsica, Chavín de Huántar, Manifestación de Samuel Matsuda Nishimura, 2 April 2001; ADP, Manifestación de Carlos Rosas Domínguez, 21 March 2001.

42. ADP, Manifestación de Máximo Rivera Díaz, 19 March 2001.

43. ADP, Manifestación de Carlos Rosas Domínguez, 21 March 2001.

44. ADP, Manifestación de Marco Miyashiro, 16 April 2001.

45. "Fujimori reitera salida pacífica al drama de rehenes del MRTA," *La República*, 31 January 1996, 4.

46. "Así no se puede negociar," *Caretas* 1453 (20 February 1997): 20–22.

47. Angel Páez, "¿De qué hablaron con el ministro Palermo y Roli 'El Arabe'?," *La República*, 12 February 1997, 2–3.

48. "El MRTA pide que conversación de fondo sea entre Fujimori y Cerpa," *La República*, 15 February 1997, 2.

49. "Néstor Cerpa y asesor del SIN frente a frente en la mesa de negociaciones," *La República*, 21 February 1996, 2.

50. "Nuestro Chino en la Habana," *Caretas* 1455 (6 March 1997): 10–13, 17.

51. "Cuatro puntos tendría propuesta del presidente Fujimori al MRTA," *La República*, 5 March 1997, 2.

52. "No buscamos ni el exilio, ni el asilo," *La República*, 5 March 1997, 3.

53. "El MRTA suspende diálogo con gobierno," *La República*, 7 March 1997, 2.

54. "La hora cero," *Caretas* 1462 (25 April 1997): 16.

55. "Cerpa se despide de su esposa ante posible salida military a la crisis," *La República*, 3 April 1997, 2.

56. "Por primera vez en 7 años mayoría del pueblo desaprueba gestión de Fujimori," *La República*, 20 April 1997, 8; "El 52.8% desaprueba a Fujimori," *La República*, 21 April 1997, 2.

57. "Por primera vez en 7 años mayoría del pueblo desaprueba gestión de Fujimori," 8; "El 52.8% desaprueba a Fujimori," 2; Silvia Rojas, "'Fenómeno Fujimori' llegó su fin," *La República*, 22 April 1997, 3.

CHAPTER 21

1. "Militante del MRTA lanza ráfaga de disparos contra camión antiminas," *La República*, 28 January 1997, 2–3; Luis Giampietri, *Rehén por siempre: Operación Chavín de Huántar* (Lima: Fondo Editorial del Congreso del Perú, 2011), 69.

2. Giampietri, *Rehén por siempre*, 79.

3. Giampietri, *Rehén por siempre*, 79.

4. Interview with Luis Giampietri, Callao, 24 July 2012.

5. "Tensa calma reinaba en la residencia japonesa," *La República*, 2 February 1997, 3.

6. Servicio de Inteligencia Nacional [SIN], Grabación secreta del interior de la embajada japonesa [audio], 22 April 1997 (personal archive of Luis Giampietri, Callao, Peru).

7. Giampietri, *Rehén por siempre*, 79.

8. "Bandera de la fe," *La República*, 20 December 1996, 1.

9. Patricia Kadena, "Un canto por la paz y la libertad," *La República*, 23 December 1996, 11–13.

10. "MRTA conmemora en residencia japonesa desalojo en Cromotex," *La República*, 5 February 1997, 3.

11. "La hora cero," *Caretas* 1462 (25 April 1997): 18.

12. "La hora cero," 18–19.

13. "La hora cero," 19.

14. "La hora cero," 19; "Cerpa recibió dos balazos en la cabeza," *La República*, 24 April 1997, 8.

15. Eduardo Torrejón, "*Especial*: La historia secreta del túnel," *La República*, 23 April 1997, VI.

16. Vladimiro Montesinos, *Operación militar Chavín de Huántar: Con el terrorismo no se negocia*, 2 vols. (Lima: Ezer Editores, 2016), 1:332–38.

17. "No hay indicios que comprueben existencia del supuesto túnel," *La República*, 8 March 1997, 4.

18. "El túnel si existe," *La República*, 7 March 1997, 1.

19. Nicolás De Bari Hermoza Ríos, *Operación Chavín de Huántar: Rescate en la residencia de la Embajada del Japón* (Lima: self-published, 1997), 152.

20. Giampietri, *Rehén por siempre*, 63.

CHAPTER 22

1. Luis Giampietri, *Rehén por siempre: Operación Chavín de Huántar* (Lima: Fondo Editorial del Congreso del Perú, 2011), 113–14.

2. Giampietri, *Rehén por siempre*, 115.

3. Giampietri, *Rehén por siempre*, 115.

4. Giampietri, *Rehén por siempre*, 115.

5. Interview with Luis Giampietri, Callao, 24 July 2012.

6. Interview with Luis Giampietri; Giampietri, *Rehén por siempre*, 115.

7. Interview with Luis Giampietri.

8. "Monseñor Cipriani lleva dos guitarras para los cautivos," *La República*, 2 January 1997, 3.

9. Giampietri, *Rehén por siempre*, 116.

10. Giampietri, *Rehén por siempre*, 116.

11. Giampietri, *Rehén por siempre*, 116.

12. Interview with Luis Giampietri.

13. Giampietri, *Rehén por siempre*, 147.

14. Giampietri, *Rehén por siempre*, 150.

15. Giampietri, *Rehén por siempre*, 153.

16. Giampietri, *Rehén por siempre*, 153.

17. Giampietri, *Rehén por siempre*, 155.

18. Giampietri, *Rehén por siempre*, 156.

19. Giampietri, *Rehén por siempre*, 156.

20. Giampietri, *Rehén por siempre*, 157.

21. ADP, Tomo 1.1, SC049501, Unidad Investigaciones 100337, Chavín de Huántar, Manifestación de Marco Miyashiro, 16 April 2001.

22. ADP, Tomo 1.1, SC049501, Unidad Investigaciones 100337, Chavín de Huántar, Manifestación de Francisco Tuleda, 3 August 2003; "Rescaten al canciller Tudela," *Caretas* 1463 (2 May 1997): 14–15.

23. Quoted in Giampietri, *Rehén por siempre*, 162.

24. Giampietri, *Rehén por siempre*, 163.

25. ADP, Manifestación de Marco Miyashiro, 16 April 2001.

26. David Hidalgo, *Sombras de un rescate: Tras las huellas ocultas en la residencia del embajador japonés* (Lima: Planeta, 2007).

27. "Incremento de la popularidad de Fujimori no significa carta blanca," *La República*, 25 April 1997, 3.

28. "Fujimori ofrece exporter tecnología antisecuestros," *La República*, 27 April 1997, 2.

29. "Afirma que un sueño le inspire la operación 'Chavín de Huántar,'" *La República*, 27 April 1997, 2.

CONCLUSION

1. Nicolás De Bari Hermoza Ríos, *Operación Chavín de Huántar: Rescate en la residencia de la Embajada del Japón* (self-published, 1997); Vladimiro Montesinos, *Operación militar Chavín de Huántar: Con el terrorismo no se negocia*, 2 vols. (Lima: Ezer Editores, 2016).

2. Umberto Jara, *Secretos del tunel* (Lima: Planeta, 2017), 12–13.

3. Cynthia E. Milton, *Conflicted Memory: Military Cultural Interventions and the Human Rights Era in Peru* (Madison: University of Wisconsin Press, 2018), 142–49.

4. Lorraine Bayard de Volo, *Women and the Cuban Insurrection: How Gender Shaped Castro's Victory* (Cambridge: Cambridge University Press, 2018).

5. Marian E. Schlotterbeck, *Beyond the Vanguard: Everyday Revolutionaries in Allende's Chile* (Berkeley: University of California Press, 2018), 135–40.

6. See Gustavo Gorriti, *The Shining Path: A History of the Millenarian War in Peru*, trans. Robin Kirk (Chapel Hill: University of North Carolina Press, 1999); Carlos Iván Degregori, *How Difficult It Is to Be God: Shining Path's Politics of War in Peru, 1980–1999* (Madison: University of Wisconsin Press, 2012); Orin Starn and Miguel La Serna, *The Shining Path: Love, Madness, and Revolution in the Andes* (New York: Norton, 2019).

7. Luis Giampietri, *Rehén por siempre: Operación Chavín de Huántar* (Lima: Fondo Editorial del Congreso del Perú, 2011).

8. CVR, *Informe Final*, 9 vols. (CVR: Lima, 2003).

Index

86–87, 88, 97, 100, 108; leftist unity sought
by, 26–27; media manipulated by, 92–93,
107; military dictatorships opposed by,
21–22; as MRTA cofounder, 72, 99–100;
MRTA-MIR merger and, 68; notoriety of,
157; overseas, 22–23, 161; radicalization
of, 24, 25; rural front organized by, 79, 80,
85–86; in San José de Sisa, 88–89, 92–93, 97;
San Martín campaign by, 86, 104; on trial,
133; truces proposed by, 53–54, 60, 154;
Varese vs., 33
Polay Risco, Víctor, 16–17, 24, 114; children
indoctrinated by, 18–19; reading and
education stressed by, 19–20
Po Lay Seng, 17
Porta Solano, Sócrates, 103
Puente Uceda, Luis De La, 23–24, 28, 47, 53, 66,
101, 221

Quechua language, 3, 4, 6, 63
Quirós, Luis, 148

Raborg, Percy, 34–35, 36, 37
Ramírez, Arce, 151
Ramírez, Felipe, 211
Ramos, Javier, 151
Reagan, Ronald, 59
Red Cross, 197, 203, 209, 224, 225, 229
Reminiscences of the Cuban Revolution
(Guevara), 44
Rénique, José Luis, 5–6
Rentería, Jacinto, 22
Renzo (MRTA leader), 186–87
Republican Guards, 62
Revolutionary Left Movement (MIR), 16, 23–28,
36, 37, 66, 95–96, 108, 117, 236; divisions
within, 67–68; insurgency of (1965), 64;
MRTA's absorption of, 67–68, 97; peasant
activists backed by, 80; youth group of
(Juventud Revelde), 45, 46, 65
Reyes, Pascual, 31
Ricardo (rebel), 121
Richard (Vargas's tenant), 130
Rincón Rincón, Miguel, 194, 196–97; arrests
of, 107, 195, 236–37, 238; as Directorate
member, 148, 178, 179; as fugitive, 183;
as ideological purist, 146, 179; Peruvian
congress assault planned by, 190–92
Risco, Clemencia, 17
Rizo Patrón, Antenor, 199–200
Rodríguez Pastor, Carlos, 30–31, 41
Rojas, Lucinda, 195
Rojas, Rolly, 187–88, 204–5, 216–17, 222, 226,
229
Romero (hostage), 206
Ronald (rebel), 186
rondas campesinas, 4, 26, 80, 105, 117, 119, 121

Rosas, Carlos, 216
Ruíz Figueroa, Germán, 55

Sagasti, Francisco, 206
Salgado, Rafael, 161
Sánchez Cerro, Luís, 17
Sandinista Front of National Liberation, 21,
33, 193
San Martín (department), 79–80, 111, 112, 179,
184, 238
San Martín, José de, 16, 28, 33, 41, 53–56
Santos Atahualpa, Juan, 37, 40–41
Sarmiento, Carlos, 31
Schlotterbeck, Marian, 236
School of the Americas, 39
Sendero Luminoso. *See* Shining Path
Sendic, Raúl, 7, 128
Sergio (rebel), 129
Sesarego, Ada, 196–97
Shining and Other Paths (Stern), 5
Shining Path (Sendero Luminoso), 3–5, 11, 44,
68, 89, 104, 158, 201, 209, 237; bombings by,
58; casualties attributed to, 238; extremism
of, 26, 60, 79, 86, 93, 111–12, 170–71, 236;
imprisoned leaders of, 127; individualism
eschewed by, 6; insurgencies launched
by, 25–26, 67; Lima controlled by, 61, 193;
massacre of, 200; missteps by, 16, 26; MRTA
vs., 36, 37, 38, 54, 86, 93, 94, 102, 105, 126;
in Pasco, 116; persistence of, 234; students
recruited by, 172; women in, 6–7, 174–75
SIN. *See* National Intelligence Service
Smith, Anthony D., 10
Solís, Domínguez, 197
Solís, Zenaida, 213
Sonia (Vargas's tenant), 130
Soviet Union, 124
Spenser, Daniela, 10
Stalin, Josef, 124
Stern, Steve J., 5
Summer Institute of Linguistics, 40, 57
SUNAT (Special Investigations Tributary Unit),
200

Tabalosos massacre, 85, 92
Tafur Ruíz, Demetrio, 112
Tapia, Bruno, 174
Tapia, Carlos, 66
Tapia, Esperanza, 8–9, 170–77, 181–83, 189,
235, 239
Telledo Feria, Jorge, 15–16
Tello Leva, Fidel, 30
Terada, Terusuke, 216
Teresa (informant), 183
Tigre (rebel), 121, 178, 183, 188, 190, 195–97;
indigenous people defended by, 117–18, 187,
235; later years of, 239

H. Eugene and Lillian Youngs Lehman Series

Lamar Cecil, *Wilhelm II: Prince and Emperor, 1859–1900* (1989).

Carolyn Merchant, *Ecological Revolutions: Nature, Gender, and Science in New England* (1989).

Gladys Engel Lang and Kurt Lang, *Etched in Memory: The Building and Survival of Artistic Reputation* (1990).

Howard Jones, *Union in Peril: The Crisis over British Intervention in the Civil War* (1992).

Robert L. Dorman, *Revolt of the Provinces: The Regionalist Movement in America* (1993).

Peter N. Stearns, *Meaning Over Memory: Recasting the Teaching of Culture and History* (1993).

Thomas Wolfe, *The Good Child's River*, edited with an introduction by Suzanne Stutman (1994).

Warren A. Nord, *Religion and American Education: Rethinking a National Dilemma* (1995).

David E. Whisnant, *Rascally Signs in Sacred Places: The Politics of Culture in Nicaragua* (1995).

Lamar Cecil, *Wilhelm II: Emperor and Exile, 1900–1941* (1996).

Jonathan Hartlyn, *The Struggle for Democratic Politics in the Dominican Republic* (1998).

Louis A. Pérez Jr., *On Becoming Cuban: Identity, Nationality, and Culture* (1999).

Yaakov Ariel, *Evangelizing the Chosen People: Missions to the Jews in America, 1880–2000* (2000).

Philip F. Gura, *C. F. Martin and His Guitars, 1796–1873* (2003).

Louis A. Pérez Jr., *To Die in Cuba: Suicide and Society* (2005).

Peter Filene, *The Joy of Teaching: A Practical Guide for New College Instructors* (2005).

John Charles Boger and Gary Orfield, eds., *School Resegregation: Must the South Turn Back?* (2005).

Jock Lauterer, *Community Journalism: Relentlessly Local* (2006).

Michael H. Hunt, *The American Ascendancy: How the United States Gained and Wielded Global Dominance* (2007).

Michael Lienesch, *In the Beginning: Fundamentalism, the Scopes Trial, and the Making of the Antievolution Movement* (2007).

Eric L. Muller, *American Inquisition: The Hunt for Japanese American Disloyalty in World War II* (2007).

John McGowan, *American Liberalism: An Interpretation for Our Time* (2007).

Nortin M. Hadler, M.D., *Worried Sick: A Prescription for Health in an Overtreated America* (2008).

William Ferris, *Give My Poor Heart Ease: Voices of the Mississippi Blues* (2009).

Colin A. Palmer, *Cheddi Jagan and the Politics of Power: British Guiana's Struggle for Independence* (2010).

W. Fitzhugh Brundage, *Beyond Blackface: African Americans and the Creation of American Mass Culture, 1890–1930* (2011).

Michael H. Hunt and Steven I. Levine, *Arc of Empire: America's Wars in Asia from the Philippines to Vietnam* (2012).

Nortin M. Hadler, M.D., *The Citizen Patient: Reforming Health Care for the Sake of the Patient, Not the System* (2013).

Louis A. Pérez Jr., *The Structure of Cuban History: Meanings and Purpose of the Past* (2013).

Jennifer Thigpen, *Island Queens and Mission Wives: How Gender and Empire Remade Hawai'i's Pacific World* (2014).

George W. Houston, *Inside Roman Libraries: Book Collections and Their Management in Antiquity* (2014).

Philip F. Gura, *The Life of William Apess, Pequot* (2015).

Daniel M. Cobb, ed., *Say We Are Nations: Documents of Politics and Protest in Indigenous America since 1887* (2015).

Daniel Maudlin and Bernard L. Herman, eds., *Building the British Atlantic World: Spaces, Places, and Material Culture, 1600–1850* (2016).

William Ferris, *The South in Color: A Visual Journal* (2016).

Lisa A. Lindsay, *Atlantic Bonds: A Nineteenth-Century Odyssey from America to Africa* (2017).

Mary Elizabeth Basile Chopas, *Searching for Subversives: The Story of Italian Internment in Wartime America* (2017).

John M. Coggeshall, *Liberia, South Carolina: An African American Appalachian Community* (2018).

Malinda Maynor Lowery, *The Lumbee Indians: An American Struggle* (2018).

Seth Kotch, *Lethal State: A History of the Death Penalty in North Carolina* (2019).

Bernard L. Herman, *A South You Never Ate: Savoring Flavors and Stories from the Eastern Shore of Virginia* (2019).

Miguel La Serna, *With Masses and Arms: Peru's Tupac Amaru Revolutionary Movement* (2020).